MIRACLE OF TIME

by Frank L. Paine

Shiloah Ministries

Shiloah Ministries
11 Beasley Court
CHARD   Somerset
England   TA20 1DX

Unless otherwise stated, all Scripture quotations are from the Authorized Version of the Bible. Extracts from the Authorized Version of the Bible (the King James Version), the rights in which are vested in the Crown, are reproduced by permission of the Crown's Patentee, Cambridge University Press.

British Library Cataloguing-in-Publication Data

A catalogue record for this book is available from the British Library.

ISBN   0-9523323-0-2

Printed in England

MIRACLE OF TIME

by Frank L. Paine

'THE KEY OF DAVID' TURNS PERFECTLY
IN THE LOCK OF ISRAEL'S ANCIENT AND
MODERN HISTORY SO AS TO OPEN THE
DOOR THAT WE MIGHT UNDERSTAND
THE SCRIPTURES IN THE CLOSING
DAYS OF OUR AGE

'The thing that is hid bringeth He forth to the light'
(Job 28: 11)

Contents

<... >

The Background to the Book

When Jesus the Messiah, the Son of God, set His face to go up to Jerusalem He knew He must die there. As the Lamb of God, He was to redeem all who put their faith in Him. His hour had come, the hour at which the Son of man should be glorified. This 'hour' was not just a metaphor, or figure of speech. It was literally true that there was just one particular day and hour, and no other in all time, when the Messiah had to die.

This book seeks to bring forth some amazing discoveries in God's Word which show the wonderful and miraculous way in which God has planned and ordered time. Many of these discoveries were made by a group of men whom God called together to study the prophetic scriptures and to understand the time measurements in His Word.

The story of this call of God began in 1917 when the Balfour Declaration was announced. Arthur Eustace Ware (1885-1978), who was working at the YMCA at the time, discerned in the Declaration a step towards the return of the Jews to their Biblical Homeland, and that the time for the return of Jesus for His Church was drawing near. Some thirty years before, Dr H Grattan Guinness, an eminent astronomer and writer, and a student of Biblical prophecy, had written books suggesting that 1917 would be a key date in God's restoration of the State of Israel. Arthur Ware then began a study of the Bible in relation to its prophetic predictions for the last days and the chronology of events contained within its pages. He was to continue this study for the rest of his life. During the 1920s he held meetings at which he spoke on prophetic subjects.

The author of this book, Frank Lawrence Paine, (1906-83), the only son of a civil servant was born in Wood Green, North London, and educated at the City of London School. His chosen career in banking had to be abandoned due to severe attacks of rheumatism; instead he worked in an Automobile Association office in London. Around 1927 he began to attend Arthur Ware's meetings, and felt the conviction of the Holy Spirit as to the reality of what he was hearing. In 1932 he married Ellen Kathleen Champion, the youngest daughter of a minister of the Gospel. At about this time Frank, and a small group of others, felt the call of God to leave their secular employment and join Arthur Ware in comprehensive Biblical research. The events recorded in this book will give the reader something of their history over the following years, and the actions they believed they were led to take by the Lord.

Over the years Arthur Ware was often away seeking the Lord in quiet places while the group of men also spent long hours in prayer and in the study of God's Word. Mr Ware believed that he was given keys to the understanding of the calendars which God uses in His Word. As the group studied these they were able to trace the dates of all the principal events in Scripture, right back to the first days of creation in Genesis 1.

Beneath the surface of Scripture lie extraordinary numerical designs. In the Hebrew and Greek languages each letter has a numerical value. When in 1890 Dr Ivan Panin, a Russian agnostic who was a brilliant mathematician living in the United States, was studying the Old and New Testaments, he was astonished to find the imprint of the divine authorship of the Scriptures. He discovered that, in every logical division of a passage, if the letters' numerical equivalents were substituted amazing designs based on the number seven came to light. God Himself is the Master Mathematician so it should not surprise us to learn that the Bible holds within its pages a perfect chronology which does not have to depend on secular chronological data for substantiation.

Returning to the little company whom God called aside to reveal to them His time measurements: in 1940 the men and their families moved to the Lake District. During the War Frank Paine and two others were eligible for military service. Against what might be thought of as normal wordly judgment, they discovered that their work on Biblical Chronology exempted them from conscription! That they were looking into fundamentally important matters was clearly the way their Lord saw it too: He was watching over His watchmen. The panel's decision seems to have been a clear case of the working of God, so that His work might continue and so be ready for the last days when its truths would be needed. Arthur Ware said in court to the judge: "Have you heard of the Person of The Holy Ghost?" The court went silent! As a result they were able to continue to pray and meet together as they followed the course of the war, the rise of the State of Israel, and the critical stages in the subsequent history of that little nation, all in relation to God's time programme. In the 1950s many of Arthur Ware's writings were published.

The manuscript of this book was written in the 1970s and early 1980s but never published in the author's lifetime. He believed it would be published at God's appointed time. Many faithful ministers of God are today speaking of the nearness of the return of Jesus for his Church, and showing that conditions on the earth are ripe for the rise of the Antichrist and the outpouring of God's wrath as the prophetic scriptures foretell. We trust that these pages will give added authority to such expositions.

It may be that not all our readers will have the mathematical skills to check the arithmetic for themselves. However, we hope that all will be excited to learn how perfectly Jesus fulfilled the Levitical Feasts of the Lord now that the true dates of His birth, death and resurrection have been restored. They will also learn how all the events of the restoration of Israel have been in accordance with God's perfect plan and timing.

My father, who was profoundly deaf by the time of his death (at the eleventh hour of the eleventh day of November, the eleventh month, in 1983!), was, owing to his affliction, often shut away from the conversation going on around him but he spent hours in the Bible and communing with the Lord over the wonders of His time measurements.

I once went into his room while he was resting on his bed, near the end of his life, to see his face aglow and to hear his lips pouring out worship to God in unknown tongues. He would have no other desire than that, with the distribution of this book, the Lord he loved and served from when he was a young man, should have all the glory. We pray it shall indeed be so.

E Joy Paine   *June 1993*

Acknowledgments

I would like to extend my grateful thanks to Penuel Christian Fellowship, Swindon for their encouragement, support and financial giving.

Most particularly my thanks are due to Christopher Barder for all his expertise and guidance — without him the whole project might not have begun and might have faltered the more at each step of the way — and to Keith Cline for many, many hours of hard work editing and checking accurately and meticulously; any mistakes are certainly no fault of his.

Jean Stockbridge has my warm and grateful thanks for checking references and working alongside me helping with the pagination for the references and indexing. Adrian Aylward's various kindnesses have also been much appreciated, as has Martin Thompson's help in drawing up the charts.

Robin and Mary Bough proof-read the text and found what needed finding with genuine skill and love. My sister, Grace Turpin, has had a heart for the book and helped when she could, and I would like to thank her and other family and friends for all their encouragement.

The information kindly supplied by Mr Simon Goulden of Jews' College, London, on the prayer Untaneh Tokef recited on the Day of Atonement (see page 100), is condensed in Note 6 on page 185. We are grateful for this and for Mr Goulden's assistance, which we acknowledge with sincere thanks.

I would like too to thank my mother for the faithful support given to my father in his study of the Scriptures during their fifty-one years together, and for her understanding and patience as I have sought to get this book into print.

Without God, quite simply none of this work would have been possible. Unto Him be all the honour, praise and glory.

E Joy Paine

MIRACLE OF TIME

FOREWORD

Peace and safety![1] Peace among nations, and safety for the individual from terrorism and violence — can anything approaching this be expected in the closing days of the twentieth century?

The major powers of the world keep their eyes on the Middle East and make efforts to impose their own solutions upon Israel, while the Israelis, on their part, are all too conscious of the final intentions of the surrounding Arab nations. Hopes are raised, and hopes are dashed, as leaders wrestle with the impossible situation, but all the while the world remains totally unconscious of the fact that the major events of history have been perfectly timed by Almighty God, 'according to the plan of the ages which He purposed in Christ Jesus our Lord'[2].

Does the Bible hold the key then, and unlock the pattern of our modern history? Did God foreknow it? Every true believer in Jesus accepts the fact that 'known unto God are all His works from the beginning of the world'[3]. And the timing of His works? This will be seen by all who study the coming pages and check the facts and figures with the Bible for themselves.

What Are 'Dry Bones'?

When I pick up the Jerusalem Post I generally glance at its humorous cartoon strip, captioned *'Dry Bones'* which touches on current topics, but I used to wonder why they gave the strip this

---

[1] 1 Thessalonians 5: 3
[2] Ephesians 3: 11 *(literal trans)*
[3] Acts 15: 18

peculiar title, until the obvious struck me — Israelis also know Ezekiel 37!

If ever their nation needed enlightenment about the 'dry bones' of this chapter, that moment has surely come in their amazing history. Truly enough, some of their leaders are taking a new interest in the Bible, and it was reported that during the Middle East War of 1973, many young Israeli soldiers made urgent calls for anyone who had understanding of the prophecies, and eagerly grouped around individuals who could offer some valid explanation as to why they had so suddenly been plunged into the bloodiest and most devastating assault Israel had ever experienced. Observers certainly rated the tank battles of that Yom Kippur War as of greater intensity than those of any preceding conflict in history.

In Ezekiel 37 we have a picture of a nation long dead. The bodies had disappeared and the bones had come apart and been scattered. But each bone told a story. Only after the disjointed skeleton of each of the dead could be re-assembled perfectly — and this, of course, with all the skeletons — could the 'sinews and flesh come upon them' and after that the 'skin'. But still, says the prophet, 'there was no breath in them'.

In these first fourteen verses we have God's own strip cartoon — a marvellous picture of the rise of modern Israel, which the whole world has witnessed this century. But the one feature which apparently neither Jew nor Gentile has observed has been the **perfect** bringing together of the 'bones', that is, the exact time-measurements of Israel, as these are concealed and now revealed in the pages of the Bible.

It is important to be very explicit about this aspect of the bones. When David wrote in Psalm 22: 14, 'all my bones are out of joint,' most Christians recognise that, with the foreknowledge of the Spirit of God, he was voicing the words of the Messiah, after the tree on which He was impaled had been dropped into the hole dug for it on the Mount of Calvary in the year AD 33. Also in verse 17 of the same Psalm we have the words, 'I may number all my bones' (literal translation).

After He had manifested Himself in resurrection, however, the Messiah of Israel declared, 'a spirit hath not flesh and bones, as ye see Me have.'[4] And He showed them His hands and His feet.

---

[4] Luke 24: 39

As the wind of the Spirit blows across this war-torn earth in the last days of our Gentile age, multitudes are being conditioned to 'see' the Messiah and, as they see Him freshly in the scriptures, they will also perceive that His bones are all in joint. No longer will the days, months and years of the Bible record remain meaningless, especially to Jews, for it is these measurements — these bones — that will be found to have perfectly survived in the sepulchre of time, so that now we may behold *the true outline* of history. Yes, it is *His story* and the story of the people of Israel (for are they not *His* people — 'the people of His pasture, and the sheep of His hand'?)[5]

He is the One who 'has the key of David'[6], and we believe this key has now turned in the lock of Bible history so that we, both Jews and Gentiles, may know the truth, the truth that 'shall make us free'. For to hold to tradition and not truth, will leave us in bondage. Jesus said, 'ye shall know the truth'[7]. Hallelujah!

'Seal the book even to the time of the end'
(Daniel 12: 4)

The Bible has remained a sealed book, as far as the 'plan of the ages' is concerned, right down the long course of history. It is not only the book of Daniel that has remained 'closed up', but the whole of the true historical record from Genesis onward which has remained sealed 'until the time of the end'.

This statement might be hotly challenged if it is not at once explained that it is in the realm of exact time-measurement that the Bible has remained sealed. The reason for this should become self-evident as the contents of the book unfold.

What Is Time?

Time, of course, is inseparable from History, for one cannot have time without history, or history without time.

An illustration of the sheer impossibility of human minds being able to obtain an accurate total of the time — even between Israel's exodus from Egypt and the crucifixion of Christ — has been sent us by a friend in Khartoum, and it discloses the following facts: It is a list of seventy five different efforts to fix the year of the Exodus, beginning with 1792 BC (Samaritan Text) and ending with

---

[5] Psalm 95: 7
[6] Revelation 3: 7, see also Isaiah 22: 22
[7] John 8: 32

the date of 1168 BC (Lipman). These various assessments by scholars made over the past four centuries show an overall difference of more than six hundred years; and so, apart from God's intervention to grant revelation on how to measure time in His Word, for anyone to come forward now and say, 'This is the true date of the Exodus' might meet with some scepticism! Clearly God had no intention of allowing this part of His Word to be unveiled by the wit and wisdom of man.

It remains true that 'the things of God knoweth no man, but the Spirit of God ... but the natural man receiveth not the things of the Spirit of God: for they are foolishness unto him: neither can he know them, because they are spiritually discerned'[8]. And in no part of the Bible's revelation is this more true than in the realm of time-measurement, or what is called Chronology.

The reason God has allowed this knowledge to be 'sealed up' is because it is now intended to throw a brilliant light upon the world events in '*the time of the end*'[9] that is, in these latter years when He has been restoring the nation of Israel to its land.

The Church and the world did not need an accurate knowledge of history in relation to the purposes of God in the time of Luther or Wesley, but now that Israel's position in the Middle East is making 'Jerusalem a burdensome stone for all people'[10] — on account of the attitude of Israel's Arab neighbours and their 'oil weapon' — it is another matter.

There is urgent need for all who are 'children of light'[11] to know about it when the Spirit of God throws light on obscure parts of His Word, but it is also certain that the 'powers of darkness' will make their heaviest assault on any revelation likely to establish the absolute veracity of the Holy Scriptures.

It has been well said that the time of the end is the time of 'fulness'— the 'fulness of the Spirit' and also the fulness of evil, corruption, violence and, ultimately, judgment. Those who take the trouble to check through with the Bible the wondrous time-pattern of the Almighty — now that at last the secret of His use of the 'Jubilee' (or 49 year) cycles has been revealed — will find their faith and their affections greatly strengthened. For they will find that 'time's long twilight' has now become illumined by the positive shining of the Bright Morning Star, and the 'shadows' are rapidly fleeing away.

---

[8] 1 Corinthians 2: 11 & 14   [10] Zechariah 12: 3
[9] Daniel 12: 4   [11] Ephesians 5: 8

MIRACLE OF TIME

INTRODUCTION

On 30th August 1970, at a large Sunday evening gathering which my wife and I were attending in the USA, an incisive prophecy stilled the congregation. It ran as follows:

'I will send thee forth, and you will see where I will send thee; by a way, and for a purpose thou hast not conceived. For I am with thee, and thou shalt know this because I shall show it to thee very clearly.

'I will cause thee to meet those whom thou hast never met, and come in contact with those whom thou hast never heard. They shall tell thee, even as the people told King Saul before he became king, where the asses were. Therefore, be on the alert … and seek … and know … and follow … and I will show thee.

'The things that are hidden must be brought to light. Things that have not been discerned must be revealed. And it is in the power of thy hand to do it, saith the Lord'.

As the speaker, a well-known Bible expositor, ended the prophecy he added, 'This is for someone in the meeting and **not** for all. The person will know for whom it is. Be like Mary and ponder these things in your heart. This is the word of the Lord. When I started to speak I had not the faintest idea what the Lord was going to say'.

When the meeting ended, a lady threaded her way across the room to my side. 'That was for you,' she emphasised. I thanked her, but replied that I did not actually need that confirmation, for it was all too clear that the Lord had spoken with reference to a matter which for many years had been deeply hidden, and the very nature of which was that it had to be written, and not spoken — hence the closing phrase, 'it is in the power of thy hand to do it'.

All who have had an acquaintance with the movement of the Holy Spirit of God in recent years will know that there are occasions when the Lord speaks by means of prophecy[1] for the specific purpose of revealing His mind to one or more of His children — in the same way, no doubt, as was common practice when the New Testament was written. The restoration of charismatic 'gifts' has been experienced by so many thousands of believers in Jesus by now that it has almost ceased to be a noteworthy phenomenon among the people of God.

Hundreds of books and articles have appeared in the past decades, telling of the wonderful works of God in healing sick minds and bodies, in deliverance from bondages of many kinds, with the consequent changing of lives, often from near despair to radiance and restored usefulness to God and man. Surely, it is difficult to ignore the fact today that God is moving by His Spirit, moving through all the earth. However, the question has been raised: Is there much which is still *hidden* — matters, perhaps, to do with 'the deep and secret things'[2] and the purposes of the Almighty — about which He, in love, would now have His children to know?

The part of the interpretation about 'the asses' had at once alerted the writer to realise that God was referring in a veiled way to certain of His children who would not only seek to enter into 'the understanding of the times' — like the men of Issachar in 1 Chronicles 12: 32, the tribe likened in Genesis 49: 14 to a 'strong ass' — but would also, as true disciples of the Master, bear the burden of opening their homes to us while our stay lasted in the United States. In Psalm 32: 9 the 'horse' and the 'mule' are said 'to have no understanding', but not so the ass. So it was wonderful shortly after this to be led to find Christian families who, for the following year or more, were to take a deep interest in our work and minister to our every need while most of the writing was being completed. The Spirit's leading was perfect and before we left Florida in November 1971 we found that God had borne witness with several that a new revelation to do with *time* in the life of Jesus had, indeed, been made available to men which would eventually uncover all those priceless secrets 'concerning

---

[1] see 1 Corinthians 12: 10
[2] Daniel 2: 22

Himself'ᵌ which have been lost over the past centuries.

The story to be told relates to figures, numbers, dates and years. After all, it is the story of *time* — God's perfect patterning of time at the beginning of things in Genesis and time now at the end of things, when no one can peer ahead into the future with any certainty. Time embraces all history, all the works of God and all the doings of men and, as we are told twenty-eight times in Ecclesiastes 3, there is 'a time' for every purpose under heaven. Small wonder then if God should in the end require the perfect timing of His works to become known with absolute accuracy — for by this means He can reveal to our present needy generation how vast has been His patience and His mercy to the race of Adam, and at the same time how certain His acts of retribution upon those who fail to fear His name, and do despite to the Spirit of grace.

Above all, He can now reveal *Jesus* — not the Jesus of the world's distorted imagination — Jesus 'the song of the drunkards'⁴ — but *His own Son*, the One who, 'after six days' took His disciples up into a high mountain apart, 'and was transfigured before them'. This is the One whom the Father would for a brief moment unveil, so that His present-day disciples might awaken and 'see His glory'. Then, the three on the mount overheard Jesus conversing with the representatives of the Law and the Prophets — Moses and Elijah — concerning His coming 'exodus', which He was about to accomplish at Jerusalem. Now, however, the same Blessed One has much to reveal from the Scriptures concerning the forthcoming *exodus* of 'the Church, which is His body'⁵ — a Church which He still finds 'heavy with sleep', as He did the disciples on the Mount. (See Matthew 17: 1-8 and Luke 9: 28-35, esp. verse 32.)

Let it be said at the start that these findings are not the work of one man, but of several called of God to study these things. However, the writer has found it necessary to obey the Word of the Lord, as quoted at the beginning of this Introduction, and to attempt to produce at least a bare outline of 'the things' which hitherto 'have not been discerned'. This 'bare outline' is, in fact, what has always been missing from the multitudinous efforts to delineate the true history of the past six thousand years, for it is the 'outline' which reveals 'the pattern' of God's own handiwork in His plan of the ages.

But in the scope of a few pages — all that a busy world has

³ Luke 24: 27
⁴ Psalm 69: 12
⁵ Ephesians 1: 22-23

time for in the present day — 'a bare outline' is all that can be attempted, and the words of Habakkuk 2: 1-3 appear to suggest only a very limited unfolding of an absolutely limitless subject. 'Write the vision, and make it plain upon tables, that he may run that readeth it' (verse 2) — this could hardly apply to an encyclopedia! But an outline which, on the surface, can be seen to bear the hallmark of being undeniably of Divine design will demand the close attention of all who revere the Word of the Living God.

Therefore, I do ask that any faults and failings due to an inexperienced writer be overlooked in favour of the facts about to be uncovered. One soon forgets the archaeologist's workmen when surveying the ancient structures their picks have brought to light. 'At last', we say, 'we have the truth, covered up as it has been with centuries of debris and the later building of men. Now we can see the foundations that were originally laid'.

This is one of the main purposes of God in laying bare the true timing of His Word: to take us all back to the first century so that we may 'see Jesus' as they knew Him then, and the true dating of His mighty work of redemption and how, in His own person He perfectly fulfilled Isaiah's prediction, 'He will magnify the law, and make it honourable'[6].

---

[6] Isaiah 42: 21

CHAPTER ONE

The Importance Today of Understanding God's Time Measurements

'There is nothing covered, that shall not be revealed; and hid, that shall not be known'   (Matthew 10: 26)

Today is a day when man's knowledge has come perilously near to the full in many fields and, where the means of mass destruction are concerned, man heartily wishes that he did not know so much!

In several directions, human knowledge has certainly overflowed its banks and the 'tree of knowledge'[1] has never spread its branches over the race with such proliferation. However, we can praise God that those who are wise have already listened to the advice of Isaiah (2: 22) when he says, 'Cease ye from man, whose breath is in his nostrils: for wherein is he to be accounted of?'

But, because of the danger of knowing too much on the human level, many Christians have taken refuge in **not** knowing and, for instance, have regarded it as extreme presumption if anyone should confess to any positive knowledge of the true timing of the many events connected with the First Advent of our Saviour into the world. For one thing, they believe it is utterly out of the question for God to have restored this lost understanding and, for another, they feel any recovery of it would only fill their heads with knowledge, when what the world really stands in need of today is love.

---

[1] Genesis 2: 9

However, there is another angle of view and that is: does God Himself desire His Church to 'know the truth'[2] concerning Jesus in the present hour? It may help us if we see the result of this lack of knowledge in the case of Israel, when Jesus was here in the flesh. He was manifestly here as 'the Bridegroom' (see John 3: 29) but Israel did not know it and in Luke 19: 41-44 we find that one thing — the one vital thing — was hidden from the Jewish nation when they crucified their Messiah. For on the eve of His death He had to warn them that a terrible destruction lay close ahead for their holy city — in fact, for their whole nation, for one sole reason — 'because', He said, 'thou knewest not the **time** of thy visitation' (verse 44).

It was the same in the days of Noah when, as Jesus reminded His disciples (in Matthew 24: 38-39), 'they ... *knew not* until the Flood came, and took them all away' and, He added, 'so shall also the coming of the Son of Man be'.

However, the 'children of light'[3] are said to be in a different category and not to be in darkness about the actual coming of the Lord. It is the purpose of this present writing to disclose that the scriptures do contain an actual *'understanding of the times'* which could only be unlocked at the ending of this age. **This** is the 'hidden' part of His Word which God now intends to unveil, for it contains a glorious revelation of His Beloved Son 'by Whom also He made the ages'[4].

For centuries past, God has called aside some of His servants to study His 'ways'. We are informed in Psalm 103: 7 that God 'made known His ways unto Moses, His acts unto the Children of Israel' — so it is clear from this that God's 'ways' are in the main 'hidden' from His people; but to some it is needful that He should reveal them for, as Amos (3: 7) says, 'Surely the Lord God will do nothing, but He revealeth His secret (*lit.* counsel) unto His servants the prophets'.

The Vision of The 'Seven Times' of Daniel 4

Over a century ago a servant of God who was also an eminent astronomer, Dr. H. Grattan Guinness, became convinced that God was fulfilling the time prophecy of Daniel 4. Studied in the light of the previous three chapters of Daniel, this vision obviously takes

---

2 John 8: 32
3 1 Thessalonians 5: 5
4 Hebrews 1: 2 *(literal Greek)*

on an importance far in excess of that which has been assigned to it by the general run of interpreters.

God had finished with the original line of the kings of Judah after bearing with their failure and unfaithfulness for over 400 years and now was determined to use a succession of pagan Gentile empires, as described in Daniel 2. He saw to it, however, that the great Babylonian king took captive four princes of Judah — Daniel and his fellows — as he subjugated Jerusalem in 607 BC. These four men he soon caused to be set over the whole province of Babylon, so that the government of the first of the four empires was on a righteous foundation. Later he established Nebuchadnezzar as supreme among the surrounding nations such as Egypt and Tyre, so that his kingdom would be unchallenged and without competitors in the Middle East.

After appointing him as 'head' of this Gentile succession, God gave Nebuchadnezzar a vision which was two-fold. Like Adam, the head of the human race before him, he would fall through pride and, secondly, the duration of his fallen state had been decreed by God. Clearly, on the basis of 'each day for a year' the *seven times* (that is 7 times 360 days)* would pass over the great king and his kingdom until the time came for the kingdom to be given up to one called 'the lowest' or 'the most abased' of men (verse 17, RV & lit. Greek). (The whole of Daniel 4 should be carefully read.)

It is obvious that God identified Nebuchadnezzar with the Gentile empires following him, in the line of Persia, Greece and Rome, for Rome was ultimately to see Jesus, hanging bloodied and naked, outside Jerusalem; but after the final count the same Jesus will be manifested 'in power, and strength, and glory', as He returns to establish a Kingdom which 'shall stand for ever'[5].

Dr. Grattan Guinness studied the history of the Captivity of Judah and measured off eras of 2,520 years from the many consecutive starting points in Biblical history when, first Israel, and then later Judah were swept away into captivity to Assyria and Babylon. On the strength of his findings he confidently pointed ahead to the years 1917, 1923 and 1934 as bound to see movement relating to the restoration of Israel to her land. (If he had measured the last period of 2,520 years from the seige of Jerusalem in 588 BC when God actually gave up Judah to judgment — see Ezekiel 24 — he would have made the closing year of the series

---

* See Note 1 on page 184, also see page 40   [5] Daniel 2: 37 & 44

1933 and not 1934.)

As the result of these predictions, which were widely read over the previous thirty years, many thousands of Christians watched through the days of the First World War and then, surely enough, in 1917 came the first real sign that the time had come for God to do two things: firstly, to begin to restore the land of Israel to His ancient people and, secondly, to allow a power to come into being which would in the end bring the great Gentile civilisation of the West tottering to its fall. For in the winter of 1917 — as is well known — the Muslim domination of the Holy Land and Jerusalem ceased, and the famous Balfour Declaration was given by the British Government to Lord Rothschild, thanks in large measure to the work of the English Zionist leader, Dr. Chaim Weizmann. At the same time, the Bolshevik Revolution swept away the last of the Czars and Communism became a force which would come to dominate vast areas of the earth.

In 1923 the passing into operation of the Palestine Mandate, under which Great Britain was the Mandatory power, formed a fitting end to the 'seven times' or 2,520* years from 598 BC when the surrender of King Jehoiachin to Babylon virtually terminated the true Kingdom of Judah.

As far as was then known, only some ten years remained to complete the predetermined era of 2,520 years which began with the fall of Judah in the days of Nebuchadnezzar. But the hand of God had designed that these 'seven times' of years should run their course from yet later starting-points in Babylon's history — not alone related to the going into captivity of the people of Judah — and these we were to learn as time went on.

---

* See Note 1 on page 184

CHAPTER TWO

Time Limited to God's Foreordained Plan

We now come to an unveiling of things which God has hidden 'from the wise and prudent'[1] and yet has 'revealed to babes', and it is these things on which we must fix our attention if we would begin to understand what has been secretly shaping the course of modern history over the past sixty years; that is, seemingly from behind the scenes.

We have just referred to a plan — a time plan — taken from the fourth chapter of Daniel. This chapter, which seems to be the only one in the Bible written wholly by a Gentile (though recorded by Daniel), is addressed to the whole human race — 'all people, nations and languages ... in all the earth'. And it is not the utterance of some minor prophet but, we find in Daniel 2: 37, that it was made by the actual head of the Gentile empires and the one Daniel calls, 'King of Kings', to whom 'the God of heaven' had given the 'kingdom, power, and strength, and glory'.

It is safe to say that without this chapter there would be no positive evidence given in Scripture as to how long God would allow the Gentile domination of the earth to continue, and the throne of Judah to remain in abeyance. For Nebuchadnezzar, in his personal experience, provides a type of the moral state of Gentile government of the earth over the past 2,520 years — alienated from the knowledge of God but, nevertheless, 'wet with the dew of heaven', which so beautifully expresses the way the blessings of true Christianity have descended upon the human race. The 'band of iron and brass', in verse 15 of chapter 4, signifies the impress of Roman civilisation and Grecian culture

---

[1] Matthew 11: 25

which would characterise Gentile rule, in the main, until the throne of Judah is restored at the return of Christ, the true 'Son of David', at the opening of His Millennial Kingdom.

This chapter shows that the essence of Nebuchadnezzar's mental illness (or call it what you will) was that it was a state allowed by God for a fixed period of time, after which illumination was to be granted, and the knowledge of Himself restored. Surely no one can read the last verses of chapter 4, recording Nebuchadnezzar's testimony, without being deeply moved. His words express the homage that this Gentile world, of which he was the fallen head, will pay to Christ when, at length, God opens man's understanding and causes him to retrace and measure the exact course of his history of pride and moral alienation from Himself, from beginning to end.

'How great are His signs!'
(Daniel 4: 3)

What then was the purpose of these 'seven times' passing over the king and his kingdom of Babylon? It is expressly stated in verse 17 of Daniel 4 that the whole matter was 'by the decree of the watchers, and the demand by the word of the Holy Ones (that is, the Godhead): to the intent that the living may know that the Most High ruleth in the kingdom of men, and giveth it to whomsoever He will, and setteth up over it *the basest (or most abased or lowest) of men'*. That is, of course, Jesus Christ our Lord.

The essence of the matter was that the **time** was strictly limited, and therefore must be accurately measured.

In the late 1920s a small group interested in these matters found themselves confronted with the fact that, although as a result of the liberation of Palestine there was much talk in Christian circles about the return of Christ, nothing was really being done to touch the world with any kind of effective warning of the peril awaiting it. The language God used in Ezekiel 24 was terrible in the extreme, when aimed at the inhabitants of Jerusalem in 588 BC, but what was to come 2,520 years later, when God had to deal with a vast Gentile civilisation that had gone astray from Him? Was no word of warning to be given to Christendom at large?

As many will remember, between October 1929 and June 1933

the world entered into one of the worst financial and commercial depressions ever known, with attendant famine and starvation and large-scale unemployment. It was with this dark background that a little group of unattached believers saw that they were faced with the evident probability that the Lord was about to come — and, if so, it looked as if the world really was going to receive no prior warning of this most tremendous event. Who, indeed, could contemplate in cold blood the closing of the door of mercy — after nineteen centuries of grace to all mankind — without some cry being raised, or some attempt to awaken the unsaved masses for whom the Churches of Christendom held little or no attraction?

For some six years prior to 1933 the Spirit of God had focused our attention on Daniel, Ezekiel, Jeremiah and those sections of 2 Kings and 2 Chronicles, which expose the state of the people of Judah as their kingdom began to collapse, at the opening of the 'seven times' in the sixth century BC. Warning after warning had been given by the prophets of impending disaster — how was it possible, then, that God could allow the whole of the Gentile world, not to mention Israel, to slide *unwarned* into the maelstrom of trouble, 'judgment and fiery indignation'[2], which the Bible forecast as preceding the return of Judah's King to set up His Millennial Kingdom?

A Secret Plan

It may be easy for us now — *after* the Second World War and the removal of 'the third part' of the Jewish people from the earth in the days of Adolf Hitler, after Hiroshima and Nagasaki, and particularly after we watched Israel in part re-gathered from over 70 different states to become a Nation again in their homeland — it may be easy now to perceive that 'the Kingdom' is 'near, even at the doors'[3], but God had preparations to make, and a 'secret counsel' to be fulfilled, before ever He could commence the work of Israel's restoration which we have seen. And He intended that, in due course, His children should enter into the knowledge of these things. But God knew that, for the moment, He would have to work in secret; for did He not have to say to Israel at the beginning of our age, 'I work a work in your days, a work which ye shall in no wise believe, though a man declare it unto you'?[4]

---

[2] Hebrew 10: 27   [4] Acts 13: 41
[3] Matthew 24: 14 & 33

One great question lay heavy on the hearts of those who realised they were watching the ending stages of the 2,520 years,* and this was: How could the Lord come for His Church in its state of utter unpreparedness? Had God some plan of action which He would reveal? Jesus called this state 'sleep' in His first parable of Matthew 25.

Oh, praise the Lord, 'and make His praise glorious'[5] — of course He had a plan and this clearly revealed in His Word, for could one single atom fail of the things that He had spoken? In due course this 'plan' began to dawn.

God had in view the ordered fulfilment of His Word. Before He could terminate His official relationship with the Gentiles — as 'grafted into the olive tree' in the place of Israel (a subject Paul writes on very fully in Romans 11) — He must warn them of His intention, in case they showed a willingness to repent. He had to do this before He could openly have dealings with the people of Israel and 'graft them in again' into their own olive tree.

Then there was the position of the Church 'which', as Paul tells us in his Ephesian letter, 'is the Body of Christ'. The Lord could not act apart from His Church, so it was necessary that it also should be given notice of his intentions.

All this was because, quite apart from the completion of the 'seven times' from 588 BC*, there were other heavily-marked eras of the Bible's chronology due to end on one particular day, in the summer of 1933. In view of this fact, those watching were, in the autumn of 1932, led into an understanding of our Lord's great resurrection miracle of John 21.

'Jesus stood on the shore'
(John 21: 4)

Every one of the eight 'signs' (as the miracles of Jesus are called in John's Gospel) throws light on His purposes at this end of our age. 'Eight' is that number in the Bible which has to do with resurrection, and it will be found that eight resurrections are recorded in Scripture (see 1 Kings 17: 17-22,   2 Kings 4: 32-36, 2 Kings 13: 21,   Luke 7: 12-15,   Luke 8: 49-56,   John 11: 44, Acts 9: 36-41 and Acts 20: 9-10).

The Gospel of John presents Jesus as the Son of God, and it

---

* See Note 1 on page 184
(This refers to both * above)

will be seen that it was at the time of His Resurrection that He received that word from His Father: 'Thou art My Son; this day I have begotten Thee'[6], for He was 'the Firstborn', or 'first begotten of the dead'[7].

As, therefore, we are now at the resurrection end of the age, it was not surprising that the one great resurrection 'sign' miracle of Jesus was used to open the eyes of those waiting on Him for instruction, and a simple revelation was made as to the real meaning of the 'two hundred cubits' distance from the land, in John 21: 8. As the 'cubit' had been used in Egypt to symbolise a 'day', and this was known to Israel, it was shown that this distance had a **time** signification — that is, '200 cubits' represented the space of '200 days'.

Clear direction was then given by the Spirit of God that, 200 days prior to the end of the age, a 'net' must be 'cast into the sea' of the Gentiles — this 'net' signifying a *testimony,* as the Gospels prove.

Light was also given as to the meaning of the '153 great fishes' and it was seen that this wonderful number signified the Church of God being brought to completion, as it will be on the resurrection shore.

Not one of us at that time had any glimpse of the enormity of the purpose that lay ahead, or of how different God's ways were from our ways — of how long the project He had before Him would really take, or of the almightiness of His arm which we should see stretched out over all the nations of the earth to bring it to fulfilment. And how little did we dream at that time that the 200 days before us would presently prove to have been the last 200 days of the '2,000 years' of 'the times of the Gentiles', as they are measured in the Chronology of Redemption — a divine method of reckoning of which we then had no knowledge. All that we were allowed to see was that around the season of Pentecost in 1933 there would be a movement of God to bring our dispensation to an end, as we thought, by the second appearing of Christ, when He would fulfil His threat, through the apostle Paul in Romans 11: 22, and *'cut off'* the Gentile nations. We had to act, indeed, like those who were 'blind', and brought 'by a way' we 'knew not'[8].

The essence of the matter was that God wanted a few people to state certain things in His Name about a coming day and date

---

[6] Psalm 2: 7   [8] Isaiah 42: 16
[7] Colossians 1: 18 & Revelation 1: 5

which, if they had known about it beforehand, they would never have been able to say.

The Positive Prediction

In simplicity of faith, therefore, a meeting was called for Christian people for the evening of 25th November 1932, at the Friend's Meeting House, Euston Road, London. The object of this was to reveal all that had come to light concerning the ending stages of the 'seven times' prophecy and to unfold the meaning of the '200 cubits' of John 21, showing how God had used it to indicate the actual time when the nations of Christendom would be 'cut off'. These 200 days would end on June 12th in the following year, 1933, and in making these facts known we desired the fellowship of other members of the Body of Christ.

It must be mentioned that in taking this step of faith in the veracity of God's Word, seven brethren acted together in obedience to the command of Jesus, as it is found in John 21: 6, 'Cast the net on the right side of the ship, and ye shall find'. There were also seven brethren acting in unison away back there on the Sea of Tiberias in AD 33, and their net was immediately filled with '153' great fishes, when they were '200 cubits' from land.

The meeting was held as advertised and, while many showed considerable interest, some were also very conscious of the presence of the Holy Spirit in this gathering. Independent witnesses were moved to count the number of those present, and the full total was found to be exactly '153'. This, understandably, was quite a sign to us as several hundreds attended further meetings on the following day. The address of November 25th was published in certain Christian papers but, as most believers in those days were members of one or other of the Christian groupings or denominations, the usual uncertainty prevailed — as generally accorded to anything not really in line with the currently held teaching.

How little did we realise how great a God was directing this simple operation, or what it was He really had in mind to do. It was not long before warnings were issued in the Christian press against any form of 'date-fixing' and this had the effect of quenching interest in the matter, except on the part of some individuals whose independence of mind carried them over this hurdle.

We moved on into the spring of 1933, still unaware of the action which God had already taken to effect this part of His endtime purpose. Prayerful research into the Scriptures continued, but it was not until April 25th that further movement was called for. Then suddenly, in the early morning, God gave explicit instruction for a large public meeting to be arranged in London, so that a final warning of *'forty days'* could be given — this time not only to Christians, but in still more positive terms and directed to the nations as a whole.

CHAPTER THREE

Events leading up to 'The World's Second Tower of Babel'

Our main purpose in writing this book was to provide as clear an outline as we could of *what God has already done.* When the magnitude of His work and the implications of it become apparent then, for all whose hearts are awakened, it will be possible to provide further light on this 'strange work'[1] of the Most High which He is performing in this 'consummation of the age'*.

God made clear on that morning of April 25th 1933 that the 'cutting off' of the nations was to be announced 40 days beforehand, and this in the most unequivocal terms. These 40 days, being the last of the 200 days from November 25th 1932 to June 12th 1933, would therefore have to commence on May 2nd or 3rd.

It was given to us to see then — but very much more clearly later on — that the 'forty days'[2] of Jonah's warning to Nineveh lay at the background of this Divine requirement. These 40 days in 1933 constituted, as we were presently to discover, the last 40 days of the 40 cycles of Jubilee years from the opening of the dispensation in AD 33 — an era which, to the day, was of the same duration as the 40 cycles of 49 years (calendar lunar years of 354 days each) which God had been reckoning, first from Adam to Abram, and then again from Abram to the death and resurrection of Christ.

Obviously, such a design as this does not show up on the surface of the Bible's chronology, but we were later to learn how positively the Scriptures prove it to lie underneath and we were to discover that without this knowledge it was totally impossible —

---

[1] Isaiah 28: 21
[2] Jonah 3: 4

* See Note 2 on page 184
and compare Matthew 13: 39

and always had been impossible   to understand or reconcile the time statements of God's Holy Word.

We had already read enough of the writings of chronologers to discover that there were difficulties in the understanding of the Bible's time records that were quite insurmountable; but now God intended to take the first steps to remedy our ignorance and reveal His ways, and the absolute perfection of them, in overruling and ordering the course of man's history on the earth.

In the spring of 1933 the scripture that was being most strongly emphasised by the Spirit of God was Romans 11: 22 and this we must briefly consider. The chapter shows the place the Gentiles have occupied in the Divine counsels since the Jewish 'branches' were 'broken off' from 'the olive tree' (which speaks of testimony for God) at the beginning of our age. It is made extremely plain that the nation of Israel was not to be cast away for ever as God's witness in the earth but only for a limited time — 'until the fulness of the Gentiles be come in', as we read in verse 25.

For their part, the Gentiles are warned not to boast 'against the (Jewish) branches', as these were broken off 'because of unbelief'[3] concerning their Messiah. So the apostle Paul says to the Gentiles in verses 20-22:

> 'Be not highminded, but fear: for if God spared not the natural branches (the Jews), **take heed lest He also spare not thee.** Behold therefore the goodness and severity of God: on them which fell (the Jews), severity; but towards thee, goodness, **if thou continue in His goodness: otherwise thou also shalt be cut off.'**

(The whole of Romans 11 should be carefully read in order to enter into the full context of these verses which were so emphasized at that time by the Spirit of God quickening them to us.)

Now the God who had given the instruction about the 40 days took particular care to see that it was carried out exactly as He required. The Queen's Hall, in the West End of London, was found to be available on the evening of Tuesday May 2nd, and was accordingly reserved for that date. Then full double-column advertisements of the Meeting had to be drawn up for insertion in all but two of the London daily and evening papers and several provincial ones. It was realised that many millions of people in all

---

[3] Romans 11: 18 & 20

walks of life, at home and abroad, would be reached by this means and full advantage was taken of this space in the press to convey the warning in suitable terms.

Although we were not to know it until some three years later, all Heaven was aware that May 2nd 1933 was a date of no mean significance! It was, in fact, the 1,900th true solar anniversary of the day our glorious Lord and Master rose in triumph from the tomb in AD 33 and it was no doubt for this reason that things were allowed to take a somewhat extraordinary course in preparation for this testimony on the Resurrection anniversary.

May 2nd 1933

In the overruling of God, none of the daily papers could find space to insert the Notice calling the Queen's Hall Meeting until the evening of May 1st and the morning of the 2nd, so the actual address, which was to be read the same evening, could not be dictated until that day arrived, when it was at once put into print. This was not what any speaker would have planned, but the way all was perfectly carried out in the time available bore witness to the overshadowing of God. The gathering of some 2,000 people at a day's notice to fill a large hall in London through an announcement of such an unusual nature was also hardly a normal procedure!

The Paper read by Arthur E. Ware to a most attentive audience in the evening of May 2nd was immediately published and tens of thousands of copies were sold in the following weeks. The 32 page pamphlet bore the title 'THE IMMEDIATE PROSPECTS OF MANKIND', with the sub-title 'As it were, forty days and Christendom shall be cut off, as forewarned by St. Paul in the Roman Epistle, Chapter 11'.

In it, not only was the 'cutting off' of the Nations comprising Christendom positively asserted, but the second appearing of Christ was also heralded as due to take place 'just before or just after June 12th'. (The reason this part of the declaration was required to be made by the One overruling the whole matter was because *in His sight* it was a true statement. This will be more perfectly understood and entered into by every spiritual mind when the chronological facts and features to do with June 12th 1933 are unfolded.)

In the course of the address Mr Ware emphasised that the facts 'which could be amplified a hundredfold ... proved beyond question that God, who mocks no man', had caused him 'positively to affirm and declare' what he did about the excision of Christendom and the Lord's warning of action on His part in 40 days' time. *Knowing what these facts are,* none of the company who stood with him have ever had any qualms about what was then said.

Predictably, during the forty days which followed this Meeting, the popular press made much of the sensational side of the matter, which was also reported in the foreign and colonial news media, so that the minds of millions were focused upon the date of June 12th.

The Hand Of God Revealed

We must now take note of the following facts which reveal the hand of God in this matter.

It was not until after the notices calling the May 2nd meeting had gone into print that a fact was divulged by the press which began to throw light on why God had so specifically caused 'June 12th' to be named, even 200 days beforehand, at the November 25th meeting. This was that on April 29th the date had been fixed for a coming 'World Monetary and Economic Conference', which the League of Nations had found it necessary to arrange in an attempt to meet the dire consequences of the great depression which had overtaken the world since November 1929. It was said that the Preparatory Commission of Experts had met for the first time in November 1932, and now the date fixed for this Conference was to be June 12th 1933.

The Significance of this Second Tower of Babel

Never before June 12th 1933 had all the nations of the earth been called to assemble themselves together in one place, the one exception, of course, being before they assumed separate nationality, after the Tower of Babel. (For the story of this, see Genesis 11: 1-9). But in 1933 a fearful necessity compelled this action, as commerce of all kinds had sunk to such a low level.

Many nations had had to abandon the gold standard, and their currencies had become utterly unstable. So alarming had conditions become that a supreme effort was needed to right them, and the result was the birth of this great conference which was to embrace all the nations of the world.

During the forty days to June 12th, that is on May 23rd, a meeting was held at the Lyceum Theatre London, when a further paper was read and afterwards published, entitled 'THE WORLD'S SECOND TOWER OF BABEL AND ITS RESULTS'. A leading article in the Daily Mail of the previous day was quoted, which is worth recalling. It opened as follows:

> 'Only three weeks remain before the World Economic Conference meets in London to deal with an emergency for which there is no parallel in history. To that gathering representatives from sixty-six countries, ranging from the Soviet Union to Guatemala, have been invited. Their task will be to **save the world from disaster.** The existing depression is the worst ever known ...'.

When the day of June 12th arrived, the World Monetary and Economic Conference duly met in the Geological Museum, Kensington, and was opened at 3 pm by King George V and the British Prime Minister (Ramsey MacDonald) who was the President of the Conference. As 'The Times' commented on the following day, it was essentially a Conference of Governments — 'of all the governments of the world'.

There were sixty-six nations that met on this twelfth day of the sixth month in 1933, and the number gathered for the official dinner that evening, so the Press stated, was six hundred. Their intention was to build an economic structure which would unite the whole world; but, like a second Tower of Babel, history has to record that this great Conference became a disasterous failure, and broke up in confusion after some six weeks. Few will need to be reminded that six years later, in 1939, the last hope of world unity was taken away with the outbreak of the Second World War — so that then, instead of the world becoming 'an economic unit', as Ramsey MacDonald had hoped, it was riven asunder, with its two great halves implacably opposing one another, and every prospect of genuine peace vanished from the minds of spiritually discerning people.

CHAPTER FOUR

The Nations Forget God

June 12th 1933

Before describing what actually took place, as the Heavens observed it, on June 12th, it is opportune to disclose the true meaning of this date, as it afterwards came to light in research which lasted some four years.

Through the writings of one of the early Brethren, Sir Edward Denny, Bart., whose works had been in print for half a century, a full understanding was granted of the divine principle governing the measurement of time by 'Jubilee' cycles of 49 years, as shown in Leviticus 25[‡]. As soon as this was applied and it was also seen that, prior to the Exodus from Egypt, the years recorded in Scripture had been lunar and nor solar[*], it became possible to trace time perfectly from Genesis 1 through to the end of those well-known 'seventy weeks' or 490 years of Daniel 9: 24-26. It was clear from this prophecy of Daniel that 'Messiah the Prince' had been proclaimed by John the Baptist seven years before he was 'cut off', that is, put to death and the year when John's testimony commenced was given in Luke 3: 1 as 'the fifteenth year of the reign (*lit.* leadership) of Tiberius Caesar'. As Tiberius had been appointed 'leader' of the army by Augustus Caesar in AD 12, his 'fifteenth year' as such was AD 26. When time was calculated, according to the Bible records, from Genesis 1 to this year, AD 26, **it was found that a total of 4,100 solar years had accumulated.**

Then came the most important seven years in history, so far as God was concerned, when His 'only begotten Son'[1] was being presented to men and 'went in and out among us', as Luke expresses it in Acts 1: 21, defining the time as 'beginning from the

---

baptism of John, unto that same day that He was taken up from us'[2]. (This period we later found was exactly seven years and seven weeks.)

After the day of Christ's Ascension, **1,900 solar years ran their course to the day of June 12th 1933.**

This meant that in 1933 — apart from the seven years just mentioned, when the sinless Son of God was heralded by the Baptist and trod this earth to the glory of His Heavenly Father — **the history of our fallen race according to the Bible had registered just 6,000 solar years.** (The exact figure of 6,000 Julian solar years from the Fall of Adam to the day and hour of the opening of the World Economic Conference on June 12th at 3 pm was eventually perfectly established from the Scriptures.)[‡]

It was mentioned in our previous Chapter that the 40 days to June 12th were subsequently discovered to be the last 40 days of an era of 40 Jubilee years from the opening of the dispensation in AD 33. This fact came to light after the great key to the understanding of the Bible's chronology had been revealed. The key was that God had only dealt with the human race, from Adam onwards, on the ground of 'Forgiveness, as the result of Redemption'. Many are familiar with the answer Jesus gave to Peter in Matthew 18: 22 concerning 'forgiveness' when He said, 'I say not unto thee, until seven times; but **until seventy times seven'** that is, until 490 times. It was found that the reason why hundreds, if not thousands, of chronologers and students of Scripture had found themselves entirely baffled when they tried to get some kind of accurate and consecutive build-up of the time periods given in the Bible was because without the use of the 'key' in reliance upon the leading of the Spirit of Truth nothing could fully fall into place. (The result was that practically every one ended up with a different set of figures.)

By the use of the key, however, the absolute perfection of the true timing of history could come to light, as should be abundantly proved in our later pages. But none of this was known to the few who had staked everything on their direct leading of God by giving the warning beforehand concerning June 12th 1933. They had simply acted in faith and obedience to the Holy Spirit.

What then happened on June 12th 1933 when, for the first time, all the separate nations of the earth (as represented by

[2] Acts 1: 22
[‡] See Appendix 8 on page 183

members of their several governments) came together into one place?

The Conference duly opened at 3 pm and it was then that God gave Britain, whose Sovereign bore the title 'Defender of the Faith' her great opportunity to be His witness to the nations of the world. In his opening address, King George V said:

> 'I believe this to be the first time in history that any Sovereign has presided at the opening of a Conference of all the nations of the world. It cannot be beyond the power of man, so to use the vast resources of the world as to ensure the material progress of civilisation'.

'All the nations ... forget God'
(Psalm 9: 17)

In those days, among so-called 'Christian' nations at such a gathering as this, there would have been at least an official, or formal, acknowledgement of the Godhead and the asking of His blessing; but it is an amazing fact that on this first occasion in history when the whole human race was representively assembled in one place, God's Holy Name and that of His Son Jesus Christ — 'the Saviour of the World'[3] — were not given so much as a single mention in all the opening speeches of the delegates of the leading Governments of the world.

Because the King's opening speech was being broadcast to hundreds of millions all over the earth, there is little doubt that it had been decided by his Government to avoid any mention of the one true God who might not be acceptable to all races — but, whatever the cause of this omission, one thing stood out in stark clarity: the nations of the World were providing positive evidence to Heaven that their leaders had 'forgotten God' and were therefore, *demonstrating to the universe that they were no longer continuing in His goodness.* We remember again the warning of Romans 11: 22 **'Continue in His goodness; otherwise thou also shalt be cut off'.**

(Very shortly after the Conference, while some of the little company were in prayer, the Lord revealed that He had fulfilled 'the counsel of His messengers'[4] and His word came clearly: 'The nations have been cut off'.)

---

[3] John 4: 42   [4] Isaiah 44: 26

Like His action then 'the fig tree' (Israel) was 'cut down', after their Sanhedrin had stoned Stephen at the end of that last 'year', which Jesus had spoken of in parable in Luke 13: 6-9, this was a judicial enactment in Heaven, but the effects of the 'cutting-off' were not long in making themselves felt upon the earth.

An important fact to note before continuing is that June 12th 1933 was **exactly four times 'seventy times seven' years** (1,960 calendar lunar years of 354 days) from the day Stephen was murdered (see Acts 7). This was October 12th AD 33 — the actual date when Israel, as a nation, confirmed by this act the rejection of their Messiah. So God had given the Gentile world His four 'times of forgiveness' from the day when He 'cut down' the Jewish 'fig tree' to the day when the Nations also were 'cut off'. We should note that it was an official governmental assembly (the Sanhedrin) that rejected the testimony of the Holy Ghost, through Stephen, and it was an official assembly of the whole Gentile world that treated its Creator as though He did not exist in spite of the warning in His Name, given in the same city just 40 days beforehand.

And what of the Christian Church? What was its reaction to this disturbing testimony and reminder of Romans 11: 22? In the main they mocked and derided the warning which had been given — some attributing it to the devil, while others later confessed that they had held their hand until after the date had passed in case, by chance, the matter was of God. This was hardly to be wondered at as, having no 'understanding of the times'[5] the masses of God's children were ignorant of His ways and oblivious of the seriousness of the days they were then entering.

---

[5] 1 Chronicles 12: 32

CHAPTER FIVE

The Consequences of 'Forgetting God'

The Consummation of The Age

'The judgments of the Lord are true and righteous altogether'   (Psalm 19: 9)

With the complete failure of the conference and with no expectation of any material benefit for Germany — the hardest hit country after the First World War — that nation's hopes became centred in the person of Adolf Hitler, who had already become Chancellor the previous January and, with a sufficiently massive vote of the German people behind him, was to be seated firmly in the saddle by November 12th 1933 — just fifteen years after the Armistice in 1918.

God's answer to the studied insult of the whole Gentile world was simple and clear. The Nations had given Him, so to speak, 'the cut direct' on June 12th 1933 and treated 'the Saviour of the world' as though He did not exist. Therefore, as these Gentiles had so positively declared to the heavens by their governments that they set no value whatsoever upon 'the goodness of God', He, for His part, would now allow them to go their own way. They would soon discover at what a cost they had ignored their Creator!

The Handwriting Upon The Wall   *(Daniel 5)*
'God hath numbered thy kingdom and finished it' (verse 26)

We must again emphasise that it was God who had caused the

most positive warning to be given to the world, forty days beforehand, in the same city as was chosen for the assembly of all these nations, concerning the ominous significance of this date of June 12th. In spite of this warning, not only the King's speech, but Ramsay MacDonald's Presidential Address which immediately followed it, in the first hour of the Conference, had carefully omitted God's Name from any reference, as did all the speeches at the inaugural dinner that same evening at which six hundred persons were gathered.

Because of this omission, our minds are inevitably turned to a counterpart scene which is recorded in Daniel 5: 23 — after the handwriting had appeared upon the wall of Belshazzar's palace in Babylon, telling that monarch that *'God hath numbered thy kingdom and finished it'*. This was at the end of the 70 years of Babylon's history, as measured from the first seige of Jerusalem by Nebuchadnezzar (Daniel 1: 1).

Belshazzar's Feast

In Daniel 5 we have picture for us a banquet at which 'the gods of silver, and gold, of brass, iron, wood and of stone' (verse 23) are the real objects of worship; but at the same time the 'golden vessels that were taken out of the temple of the house of God' (verse 3) are being used, showing the same mixture of materialism and religion and an acquaintance with the things of the true God, as characterises Christendom today. In his interpretation of the mysterious 'handwriting', the prophet Daniel recalls Nebuchadnezzar's experience during the 'seven times' of his alienation from God (see verses 18-23) and continues — 'And thou ... O Belshazzar, hast not humbled thine heart, though thou knewest all this'. But the solemn words of Daniel, to which we have to draw particular attention, are these: 'Thy God in whose hand thy breath is, and whose are all thy ways, *hast thou not glorified'.*

Belshazzar's sin was the sin of omission, the sin of 'forgetting God' and with this king, as we know from the end of the chapter, judgment was executed without delay, for 'in that night was Belshazzar the King of the Chaldeans slain'.

As we have said, the result of this 'apostasy' — that is, ignoring God and leaving Him out of their counsels entirely — was that in six weeks the World Monetary and Economic Conference had broken down and had to adjourn *sine die*. Several years later, Viscount Bruce of Melbourne, commenting on this breakdown in a broadcast, said:

'The economic and financial crisis of 1929 spread throughout the world. It lasted for some years, and in 1933 the Monetary and Economic Conference was held in London. This Conference was one of the major tragedies of history. It achieved nothing'.

What then had really taken place with the passing of June 12th 1933 and what was the true significance of this obvious turning-point in world history, as we can now look back upon it in years of further economic crisis?

The Ending of a Dispensation
'The thing that is hid bringeth He forth to light' (Job 28: 11)

The thing that had been hidden from the little company whom God had called together to 'watch' His actions at the end of this age was that there was 'a time to every purpose under heaven'[1]. God, in other words, was a God of perfect order and had ample leisure for everything He did. And yet, not one of His purposes would be one day late in fulfilment.

The first thing that was shown was that there was a 'time of harvest'[2] and that **'the harvest is (lit.) the consummation of the age'***(Matthew 13: 39). *(Most emphatically this has nothing to do with 'the end of the world', as the King James Version erroneously translates verses 39 and 40.)* That a period of time was involved, over which the age would end, became clear from the words of Jesus in verse 30 of the same chapter: 'And in the time of harvest I will say to the reapers, "Gather ye together **first** the tares and bind them in bundles (in order) to burn them: but gather the wheat into My barn"'. And the expression 'gather the wheat' was literally 'bring together' or 'lead in' the wheat — a purpose which obviously requires time to perform. Our Lord perfectly explains what both 'wheat' and 'tares' signify in this parable.

It was quite clear, when we looked back to the first century of our era, that God had brought about a 'consummation' of what we might call 'the times of Israel', or Jewish history, over a period of

---

forty years, that is, between AD 33 and AD 73. It was then, as Josephus informs us, that the Roman War terminated with the fall of the fortress of Masada. Nothing, perhaps, is more poignant than to learn that the garrison of the last 960 Jews, holding out against the Romans, commited suicide to a man 'on the fifteenth day of the month Nisan' in AD 73 (see Whiston's Josephus; Wars of the Jews, Book VII, Chapter IX). This was, to the day, forty years after the suicide of Judas Iscariot, following the crucifixion of Jesus in AD 33.

The 'Days of Vengeance'

Another most significant fact is that the Roman War lasted for seven years, commencing after the Passover in the twelfth year of the reign of Nero, which was AD 66 — forty years from the beginning of the Baptist's ministry — and it is only too clear that Luke was referring to these seven years in his Gospel in the words 'For these be the days of vengeance, that all things which are written may be fulfilled'.[3] We may also recall the words of Jesus in John 2: 19: 'Destroy this temple ...'. This was said at the time of the Passover in AD 30 and, as is well known, it was **forty years later**, at the Passover in AD 70 that the Jews of Jerusalem and their temple were shut up to the desolating destruction that followed that very summer and of which Daniel himself had prophesied in his day.[4]

None of this, however, occupied the minds of those who had given the warning in 1933; only the dawning realisation that the world had entered a new phase in its history and that it was essential to understand all that God had concealed in His Word concerning *time*. We certainly knew well enough that if, as the writer of Proverbs 25: 2 has said, 'It is the glory of God *to conceal a thing'*, then whatever He had concealed would have to remain hidden until He, in His sovereignty, **revealed** it. But the Scripture did go on to say: 'the honour of kings is to **search out** a matter'!

So our course was clear — we must wait upon God until we received so positive an 'understanding of the times' that it would be possible to provide proof to all men that the warning we had given as to His action on June 12th 1933 had been a matter accomplished entirely under His direction.

---

[3] Luke 21: 20-24, esp. verse 22
[4] Daniel 9: 24-27, esp. verse 26

The Wonderful Key of The Principle of Forgiveness in Time Cycles

As has been stated, the key which began to unlock the Bible's time secrets was the fact the God measures the course of man's history on the earth according to the principle of *forgiveness* — that is, in cycles of 'seventy times seven'[5] years. In order to prove this He provides us with an apparently insoluble difficulty in 1 Kings 6: 1, for we are told here that it was 'in the 480th year' after the Exodus that Solomon commenced to build the house of the Lord.

It has been found quite impossible to reconcile this statement with that of Paul in Acts 13: 20, where the apostle says that, after the dividing of the Land of Canaan among the tribes (some 47 years after the Exodus) God 'gave unto them judges about the space of 450 years, until Samuel the prophet'. He then goes on to speak of the 40 years of Saul after which, as we know, David reigned for 40 years before Solomon came to the throne. Paul's statement also confirms the actual total of years which can be traced through the books of Judges, 1 Samuel and 1 Kings and which clearly amounts to a very much greater span of time that '480 years'. There is obviously a very large error somewhere in one or other of these inspired statements, if we are expected to take them both literally as recording the time which elapsed between the Exodus and the foundation of the Temple of Solomon.

The critics of the Bible, of course, have always rejoiced to see a 'contradiction' like this and have viewed it as a devastating blow for those who held to 'the Divine inspiration of the Holy Scriptures', but God had quite a definite purpose in bringing man's natural understanding of the Bible's chronology to a sudden halt at this point in the sacred Record. He had something wonderful to reveal.

The Key to The Enigma

Over a century ago, the servant of God we have already mentioned, Sir Edward Denny, was allowed to see the simple solution to the conundrum. Having made a study of the 25th chapter of Leviticus, he knew that it was God's practice to measure time in Jubilee cycles of 49 years[‡]. He also saw that the last ten

---

[5] Matthew 18: 22
[‡] See Chart 5 on page 190

cycles of 49 years (490) to the crucifixion of Christ had been the subject of a revelation by the angel Gabriel to the prophet Daniel *(see the closing verses of Daniel 9, and Chart 1 on page 186)*.

So, Sir Edward argued that if the last 490 years to Christ (spoken of as 'seventy weeks' of years) had marked off the time from the restoration of Jerusalem under Nehemiah, then it looked clearly as if the first 490 years of Israel's national history, from the Exodus to the dedication of the Temple in the 14th year of Solomon (ten years after the foundation was laid), would just as definitely have been patterned out by God.[‡] At any rate, the Scripture stated quite unequivocally 'the 480th year' was the 4th year of Solomon[6].

But how could Paul's '450 years' be a true statement of fact? Sir Edward was led to the words of Jesus in Matthew 18: 22 where the Lord answers Peter's question on the subject of forgiveness:

'Jesus saith unto him, "I say not unto thee, until seven times: but, until **seventy times seven**"'.

Here was God's answer to the difficulty. The 70 times 7 years had relation to *the forgiveness of God,* while He was in the midst of His people and accepting their sacrifices — all of which were a foreview of the sacrifice of Christ. Not a moment of this time could He be **punishing** them in the same way as when He gave them up into the hands of their enemies; and time and again He had had to do this in the days of Judges.

Sir Edward Denny then calculated the total of the seven periods of servitude recorded between Judges 3: 8 and 1 Samuel 7: 2-3 and found it to be 131 years. **All this he saw was time outside of the Jubilee cycles of Redemption and Forgiveness.** This was a revolutionary concept and meant that the whole era from the Exodus to the dedication of Solomon's Temple was actually 621 years. Paul's '450 years' clearly referred to *the actual time that had elapsed* and reckoned in the years of punishment and servitude as well.[‡]

So God had used a 'contradiction' for the purpose of revealing a secret. He had brought to light a *key* and the question was, would this same key turn in the lock in other parts of the Chronology and what would it reveal?

[‡] See Chart 3 on page 188   [6] 1 Kings 6: 1
(This refers to both [‡] above)

CHAPTER SIX

Some Keys to the Understanding of God's Calendar

It was obvious that the next part of the Bible's time structure to be examined was the era of the Kings of Judah and the period on to the beginning of the 'seventy weeks'[1] or 490 years to Christ, which commenced in Nehemiah's day. Would this second division of Israel's national history also turn out to be 'seventy weeks' of years? After light had been received as to the Divine principles of measurement employed, there was little difficulty in reckoning up the regnal years of the kings of Judah and calculating this era with accuracy. The total was found to be 560 years.

With the Key in hand, it was not difficult to unlock this part of the Bible's chronology, for who could be ignorant of the great 'seventy years'[2] of the Babylonian Captivity? Plainly these were years of punishment **outside** of God's 'seventy times seven' or 490 years of forgiveness; so once again in the Chronology of Redemption there stood out a clear 490-year period.

This meant that the God of Israel had been in relationship with His people, on the ground of Redemption, for *three times* 490 (or 1,470) years between the Exodus from Egypt and the Cross of Calvary.

It was interesting to see that Jacob, whose name was changed to *'Israel'*[3] was the one who said to God that of all he possessed he would surely 'give *the tenth* unto Thee'. We are told that 'the whole age of Jacob was 147 years'[4]. So his age was exactly the tenth part of the length of Israel's national history, while they were in covenant relationship with God. God is evidently the God of design in history as He is in nature.

---

[1] Daniel 9: 24
[2] Daniel 9: 2
[3] Genesis 32: 28
[4] Genesis 28: 22 & 47: 28

(It should be mentioned that the date of the Exodus, which is somewhat earlier than is generally held by modern historians, has been abundantly confirmed in a multiplicity of ways by the Bible's chronology and also by research into Egyptian Chronology in recent years — see 'Ages In Chaos' by I. Velikovsky.)

The next question was whether this same time-scene of reckoning by Jubilee was carried back prior to the Exodus, that is, to the birth of Abram, the father of the Jewish race.[‡] The well-known total of 505 years (which was simple to calculate) was, of course, 15 years more than the required 490 years, but it did not take long to be shown by the Spirit of God that there was a break in the continuity of this period — a delay in the purpose of God, brought about by an act on Abram's part which was to have disasterous consequences right down the course of history even to our own day. This was when Abram 'hearkened to the voice of Sarai'[5] and married Hagar the Egyptian when he was 85 years old.

It was 15 years that Abram had to wait before Isaac, the son of promise, came and no reader of Scripture can be ignorant of God's thoughts concerning Isaac, and concerning Ishmael also (see Genesis 16 to 21). Isaac was *the seed* through whom the Redeemer was destined to come[6], and for Abram to take Hagar and beget Ishmael was an attempt to fulfill the promise of God by natural means, and by so doing to leave the path of faith and obedience. So these 15 years too, fell *outside* the 10 Jubilee cycles which measure the first of the *four* periods of 490 years from the birth of Abram to the Cross of Calvary. (Isaac was born when Abram was 100 years old[7].)

The establishing from Scripture of these four exact divisions of 490 years was a tremendous discovery but where was it going to lead? Were we going to see that God had planned **all history**, right down from Adam, on the basis of these Jubilee cycles of 49 years? Were we, in fact, going to find that the Bible — the immutable Word of the Living God — contained within its covers *the answer* to the everlasting search of man for his Creator? 'How can there be a God?' asks the scientist, 'We can't find one and we certainly are not interested in the subjectionist who can only talk about his own experience. Where is there positive *evidence of God as a person* and not just a creative force — that is what we want to see?'

As we pondered these things in the middle 1930's, the

[‡] See Chart 2 on page 187
[5] Genesis 16: 2-3
[6] Genesis 21: 12 & Romans 9: 7
[7] Genesis 21: 5

evidence began to mount. The terminal datings of the First World War of 1914-1918 and such interpositions as the great Quetta earthquake of 1935‡, were to be seen exactly timed as part of the Plan of the Ages which was beginning to come into view, and we realised that we must press on and leave no stone unturned, so as to be able eventually to present to our fellow men the proof that the Bible's figures were 'true from the beginning'.

But far more than this was in the mind of Almighty God.

'The Eternal Purpose'

The 'plan of the ages' or 'purpose of the ages', as the words in Ephesians 3: 11 should be translated, was centred 'in Christ Jesus our Lord', and it is the purpose of God to reveal His Son to our dying civilization — and particularly to His restored Israel — and also to reveal all those secrets concerning time to do with His birth and ministry and His sacrificial death and resurrection which had been lost to memory by His Church after the apostles departed. Perhaps more important still for our generation was the fact that, until this priceless knowledge was restored to the members of His Body, the Church, it would be impossible for knowledge to be released concerning the timing and manner of His return — a subject which is increasingly occupying the thoughts of all who 'love His appearing'[8] in the present day.

So the research went on and, as is usual with those who find themselves in 'the school of God', from the first it was necessary to abide by the rules of the school — that is, to live like the early disciples of the first century who were in the main unencumbered by their possessions. For ourselves, this meant living in furnished houses and being in dependence upon God for all resources, as we also were for the wisdom necessary to understand His Word alright.

About The Calendar

As already mentioned, one basic reason why none had ever been able to produce from the Bible a record of time which could be seen to be accurate to the day, as well as palpably true — that is, perfectly revealing the Plan of Redemption — was that God's use

---

‡ See Chapter 20
[8] 2 Timothy 4: 8

of the 49-year cycle and the 'fiftieth year' (called the 'Jubilee' in Leviticus 25) had never really been understood[‡].

A second 'secret' was the Divine use of the Calendar Lunar Year of 354 days throughout the whole course of time. Of course, it was clear that Israel kept their Passovers in the Spring, as they do today, and this demands the insertion, or 'intercalation' of months (or 'moons') every three or two years. Reference to a modern Jewish calendar will show that generally, in the third, sixth and eighth years, one of these intercalary months has to be inserted, so as to keep the first month, Nisan, in the Spring season. This is because our solar year of 365¼ days is 11¼ days longer than the 12 lunar months.

But the Bible never acknowledges the existence of a 'thirteenth' month and it is clear that with God the year is always one of twelve 'moons' (the Hebrew word for month is literally 'new moon'). The order of days in the 12 months is, invariably, 30 days in the first month, 29 in the second, 30 in the third and in that alternation throughout the year. Between the Exodus and New Testament days the 'intercalary' 13th months were simply gaps of 30 (or often 31) days in the Calendar, while Israel waited to see the New Moon which signalled the incoming of their New Year. This had to be when the barley was ready — the first month being called 'Abib' or 'green ears'[9] but later, 'Nisan'. The present fixed Jewish Calendar, with many innovations, such as 353 or 355 days in their 'Common' years, has no warrant in the Bible and was brought in around the fourth century AD. It has been acknowledged that this present system often has the Nisan or first month positioned too early in the Spring and that in Bible times the year would have commenced a month later.

There is a divine reason why God kept to the 354-day year in His reckoning of time in Scripture and this will be discussed in later pages.

During the past century many thousands of Christians have followed writers who have attempted to build up a chronology with 'years' of 360 days. Nowhere in Scripture, however, is a period of 360 days ever called a 'year' but always a 'time' — like the seven 'times' of Daniel 4, or the 'time, and times, and half a time' of Revelation 12: 14. In verse 6 of this chapter, the other three and a half 'times' are shown to be equal to '1,260 days', which confirms

[‡] See Chart 5 on page 190
[9] Exodus 13: 4

that a single 'time' is 360 days.[*]

An interesting and instructive illustration of the 'year' is to be found in the Genesis account of the Flood, this being the first occasion where 'months' (*lit.* 'new moons') are spoken of in the Bible. The Flood commenced on 'the 17th day' of 'the 2nd month'[10] and Noah left the Ark on 'the 27th day' of 'the 2nd month'[11], exactly one solar year later, that is, inclusively, one 354-day year and 11 days from the Flood's beginning.

---

[*] See also Note 1 on page 184   [11] Genesis 8: 14
[10] Genesis 7: 11

CHAPTER SEVEN

The Week of Creation Patterns All Time

'Ye shall hallow THE FIFTIETH YEAR, and proclaim liberty thoughout all the land ... it shall be a Jubilee unto you'
(Leviticus 25: 10)

As soon as we begin to consider what lies at the heart of the Bible's chronology, we find it is the subject of **redemption**. And whenever 'chronology' is divorced from redemption and the great purposes of God, and made a matter of interest and intellectual curiosity, it loses its value for the spiritual life. But, conversely, it is true to say that without being in possession of the real time-programme of God's works, it is never possible to see redemption clearly in His light, for it is positively related to time in the Bible; a fact few have recognised.

In exactly the same way as the bones — when they are in joint — are necessary to keep the flesh of the body in its perfect form and stature so, obviously, is a true chronology a necessity to history. Once history is deprived of its true timing, it is often liable to be dismissed as a fable, and we know this is how the world, the religious world not excepted, has treated much of its sacred history, especially in Genesis. Also, when it comes to understanding the Bible's prophecies, what are these, if not history written beforehand? If the knowledge of time is necessary to perceive the true outline of history, then it is just as necessary for the understanding of prophecy.

We all, however, can appreciate the need for God to keep the true timing of His purposes secret until the moment of their fulfilment, or even to hide it until the events have passed into history, and we can look back upon them and glorify God for the perfection of His working.

If we are then to begin to understand *time* in the Bible, we must study Leviticus 25, where the Mind of our Creator-God is unfolded on this infinitely important subject. And the very first question we must ask is: Why was it so important for Israel to count time accurately and, not only to observe each *sabbath day*, but also to keep each *seventh year* as *'a sabbath of rest* unto the land'? And why also, when this whole system of things has apparently passed away, should it be so important for the present-day, Spirit-filled members of the Church of God to know anything about such matters? Are these things really so vital that they should occupy our time and attention in a day of desperate world crisis like the present?

Those who have given any credence to what we have already written will have some idea at least of the reason but it may be wise to answer the above questions with the actual words of Barnabas, who was the Spirit-filled companion of the apostle Paul, and who is first mentioned in Acts 4: 36. (The Epistle of Barnabas lays a greater claim to canonical authority than most other writings in the Apochryphal New Testament and we quote it now to show what was current teaching in Apostolic times.) He writes in chapter 15 of his Epistle:

> 'Also keep the Lord's sabbath holy, with clean hands and a pure heart ... what is said at the very beginning of Creation about the sabbath, is this, "In six days God created the works of His hands and finished them on the seventh day; and He rested on that day, and sanctified it".

> 'Notice particularly, my children, the significance of, "He finished them in six days". What that means is, that He is going to bring the world to an end in six thousand years, since with Him one day means a thousand years; witness His own saying, "Behold, a day of the Lord shall be as a thousand years". Therefore, my children, in six days — six thousand years, that is — there is going to be an end of everything.

> 'After that, "He rested on the seventh day" indicates that when His Son returns, He will put an end to the years of the Lawless One, pass sentence on the godless ... and then, on the seventh day, enter into His true rest'.

This is an amazing statement for apostolic times, when 4,000 years had only just reached their close! Could the great secret really have been disclosed **then** — that the end of 6,000 years was to bring in the Millennial Kingdom of Christ — God's *sabbath 'thousand years'* that John later refers to no less than six times in Revelation 20? Well, we can only see how forcibly the Holy Ghost affirms in 2 Peter 3: 8, that we should *'be not ignorant of this one thing'* — that is, 'that one day is with the Lord as a thousand years and a thousand years as one day' — whatever else we may be willing to be ignorant of! *(See Chart 4 on page 189.)*

This is truly a powerful commentary on June 12th 1933, when the whole world and the whole Church were together *ignorant* of the fact that *six days* of *1,000 solar years* had come to completion and that 'the day of the Lord' (as far as the solar measurement was concerned) had indeed come 'as a thief in the night', exactly as both Peter (2 Peter 3: 10) and Paul (1 Thessalonians 5: 2-3) had warned would be the case!

Leviticus 25 begins with instruction concerning the 'seventh year' or the 'sabbath of rest' for the land. God evidently wanted Israel to be on the watch for the end of the six thousand years and so made them keep 'sabbath' days and years continuously throughout their generations. But after this the chapter goes on to unfold a further seven-fold measurement: 'Thou shalt number *seven sabbaths* of years unto thee, seven times seven years; and the space of the seven sabbaths of years shall be unto thee *forty and nine years'* (verse 8). *(See Chart 5 on page 190.)*

We have had to focus attention upon the seven-fold principle of divine measurement in order to learn just how God regards 'the fiftieth year' and what its place is in the scheme of time.

First of all, we have to answer the question, *why* does God have everything to do with *time* measured in *sevens?* We see 7 days, 7 weeks, 7 months, 7 years, and then 7 times seven years, 70 times 7 years — obviously, there is a reason for such a design. Well, as we have seen, it was accepted in Apostolic times that 7,000 *years* was the limit with God, and that after this great *week of time* there would be 'a new heaven and a new earth'[1], where the sun and moon would no more be needed, as the last two chapters of the Bible so clearly show. Peter, in his second epistle (chapter 3: 10) actually describes what the astronomers call a 'Nova', which is

---

[1] Revelation 21: 1

the sudden flaring up of a bright star (such as our sun); this is undoubtedly the means by which our present earth will be brought to an end.

We have gone into all this because 'the *eighth day'*, or all that follows the 7,000 years, is what we call 'eternity to come', as distinct from eternity that is past. It is not measured by 'time', it is *everlasting*, and we certainly cannot measure 'everlasting life'! *'Eight'* is the number related to 'resurrection' in the Bible and, as already mentioned, there are eight resurrections recorded in Scripture.

At the end of 'the day of the Lord' — the seventh thousand solar years which the Bible's chronology shows the world has already entered — we read in 1 Corinthians 15: 26, 'the last enemy' shall 'be destroyed', that is 'death'. So *seven* is the number related to *time* and *death*, and *eight* to resurrection and eternal life.

Now the year of Jubilee is *'the fiftieth year'*[2], just as the day of Pentecost is the *fiftieth day*. As it follows 7 times 7 years, the Jubilee is an *eighth* year and it has this most remarkable feature in the Chronology of Redemption, as we will call the Jubilee Chronology — **it cannot be measured as forming an addition to time**. We see from the chapter (Leviticus 25) that this 'fiftieth year' starts in the seventh month of the forty-ninth year of the cycle, and it runs its course as 'a full year' (verse 30), thus ending in the seventh month of the first year of the succeeding forty-nine. The result is that, while man measures only 49 years, God looks upon each cycle as containing a '50th year' **which only *He* reckons**.

From the foregoing we can see that each 490 years we have outlined in earlier pages, from the birth of Abram onwards, was to God 500 years, so that the four such divisions of Israel's history to the death and resurrection of Christ were reckoned by God as *2,000 years*, or *forty Jubilee years*.

Without stopping now to go into the wonderful astronomical and calendar design of the Jubilee cycle, we must continue our search and discover how God has concealed the first great era of *2,000 years* or *forty Jubilee years* in the Bible's chronology, from Adam to Abram.

It is, indeed, a sobering thought that God has managed to hide the true course of time in His Word by so simple a method as to use two different chronologies which, unless they were discerned

---

[2] Leviticus 25: 11 and
   see Chart 5 on page 190

and separated from each other, rendered it totally impossible to compute time accurately and measure the true age of our race from that far-off beginning in Genesis 1.

CHAPTER EIGHT

The Beginnings in Genesis

Before attempting the simple reckoning of years, as given in the two chronological tables of the 5th and 11th chapters of Genesis, we must observe the way the Spirit of God has presented the facts relating to our present creation, because of what lies concealed beneath the surface of the Scriptures.

'Darkness was upon the face of the deep'

The first picture that we are given of this earth in Genesis 1: 2 is that of a complete overthrow — an absolute desolation — and it is of little use for us to embark upon the exact measurement of *time* in the Bible unless we understand that God, in His Word, is describing for us a new beginning, after drawing the curtain of obscurity over a past which He intends to blot out completely from our view.

When we read in verse 2 that 'the earth was without form, and void', we can find the same Hebrew words used in Jeremiah 4: 23 where a scene of unmitigated judgment is described. Why has God had to judge the earth and make it 'waste' and 'desolate' (as the words translated 'without form, and void' really imply). Why was there 'darkness' and why has the whole planet been baptised in water, so that every trace of the former world has been submerged? We know that God had to do this a second time in the days of Noah, on account of the total corruption of the human race — the difference in that case being that 'eight souls were saved by water', as we are told in 1 Peter 3: 20.

We have to refer to other parts of the Divine revelation for the answer. In Isaiah 45: 18 we find that God did not originally create the earth a waste (or 'in vain') for 'He formed it to be inhabited'. And if we study the glimpses we are given in Isaiah 14: 12-14 and Ezekiel 28: 1-19, which describe the former office of Satan, we find that this greatest-of-all created intelligences once bore the name of 'Lucifer', which means 'Light-bringer'. Very clearly, this appointment was to a former creation, before this great angel fell through pride, for we are told that it was his very 'brightness' which was his undoing (v 17), as he drew attention to himself, and not to God.

In 2 Peter 3: 3-7 we are briefly informed that the 'scoffers' of 'the last days' of our age think in terms of an ordered progression of all things continuing 'as they were from the beginning of the creation'. This is, of course, a reference to evolutionary teaching, as it covers the earth today. But this they ignore, that 'by the word of God the heavens were of old, and the earth standing out of the water and in the water: whereby the world that then was, being overflowed with water, perished'. After this we are told about the ultimate destruction by fire of 'the heavens and the earth, which are now'.

From all this we see that when Satan fell he brought down a former creation which he has corrupted into darkness, judgment and death; and God would have the very memory of it blotted out before He commenced the new purpose with Adam and Eve. In other words, we have to think in terms of a *baptism — followed by a new creation*, as we read the account in Genesis 1. (There is little doubt that the origin of demons may be traced to the former creation, for these are earth-bound disembodied spirits, under Satan, which are ever seeking to find an entry into the bodies of the inhabitants of this world.)

The New Order in Genesis

As we have said, God had in view a New Creation, and so He pictures what He has in view in the first seven days of the Bible's narrative. These days are indeed the ground plan, so to speak, of His actings in the following 7,000 years. The whole Bible witnesses to this fact and, once the Church of God has awakened to the reality that the great 'six days' (that is, 6,000 years) are now at an end, and that 'the Kingdom' which millions have prayed for is about to 'come' and translate this planet from being a shambles into a scene of blessing and enlightenment for the whole of our race, a vast transformation will take place in the lives of Christians the world over — if we may judge from the wording of Matthew 25: 1-13, which is one of several of our Lord's end-time parables now about to be fulfilled.

So in the first six days of the Bible we see God at work to prepare the earth for two persons (Adam and Eve) who prefigure Christ and the Church which is His Body, and revealing exactly what He intends to perform in 6,000 years — and here we must carefully note that the six days of Genesis typify the 6,000 years of the Chronology of Redemption — the one measured by Jubilee cycles and not the 6,000 solar years which terminated in 1933. (We have to accustom ourselves to seeing time in different aspects, as God does, and to realise that in the realm of Chronology, as in every other of Holy Scripture, we need the assistance of the Holy Spirit to 'guide' us 'into all truth'[1].)

It is glorious to behold God's culminating work at the end of the six days in Eden, for it pictures so wonderfully the coming together of Christ and the Church. We find this all described in 1 Thessalonians 4: 13-17 and 1 Corinthians 15: 51-54. It is the final 'work' of God which brings the Christian dispensation to an end; for, just as He made the body of Adam from 'the dust of the ground'[2], so will God raise up from the dust every sleeping member of the Body of Christ. Yes, we believe God will take the actual 'dust' of those who have departed over these past two thousand years. We must see clearly that this precious 'Body' will not be complete until the Lord Jesus — 'the Head' — descends from heaven to be united with His members, every one of them, before the translation of the whole Church into Heaven. When He descends and 'the dead in Christ ... rise first[3], then 'the last Adam' — God's *second man ... the Lord from Heaven*'[4] — will, for the first time, stand complete, head and members, on this earth.

'It is not good that the man should be alone'

This wonderful picture in Genesis[5] would be totally incomplete without a '*Bride*' and so we see God has to make (or 'build') a woman, 'meet for him', from the very body of Adam, and His actual last 'work' of the six days is not accomplished until He has

---

[1] John 16: 13
[2] Genesis 2: 7
[3] 1 Thessalonians 4: 16
[4] 1 Corinthians 15: 45, 47
[5] Genesis 2: 18

'brought her unto the man' (verse 22). The name Eve in Hebrew means '*living*' and who can doubt that she is a vivid type of those 'which are alive and remain unto the coming of the Lord'[6]. No wonder God has to portray the grand objective of the 6,000 years at the very beginning of the Bible, for it is an event which will stagger the universe by its sheer immensity when it does take place. In preparation for it we behold the Spirit of God already at work, all over the earth, 'bringing the woman to the Man' — in other words, leading those who are to form the Bride of Christ into a wondrous love-union with Himself and separating them from everything else on earth as they are, one by one, 'filled with the Holy Ghost'[7]. Let all who are watching the speed of this final work of God remember that it is in preparation for the great marriage of Matthew 25 and that 'the time is at hand'.

There will be more to say about this swift work of the Spirit in later pages but we mention it now as we survey the end of the great six 'days' of 1,000 years. We hear the closing petition of Jesus, as His eyes looked on beyond Gethsemane and Calvary, to the glorious union now so shortly to be consummated: 'The glory which Thou gavest Me I have given them; that they may be one, even as we are one; I in them and Thou in Me, that they may be made perfect in one; *and that the world may know that Thou hast sent me'*. This prayer of John 17: 22-23 is the echo of Adam's words in the Garden: 'This is now bone of my bones, and flesh of my flesh'[8], and the same almighty hand that fashioned Eve at the end of those six days is now committed to the task of which the creation of this first woman was typical. 'Known unto God are all His works from the beginning of the world'[9].

The more it is realised that God performs all His works according to a timetable or 'purpose of the ages', the more amazing a Book does the Bible become and the smaller does man become, and the more is God glorified in all His works.

The Atonement (or Covering) in Eden

'Unto Adam ... and to his wife did the Lord God make coats of skins, and clothed them' (Genesis 3: 21). As this work of atonement (or 'covering') involved the shedding of blood, it marked the first step in the Plan of Redemption. This was in the

---

[6] 1 Thessalonians 4: 15　　[8] Genesis 2: 23
[7] Acts 2: 4　　[9] Acts 15: 18

evening of the day of Adam's fall. Death — the death of a clean animal — once again entered the Creation and so it was at this point that the years of Adam were timed to begin and the Chronology of Redemption began to run its course.

It is not now our purpose in this brief survey to go into the exact dating of events in this first part of the Bible's chronology — all of which, however, are possible for any to prove and check in due course, when the astronomical position has been laid bare. But it will be needful to mention certain time-patternings of God as we go forward from the fall of Adam and Eve on our chronological journey to the birth of Abram.

After a careful computation of the years given in the two genealogical tables of Genesis chapters 5 and 11, it was found that the years from Adam to the birth of Abram totalled 2,008. This showed that the excess above 4 times 490, or 1,960 years, was 48 years. Here was a place where it became necessary for light to be given 'from above' in order that we might know where, and why, God refused to reckon 48 years in the course of the Jubilee cycles.

In answer to prayer, this light came. It was, of course, between the death of Abel — when the first murder in history was committed — and the birth of Seth, when 'the seed' through whom the Redeemer was ultimately to come was restored, that these 48 years found there place. Now, although **faith** might accept and enter into the above fact, only the perfect and miraculous design of God in the chronology could demonstrate and prove it. Without going into too much detail, this is what the **design** brought to light.

The murder of Abel occurred some time during the course of Adam's first 130 years[11] but, unless our eyes are opened so that we see who it is that is pictured and typified in this first 'good shepherd' of Bible history, we shall be unable to uncover the chronological plan which God has concealed in the period up to the birth of Seth. God has not made His time-keeping a subject of interest for the mind, however fascinating this might be — it is by exact chronology that He has taught vital truth and confirmed the accuracy of the Holy Scriptures so that, in a day of apostasy and corruption such as the present, He might be able to face the world with proof, from within its own pages, that His 'Word is true from the beginning'[12], seeing that it is by the same Word that the world

[11] Genesis 4 — 5: 3
[12] Psalm 119: 160

is about to be judged.

As most will agree, Abel is a wonderful type of Jesus, 'the Good Shepherd'[13]. Just as Abel was slain by his own brother Cain, the Lord Jesus, as the Lamb of God, also became the antitype of Abel's offering of the firstlings of his flock by being put to death by His own brethren, the Jews. After what God Himself did at the fall of Adam and Eve, the sacrifice and death of Abel is thus the first representation of the sacrifice of Christ we find in the Bible.

When light was given on the timing of it, it was wonderful to see the dates and measurements confirm that Abel was born at the first *Jubilee* — that is, at the end of 49 years from the Fall of Adam — and that his life was *to the day* identical in length to that of Jesus up to His death on Calvary. The 48 years which then elapsed and which are *unreckoned* in the Redemption Chronology up to the day of Seth's birth, were an expression of the 48 hours, or two days, between the day of Christ's death and the opening of 'the third day' when He was raised up. It was very clear that if Abel was a type of Christ slain, then Seth — 'another seed instead of Abel, whom Cain slew'[14] — was a beautiful type of Christ restored, or risen from the dead.

When the whole plan was drawn up, there were even more striking features standing out plainly to prove that the truth had come to light, but it would not be fair to mention them now until it becomes possible to go into the calendar and astronomical details in full, enabling everything to be checked and measured with both solar and lunar years. The 48 years have had to be mentioned however, because they form an unreckoned excess over the first 1,960 years from Adam to Abram.

It was also found that the five months during which the waters of the Flood prevailed above the earth in Noah's day were not reckoned in the Chronology of Redemption because this was a period of universal judgment (see Genesis 7: 11 and 8: 14).

The Great Four Days or 4,000 Years of Redemption

With this discovery — that is, that between Adam and Abram the Redemption Chronology recorded exactly 1,960 years — the importance of the Bible's hidden time programme at last began to dawn. As we have seen above, God, who counts the 'fiftieth' or

---

[13] John 10: 11
[14] Genesis 4: 25

Jubilee years in His reckoning, looked upon these 1,960 years with their 40 years of Jubilee as making up a total of 2,000 years. This meant that from Adam to the death of Jesus at Calvary was a period which, *with God,* was precisely **four thousand years** in His concealed Chronology of Redemption. This was what a multitude of chronologers had been waiting to see — for the following reason.

This fact at last explained why at the Exodus God gave instruction that the lambs for the Passover were to be chosen and set apart on 'the tenth day of the first month' **to wait four days** before they were sacrificed in the evening of the fourteenth day. This keeping of the lambs four days before each Passover was to typify the *great four 'days' of a thousand years* that Jesus Himself would wait before, exactly at the appointed time, He would offer Himself up as 'the Lamb of God, which taketh away the sin of the world'[15] (see Exodus 12: 3-6).

It was no wonder that Almighty God required time in the Bible to be searched out and calculated with absolute precision. It was going to be by this means that He would glorify His Son, Jesus — causing both sun and moon to bow down before Him and fulfil their primary purpose, which was to be *'for signs'* [16] in relation to the person and work of Him, by whom and for whom all things were created. We must not forget also that the light of a perfected knowledge of *time,* as it shines out from the sacred record to illuminate the mighty work of Redemption, would have been revealed to no purpose nineteen hundred years ago when Israel was being cast off as a nation, but has obviously been reserved *for now* when she is being nationally restored and is yet destined to be God's light-bearer to the farthest corners of the earth. (Romans 11: 15 and 30-33 make it abundantly clear that, as we Gentiles have received mercy through the defection of Israel, this 'mercy' must now be restored to that people. In other words, *they* gave us the truth concerning *their Messiah, and now it is our turn to return the truth to them.)*

'Hath God cast away His people?' *(Romans 11)*

So that we may see at a glance the simple time-pattern of God's purposes for Israel, since they committed the terrible offence of rejecting their Messiah at His first Advent, let us turn to

---

[15] John 1: 29
[16] Genesis 1: 14

Hosea 5: 15 where we hear the Lord say:

> 'I will go and return to My place, till they acknowledge their offence, and seek My face: in their affliction they will seek Me early'.

Then in chapter 6: 1 we get the response of Israel:

> 'Come, and let us return unto the Lord: for He hath torn, and He will heal us; He hath smitten, and He will bind us up. *After two days* will He revive us: *in the third day* He will raise us up, and we shall live in His sight'.

What we learn from this passage is that, after the *four days*, or four thousand years from Adam to the crucifixion of Christ, there would be a further waiting period of '*two days*', or two thousand years, before '*the third day*', or 'the thousand years', of our Lord's glorious Kingdom would come — in which He would raise Israel up, that they might 'live in His sight'.

So we can plainly see that *seven 'days'*, or seven thousand years, are accounted for in the Bible, no more and no less. And if, through the grace of our Lord Jesus Christ, we are among those who 'love His appearing'[17] we shall be obeying His command to 'watch' — which means to show a real interest in the time of His return; for we are warned not to 'sleep, as do others', but to 'watch and be sober'[18]. This is because '*the day* of the Lord so cometh as a thief in the night', as we are told in 1 Thessalonians 5 — 'The day of the Lord' could hardly come until the 'two days' of Hosea 6: 2 had reached their close; hence the need to 'watch' and not be 'in darkness' lest that day should overtake us 'as a thief'.

It is because this command of Christ to 'watch' was not taken seriously by His Church that, as we have had to record earlier, 'the day of the Lord' **did** 'come as a thief in the night' on June 12th 1933, when 6,000 years of human sin and failure ended with a universal demonstration of man's complete disregard for his Creator.

---

[17] 2 Timothy 4: 8
[18] 1 Thessalonians 5: 6

CHAPTER NINE

The True Passover

In the previous Chapter the simple fact was revealed that, in the reckoning of God, *four thousand years* had elapsed from the fall of Adam and Eve to the death of Jesus Christ, 'the Lamb of God, which taketh away the sin of the world', in AD 33. God's Lamb, in other words, had been kept for '*four days*' awaiting His sacrifice at the one and only *Passover* in all time or eternity which gave full meaning and fulfilment to all the previous ones. Every other Passover which Israel had observed had, of course, looked back to the time of their exodus from Egypt, when the first passover feast was instituted. That was as far as the Jews were concerned. But with God, the Exodus Passover had simply looked forward — it was a **type** which required an **antitype**.[‡] The same, of course, has to be said about every one of the multitudinous sacrifices of the Levitical law — all were meaningless to God, except as they foreshadowed the One who was yet to come and give them their antitypical fulfilment. The antitype's appearance **had** to be according to God's exact time programme. (Oh let the people of Israel recognise this!)

So, in AD 33, Jesus approached the close of His ministry in Israel. He had come to His people as *'the Bridegroom'* [1] and as such He had revealed Himself to those who had received Him, for John had declared: 'He that hath the bride is the bridegroom'; and a number of believers, mainly from Galilee, had attached themselves to Him. The great 'bridegroom' of the Old Testament, King Solomon, had had to confess in his day: 'One man among a thousand have I found, but a woman among all those have I not found,'[2] but now the 'greater than Solomon'[3] had come seeking a *bride* — that is, a remnant of His own people in Israel — and we can learn much from the example of the one woman He *did find*.

[‡] See Charts 6 & 7, pages 191–192
[1] John 3: 29
[2] Ecclesiastes 7: 28
[3] Matthew 12: 42

In the course of His ministry, Jesus had come upon one woman, Mary of Bethany, who chose to sit at His feet and *hear His word*[4]. It was she (the record shows), and she alone, who was ready, when the hour arrived, to perform that 'good work' on Him — without the telling of which, He said, the Gospel could not be preached throughout the whole world! Let us repeat exactly what He said:

> 'She is come aforehand to anoint My body to the burying. Verily I say unto you, wheresoever this gospel shall be preached throughout the whole world, this also that she hath done shall be spoken of for a memorial of her'[5].

Why was this action of Mary so important? We can hear the disciples also asking the same question: '*to what purpose* was it done?' What was the reason why it was done just then? To answer this fully would require a comprehensive understanding of the meaning of the days surrounding our Lord's passion but a partial answer can be given in the light of the knowledge we have already gathered in the previous pages. For the present we can only look at Mary's act in relation to *the Passover*.

'Then Jesus six days before the Passover came to Bethany'

The 'Passover' spoken of in John's Gospel[6] is always the 'feast of the Jews' and must never be confused with the *true Passover* which Jesus took with His disciples twenty-four hours before the Jews kept theirs. The other three gospels refer exclusively to the Lord's Passover which He took the same night when He was betrayed. Once it is appreciated that the Bible makes a sharp distinction between the true 'Feast of Unleavened Bread' which Jesus kept and the Jewish one a day later (which was only opening as the Lord's body was being laid in the Sepulchre), many difficulties begin to depart regarding the calendar of Passion Week.

We now focus upon the true Passover which Jesus kept. This was *five days* inclusively after the day on which He arrived in Bethany when 'they made Him a supper'. So, *at a space of exactly four days* from the time of the supper when Mary anointed Jesus in Bethany, He and His disciples were gathered in the Upper Room partaking of the Passover meal. In other words, the supper in

---

[4] Luke 10: 39
[5] Mark 14: 8-9 (& Matthew 26: 13)
[6] John 12: 1

Bethany was at the opening of *the last four days* of the exact *four thousand years* (in the Jubilee Chronology, or Chronology of Redemption) from the fall of Adam and Eve. Jesus the true 'Lamb of God' had now come to the end of the great *'four days'* of His waiting — *waiting for death.* According to the instruction given in Egypt (see Exodus 12: 3-6) it was now the duty of *someone* in Israel to take action and choose the lamb for the household four days before it was to be slain.

This was the day God had had in mind from the beginning. If it was necessary to obey His Word and set aside typical lambs for four days prior to each typical passover all down Israel's history, what was to be done now when, not a typical lamb, but the Son of God Himself — the great *antitype of every paschal sacrifice* Israel had ever offered — was ready to be chosen out and set apart to die?

Was Caiaphas, the high priest, to be called for? As we learn from John 11: 50 he had just prophesied that it was 'expedient for us, that one man should die for the people, and that the whole nation perish not'.

No! Here we believe was the one occasion in the whole history of man when God needed help! Why so? Well, He required the co-operation of some person in Israel who would act for the nation and set apart the Lamb of God at the right time — and where was He to find that person? It was no good looking to the apostles, for it is clear from the gospel accounts that they had no understanding at all of what was to transpire that night. To whom then did God look?

> 'O the depth of the riches both of the wisdom and knowledge
> of God! How unsearchable are His judgments, and His ways
> past finding out!'[7]

God knew — He had known from the beginning how this position would be met. It was *'the woman'* (who) being deceived was in the transgression, that evening, just four thousand years before in Eden (see 1 Timothy 2: 14) and it was that act of Eve which must now be undone — yea, blotted out with blood, the blood of His own Son. *And Mary knew it* — she knew that He was about to die, and she knew He was about to die for her!

She brought it (the ointment of spikenard) *beforehand* 'to anoint My body to the burying'[8], said Jesus. It had not been for

---

[7] Romans 11: 33
[8] Mark 14: 8

nothing that the Son of God had called in at the little house in Bethany and found a quiet listener in Mary. Praise God, though Solomon himself had failed to find 'a woman', Jesus (his greater Son) had discovered the very one whose words Solomon recorded in prophetic utterance, in the opening chapter of his 'Song' (verse 12):

'While the king sitteth at his table, my spikenard sendeth forth the smell thereof'.

Yes, at the beginning Eve had been fashioned by the hand of God to be a 'help meet' for Adam. But when she fell and Adam with her, the blood then shed by the hand of God, as He clothed the naked pair 'with coats of skins'[9], could not by any means alone atone for sin. Mary had learned this, sitting at the feet of Jesus there at home in Bethany. 'Her sins' which were 'many' had been 'forgiven' — Mary knew this from the time of her first encounter with the Saviour, which we find recorded in the seventh chapter of Luke (verses 36-50). She had had a box of ointment then (perhaps it was two years before, as an understanding of the time-structure of Christ's ministry might lead us to imagine) and had poured it on His feet after washing them with her tears and wiping them 'with the hairs of her head'.

Already then, she had 'loved much' (verse 47). Jesus had said so to the Pharisee but, on those later visits which He paid to Bethany, Mary had learned to listen and to *hear His Word*. She now knew He was the Redeemer, first promised 4,000 years before in Eden (Genesis 3: 15) and that the days of His waiting were now accomplished. She knew He was 'the Lamb of God which taketh away the sin of the world'[10].

Far more than this, here was her brother Lazarus, seated at the table with them — Lazarus, who had been dead four days, 'whom He raised from the dead'! The words of Jesus rang on in Mary's ears: 'I am the resurrection, and the life'[11]. Mystery of mysteries, who could then fathom the coming tragedy of Calvary — who could foresee it?

It was the Spirit who led Mary to perform this final act of worship in the house of Simon and, in so doing, she singled out — before the watching eyes of the whole universe — God's **Lamb** and God's Anointed **King**. Yes, it was not only as the Lamb but as the King that Jesus was anointed — and this at the very opening of the

---

9 Genesis 3: 21   11 John 11: 25
10 John 1: 29

day He would appear as 'King' — for it was the very next morning that the prophecy of Zechariah 9: 9 received fulfilment (see John 12: 12-16).

From the Bethany Supper *four days* ran on to the true Passover that Jesus kept with His disciples in Jerusalem and 'when the even was come, He sat down with the twelve'[12].

Until the whole calendar and astronomical position has been laid bare and the actual weekdays established, it will not be possible for us to go more deeply into the hidden significance of the days and hours surrounding the death and resurrection of God's Son but we must at least state most positively that the days of the coming out of Egypt, following the Exodus Passover, were found to be exactly typical of the days that followed our Lord's Passover in AD 33.[‡]

A glance at Numbers 33: 3-8 shows that the Exodus took place on 'the fifteenth day of the first month', when 'the children of Israel removed from Rameses, and pitched in Succoth'. After this, 'they departed from Succoth, and pitched in Etham' — that is, on the second day after the Passover. Following this, 'they removed from Etham ... and ... pitched before Migdol', — that is, on the third day after the Passover. This brought them to a place called Pi-hahiroth and, in that night, as Exodus chapter 14 so graphically describes, they passed through the midst of the sea. 'When the morning appeared ... the Lord overthrew the Egyptians in the midst of the sea' and the people of Israel 'saw the Egyptians dead upon the sea shore. And Israel saw that great work which the Lord did upon the Egyptians: and the people feared the Lord, and believed the Lord, and His servant Moses' (verses 27, 30-31).

Type and Antitype

What has just been shown is that between the Passover in Egypt and the triumph of Israel 'when the morning appeared', after they had passed through the sea, is revealed in Scripture to be *three days and a half**. If this was then *the type* of the great work of Redemption, ultimately to be enacted in AD 33, how is it that Christendom has managed to mar the *antitype* completely — by deluding the world into thinking that Jesus was raised from the dead after only *two days and a half* from the Passover which He

---

[12] Matthew 26: 20
[‡] See Chart 7 on page 192
* See Chart 10 on page 195

kept with His disciples, and after His body had been only *one clear day* in the grave?

Let us repeat the question. How in any conscience can '*three days and three nights*' be only 36 hours? All who have read Matthew 12: 39-40 will remember the one and only sign that Jesus gave to His generation. These are His words: 'There shall no sign be given to it, but the sign of the prophet Jonah. For as Jonah was three days and three nights in the whale's belly; so shall the Son of Man be three days and three nights in the heart of the earth'.

As we have said, it is not possible just now to unravel to the full the precious secret of the exact timing of our Lord's death and resurrection but it has already been plainly stated that He was raised from the dead on 'the third day'[13], after two full days in the tomb. These days, like the 'two days' and 'the third day' of Hosea 6: 2, (as we have shown) are, of course, typical of the two thousand lunar years of our past dispensation and the third 'thousand years' of our Lord's glorious resurrection rulership of this earth which we call the Millennium (see Revelation 20).

---

[13] 1 Corinthians 15: 4

CHAPTER TEN

Daniel's Seventieth Week

'Seventy weeks are determined ...' (Daniel 9: 24-27) ‡

It is sad, but safe, to say that the confusion that has abounded through man's trying to interpret 'the things of God' with his natural mind has shown up more in what has been taught and written on Daniel 9: 24-27 than perhaps on any other prophecy of Scripture. This is not surprising, when the paramount importance of this revelation for both Israel and the Gentiles is considered, and few parts of God's Word can be more hated by the prince of darkness.

Verse 24

'Seventy weeks are determined upon thy people and upon thy holy city, to finish the transgression, and to make an end of sins, and to make *(lit.)* atonement for iniquity, and to bring in everlasting righteousness, and to seal up the vision and prophecy, and to anoint the *(lit.)* Holy of Holies'.

The first thing we have to consider is that Gabriel had been sent from the Throne of God in answer to Daniel's prayer and intercession on behalf of his people and the 'holy city'. Whatever was going to transpire centuries ahead would certainly not be an answer to Daniel's question regarding the 'seventy years' of desolation referred to in verse 2 of the chapter. Therefore, the prophet is told of a period of 'seventy weeks', or 490 literal days, which were to elapse from the very 'evening' when Gabriel arrived (verse 21) to a day in the following year, 536 BC, when God would once again accept His restored people in the holy city, after an

---

exile which had first begun with Daniel's own captivity, seventy years before, in 607 BC (see Daniel 1: 1-6 and Jeremiah 25: 1-11).

Much could be said as to the significance of the date — June 22nd 537 BC — when Gabriel came to Daniel (but we cannot enlarge on this here). From this very 'evening', however, to the opening of the Day of Atonement (Tishri 10th) in 536 BC (Oct. 26th) we can trace the exact span of 'seventy weeks', or 490 days. As we see from Ezra 3: 1-6, the Jewish exiles had by this time returned from Babylon and were once again offering their sacrifices in the holy city; for in the previous spring, Cyrus, King of Persia had been moved to issue his famous decree concerning the restoration of the temple in Jerusalem, thus bringing to an end the 'seventy years' of Jeremiah's prophecy (Daniel 9: 2 and Ezra 1: 1-5).

However, neither this 'decree' nor any of the other decrees that followed relating solely to the building of 'the house of the Lord', were in view in the prophecy of Daniel 9: 24-25. This had specific reference to the full-scale restoration and building of the 'holy city' Jerusalem and seventy-eight long years had yet to elapse before this 'building' could commence.

Daniel was therefore to 'know and understand' that his seventy weeks of days were but a token — a type, in fact — of a coming seventy weeks of years which were to reach, not just to a Jewish Day of Atonement when God would — in the immediate future — restore His exiled people after they had gathered together 'as one man' to Jerusalem in the following year (Ezra 3: 1), but to the great all-atoning sacrifice of Messiah Himself, when He should 'finish the transgression ... make an end of sins and ... make atonement for iniquity' bringing in 'everlasting righteousness' in His own Person — that is, for all who should believe on His name.

How anyone could suggest (as so many have done) that there would be no actual 'seventy weeks' or 490 years reaching fulfilment at the Cross of Calvary is hard to imagine, but this error is due to a secret which God allowed to exist in the wording of verse 26.

In verse 25 it is shown that 'seven weeks' (49 years) and 'three score and two weeks' (434 years) from 'the commandment to restore and to build Jerusalem' would measure 'unto the Messiah the Prince'. This could only mean to the time when He would be presented to Israel by His herald, John the Baptist, 'in the fifteenth year of the *(lit.)* leadership of Tiberius Caesar', as we are shown in Luke 3:1. No date in the New Testament receives greater emphasis than this, because it is here that the Bible's chronology *must* be linked securely to a Gentile calendar — the Roman one — which would carry time forward with perfect accuracy down to our own day. (As mentioned in Chapter 4, this 'fifteenth year' was found to be AD 26, as Augustus Caesar made Tiberius, his adopted son, 'leader' of the army in AD 12.)

AD 26 was therefore 69 'weeks' of years from 'the commandment to restore and to build Jerusalem' (verse 25, and see Nehemiah 2), and AD 33 was the end of 490 years. However, it is here that the difficulty (to our natural way of thinking) stands out because we are told in verse 26 that '*after* (seven weeks and) three-score and two weeks *shall Messiah be cut off'.* This statement has thrown interpreters into great confusion. Does it mean immediately after, three and a half years after, or seven years after? Without the aid of the Spirit of Truth (and, we might add, common sense) how can we tell? We can tell by reading verse 24 again, where it is plainly stated that the whole 490 years were to run their course to the finished work of Jesus the Messiah when He was 'cut off' upon the Cross of Calvary.

Verse 26 therefore tells us that seven years *after* the 'threescore and two weeks (i.e. when the 490 years were complete) shall Messiah be cut off, and (literally translated) there shall be nothing for Him'. In other words, He would not **then** be able to bring in the Kingdom for Israel.

Following this, we read in verse 26 of the destruction of Jerusalem and the temple by the Romans in AD 70 and of the 'desolations' which would exist 'unto the end of the war'. This is no doubt a reference to the end of the Roman War of AD 66 to 73, after which Jewish history in the land officially ceased until the end of 'the times of the Gentiles'[1] and the long age of Jewish dispersion.

Verse 27: 'One Week'

We now come to the mention of the 'one week' of seven years which is needed to complete the 490 to the Kingdom. It will be seen at once that this cannot possibly be the seven years from

---

[1] Luke 21: 24

AD 26 to 33 again alluded to, but that this 'one week' must refer to a time yet to come. This is because in the preceding verse another 'prince' or *(lit.)* 'leader' has been spoken of — 'the prince that shall come'. 'The people of the prince that shall come' are clearly stated to be the ones who would 'destroy the city and the sanctuary' — that is, the Roman armies under Titus in AD 70.

So it is a Roman 'prince' or leader who is yet to appear on the European stage who, as stated in this final verse of the prophecy, will 'confirm a covenant with *(lit.)* the many (that is, the majority of the people of Israel) for one week', or seven years. In the middle of the seven years we read, he will break faith with Israel and 'cause the sacrifice and the oblation to cease' producing desolation, 'even until the consummation' which will be visited upon him. (The last word in this verse should be translated 'desolator', that is, this Roman leader.) Many other scriptures refer to this individual in whom Israel will put their confidence for a while until they discover their fatal mistake. There is no doubt that Paul is also referring to this same person in his warning in 2 Thessalonians 2: 3-10.

The Two 'Weeks' of Seven Years

We referred earlier to a 'secret' existing in verse 26 and by this we mean that God, whose 'thoughts are not our thoughts'[2], was expressing exactly what **He** foresaw about the seven years of the gospels.

He foresaw that they would be *lost to Israel.* They certainly were not lost to the Church of God — which is the Body of Christ — but to Israel as a nation they were *lost*, for their Messiah was 'cut off' and had 'nothing'.

This is, of course, perfectly illustrated by Pharoah's dream which, for emphasis, was repeated twice in Genesis 41. The seven years 'of great plenty' were clearly figurative of the seven years of the gospels — AD 26 to 33 — but, as we have said, they were *lost* to Israel. The Genesis type show us that the good seven years were *'devoured'* or swallowed up by a very evil seven years that followed them. In other words, the evil years replaced the good years. This is precisely what we see takes place with the 490 years of Daniel 9, that is, with the last 'week' of the period.

---

2 from Isaiah 55: 8

Because the Jews slew their Messiah and *lost* the Kingdom that He came to set up, God set the nation aside and brought in the Gentiles, as Paul's Epistles to the Romans and Galatians so graphically reveal.

But God must still complete the 'seventy weeks' and bring in for Israel — and the whole world with them — that which they lost in AD 33. So, in effect, *He cancelled from reckoning* the seven years of the gospels but allowed all the precious store of light and truth concerning the Messiah, and all that He accomplished through His death on Calvary, to be 'laid up' in store for Israel for the seven years to come. Those years, indeed, will be 'very evil' and a more literal translation of Daniel 9: 27 — the latter half of the verse — can read: 'And upon the wing abominations making desolate, even until a consummation, and that determined, shall be poured upon the desolator'. Has not the world already experienced 'abominations upon the wing, making desolate'? What of Hiroshima and Nagasaki and the cities of Europe in the Second World War?

We must not forget that Jesus Himself spoke of 'the end' of these coming seven years in His great unfolding of what lay ahead for His Jewish brethren in Matthew 24: 14-44. He said, 'For then shall be great tribulation, such as was not since the beginning of the world to this time, no, nor ever shall be. And except those days should be shortened, there should no flesh be saved: but for the elect's sake those days shall be shortened' (v 21-22). There is little reason to doubt that the final unleashing of nuclear war, at 'the end' of the time of 'tribulation', will create so dire a threat to the very continuance of life in the areas of conflict that only the personal return of the Son of God, 'with power and great glory', will be sufficient to deal with this last effort of Satan to wreak destruction upon the planet.

We see then that the final 'one week' of Daniel 9: 27 is the last seven years of this age‡. Graphically described in the visions of John in Revelation 4 to 19, they will constitute the prelude to the 'kingdom' of 'a thousand years', of Revelation 20, which will be measured in terms of the Redemption Chronology — as 980 lunar years, with their 20 years of Jubilee. 980 years are, of course, twice 'seventy weeks' of years and a glance backward over the whole course of *time*, as the Bible's Chronology has revealed it, has

---

‡ See Chart 1 on page 186

shown us that *forgiveness* — 'the forgiveness of God' — is the only basis upon which the Most High has been able to bear with the human race, from the fall of Adam onwards. 'Until seventy times seven'[3] has been His measuring rod and 'four' — the number of universality — times 'seventy times seven' years, that is, 1,960 years, has been shown (however briefly in these pages) to be the length of each of the three main 'dispensations'. During these dispensations God has dealt, first, with the patriarchs (from Adam to Abram), then with Abram and his seed to Christ and, finally, with the Gentiles, so that 'out of them' He might take out 'a people for His name' (Acts 15: 14), that is, true Christians.[‡]

And what of the last two periods of 'seventy weeks' that are yet to come? These 980 years, with their 20 years of Jubilee, will bring to fulness the forgiveness and forbearance of God, with a display of His 'goodness' to both Jew and Gentile, in the Messianic Kingdom of our Lord Jesus Christ, which will surpass all that has ever entered the imagination of man. For God must yet, 'in very deed dwell with men on the earth'[4] and commune with them as He did with Adam on that first 'sabbath' in Eden.

So at the outset of these last 'thousand years' — that is, at the close of the 'one week' of Daniel 9: 27 — we see, in the vision of John in Revelation 19, the return of Messiah the Prince as 'King of Kings, and Lord of Lords'. But His coming then will spell the extirpation of every rebellious element on the earth, the binding of Satan for the whole period of the Kingdom, and thus enable this world to settle down to an era of peace and rest and the full enjoyment of 'the forgiveness of God'.

The Vision of The Last Seven Years

The measurement of this 'one week' we find perhaps most clearly given in the vision of Revelation 12. In this and the preceding chapter the seven years are divided into two halves: 'a thousand two hundred and three score days' and either 'forty two months' or 'a time (360 days) and times (2 x 360 days) and half a time (180 days).' The 1,260 days will be found on examination to refer only to the first half of 'the week' and the measurement in 'months' or 'times' only to the last half.[*] The reason for this is that, as He looked on to the time of His return, Jesus foresaw that those

---

[3] Matthew 18: 22
[4] 2 Chronicles 6: 18

[‡] See Chart 4 on page 189
[*] See Note 1 on page 184

last 'days should be shortened' otherwise 'there should no flesh be saved'. Therefore, the second 3½ years are never spoken of as 1,260 days — only in the looser terms of 'months' or 'times'. It is in reference to **this coming** 'with power and great glory' that our Lord introduces His one prohibition: 'But of that day and hour knoweth no man, no, not the angels of heaven, but My Father only'[5].

Why? Because all else will by that time be known! Certainly, the start of the measured '1,260 days' will be known and the great crisis at their close (see Revelation 11: 7-13) after which the '42 months' of Revelation 11: 2 and 13: 5 will take their course.

It is an amazing fact that because of this one prohibition of knowledge (i.e. 'of that day and hour') the devil has sown a fear in the hearts of the vast majority of the people of God, lest by any means they might 'know' anything positive in regard to *time* in the Bible!

In Revelation 12: 5 we are given an amazing vision of Israel as 'a woman' who brought forth *(lit. Greek)* 'a son, a male'. This we see clearly figures Christ, who is 'to rule all nations with a rod of iron' (see also Psalm 2: 7-9). Then we see her 'child' — a perfect type of the Church which is the Body of Christ — *'caught up to God and to His throne'.* This part of the vision beautifully illustrates the catching up described in 1 Thessalonians 4: 14-17 and 1 Corinthians 15: 51-52. (It is interesting to note that the word for this 'child' is neuter in the Greek, for it typifies the Church which is 'neither male nor female'[6] and this is in marked contrast to the 'son, a male' which typifies Christ the Head.)

Now, if 'the woman' is a figure of Israel, 'of whom as concerning the flesh Christ came'[7], and we see in this vision her 'child' being 'caught up to God and to His throne' *before* **the measurement of the seven years commences** (that is, the 1,260 days and 3½ times) why should a pernicious teaching cover the earth today that the Church is going to pass through 'the great tribulation' of Matthew 24: 21?

Let all who have held this doctrine re-examine the facts and, if they are convicted that they have taught what is error, let them confess it and seek readjustment before God.

Of course, the 'feeding' of 'the woman' during the two periods of 3½ years[8] prefigures the way the believing Jews (otherwise referred to as the 'sealed' remnant of 'an hundred and

---

[5] Matthew 24: 22-36
[6] Galatians 3: 28
[7] Romans 9: 5
[8] Revelation 12: 6 & 14

forty and four thousand of all the tribes of the children of Israel')[9], will be nourished upon 'unleavened bread' (i.e. the pure truth of God) right through until the time of tribulation is over. The first seven days following the Exodus and midnight 'cry' in Egypt were the original seven days of unleavened bread which were also divided into two periods of 3½ days, as Exodus 8: 27, 15: 22, Numbers 33: 1-9 and their context will show[‡].

We cannot stay to look further into these facts now, except to say that it should be obvious that *Christ* — both head and members — must be complete in resurrection before the terrible seven years of judgment can commence, and the testimony of Scripture appears to be conclusive on this point.

[9] Revelation 7: 14
[‡] See Chart 10 on page 195

CHAPTER ELEVEN

The 'Parousia' and The Rapture of The Church

'The 'parousia' (lit. being alongside) of our Lord Jesus Christ with all His saints'   (1 Thessalonians 3: 13)

The vision of Revelation 12 has shown us the resurrection of Christ being gloriously completed by the catching up of the Church 'which is His body' before the commencement of the '1,260 days' and 3½ 'times' which the elect of Israel will be called to pass through on the earth. When this union of Christ the Head with the members of His body has been consummated by the raising of 'the dead in Christ'[1] and the translation of the living to Heaven, then — and not until then — can the events described in the visions of John, from Revelation 4 to 19, have their fulfilment. In fact, when John is called to 'come up hither' at the opening of chapter 4, he then sees the Church — symbolised by the four 'living ones' and 'elders' — around the Throne, before any of the seals of the Book of Judgment are opened.

If it is a fact that this most stupendous ending of the Church's earthly history is lying just ahead of us now, surely we should ask whether the Bible holds any clear information as to the order of events when it actually takes place. It certainly does, for when Paul was given 'the word of the Lord' concerning the translation of the Church in 1 Thessalonians 4: 15-16, he was shown that a *positive space of time* would elapse between the descent of our Lord, when He comes 'from heaven with a shout ... and with the trump of God' (at which moment 'the dead in Christ' would 'rise

---

[1] 1 Thessalonians 4: 16

first') and the event which was to follow this, described in verse 17. Correctly translated, this should read '**afterwards**, we which are alive and remain shall be caught up together with them in the clouds'.

How long is it between *'first'* and *'afterwards'?* Most have said "No time at all — it is all to be accomplished 'in a moment, in the twinkling of an eye, *at the last trump'"* (1 Corinthians 15: 52). No wonder there is confusion in the minds of the saints, if this is the way they handle the Holy Scriptures!

How can the **first** and **last** trumpets be blown 'in the twinkling of an eye' when the Word of the Lord is clear that, when *the first* has been sounded, *'the last'* is *'afterwards'?* Language could not possibly be plainer. So we have to face the fact that for a brief while, however short, our wonderful Saviour and Lord is to be here on earth *'alongside'* us who are alive, 'with all His saints', in the same way as He was with His disciples in those forty days after His Resurrection.

After it has been taught for over a century that Christ might come 'at any moment', and we at the same instant be removed from earth to the heavens, it is good to pause and let the truth of God soak in.

We have to see this coming event in its true perspective. It is, indeed, the second part of the Resurrection of Christ. The first part was perfectly fulfilled when He, the head of the Church, was raised up on 'the first (day) of the weeks'[2]* - that is, at the opening of the seven weeks to Pentecost. His first act on rising from the dead, it would appear, was to wrap up 'the napkin, that was about His head' and put it aside 'in a place by itself'[3], but to leave the linen clothes which had enwrapped His body, lying as they were. He had passed from them, without disturbing them, because this whole action was to signify that He, 'the Head', had finished with death, while the turn of the Church 'which is His body', would come later!

The seven 'weeks' to Pentecost were, of course, the harvest season of the year. They began with the barley harvest and ended with the wheat harvest. The whole harvest was an expression of *resurrection.*

---

[2] Matthew 28: 1   * See Note 3 on page 184
[3] John 20: 7

'Now is Christ risen from the dead, and become the firstfruits of them that slept'
(1 Corinthians 15: 20)

We must now examine this great annual type of the resurrection of Christ which is pictured for us in Leviticus 23: 9-21 for, if we fail to grasp its meaning for the Church now, at the climax of the age, we shall find ourselves deprived of a vital part of 'the armour of light'[4] just at the time when it is most urgently needed.

Those who have read these verses with understanding have seen that the harvest has special reference to the *Church*, which is the Body of Christ — springing forth, as it were, from that *one* *'corn of wheat'* which fell into the ground and died (John 12: 24) — and that the seven weeks begin with *'a sheaf of the firstfruits'* and end with *'the bread of the firstfruits'* being 'waved', that is, ascending to the Lord.

Nothing is more wonderful than to see the way Jesus fulfilled the beginning of this typical picture of the harvest. He had, indeed, died and fallen into the ground but, in resurrection, He 'bore much fruit', for we read in Matthew 27: 52-53 that 'many bodies of the saints which slept arose, and came out of the graves after His resurrection, and went into the holy city, and appeared unto many'. Had He not promised, at the graveside of Lazarus, that 'he that believeth in Me, though he were dead, yet shall he live'[5]? And had not many, who had believed in Him in the years of His ministry, already passed on and predeceased Him? Were these to remain in their graves when He, the Prince of Life, had conquered death and already 'led captivity captive'[6]? No, a thousand times, No! For the harvest meant that all that had sprung from that one corn of wheat must be raised up together — none could continue to remain in death.

What would have been more unnatural than if these, who had recently died, should keep to themselves the glorious fact that both He and they had been loosed into everlasting life?! Of course, they went and manifested themselves to their bereaved friends and relatives still gathered in the holy city!

And so we come to the early morning of 'the first (day) of the weeks'* and the account of it, as given in John 20.

As soon as Mary Magdalene recognised the Lord and heard

---

[4] Romans 13: 12
[5] John 11: 25
[6] Ephesians 4: 8
* See Note 3 on page 184

Him call her name, she naturally wanted to do what the other women did, an hour or two later, when 'they came and held Him by the feet, and worshipped Him'[7], but this Jesus could not allow, and He tells her why it was impossible at that hour. He said 'touch Me not; for I am not yet ascended to My Father'[8].

This was the reason. He, and those raised up at the time of His own Resurrection, were to constitute the sheaf of the firstfruits, which must now be presented to God. We read in Leviticus 23: 14 that it was expressively forbidden for anyone to touch the new harvest until this first sheaf had been offered to the Lord. This was to be in the morning, as Deuteronomy 16: 9 clearly implies, and without a doubt Jesus ascended to His Father at the hour of the morning sacrifice. This, to the Jews, was the 'third hour of the day' — that is, from 8 to 9 am.

The Seven Weeks of Harvest [‡]

It was from this hour that the 49 days to Pentecost began to run, according to the divine instruction in verse 9: 'begin to number the seven weeks from such time as thou beginnest to put the sickle to the corn', and we know that it was at this hour (the 'third hour') that 'the day of Pentecost' was marked at its opening by the descent of the Holy Ghost in Acts 2: 1-15.

So Jesus ascended to His Father, 'the firstfruits'[9] of a mighty harvest that is even yet to be completed by the quickening of myriads of souls whom the Holy Spirit is silently gathering out from the teeming multitudes of the earth. 'The harvest' had begun, a resurrection scene from which death had for the moment been banished, and no doubt sickness also. But He who was 'the resurrection and the life'[10] must needs be present with His own throughout this glorious season after His Resurrection, and so He soon returned, in time to greet the women who came after Mary Magdalene, as they ran 'with fear and great joy' to carry the news to His disciples. These He did not forbid to touch Him[11], for 'the weeks' of harvest had began.

For nearly six weeks Jesus continued in the earth sphere, and at stated times He was seen by his disciples — on one occasion, by 'above five hundred brethren at once', many of whom were, no doubt, known to the apostle Paul, who recorded these appearances in 1 Corinthians 15: 5-8.

---

[7] Matthew 28: 9   [9] 1 Corinthians 15: 20-23   [11] Matthew 28: 8-9
[8] John 20: 17   [10] John 11: 25   [‡] See Chart 8 on page 193

But *Jesus broke the type,* that Is, after 'forty days'[12] He ascended back to Heaven, leaving His disciples with the promise (through the 'two men' who stood by) that He would return 'in like manner'[13] as they had seen Him depart.

'In like manner' certainly could not mean 'with power and great glory' — nor could it mean 'as the lightning cometh out of the east, and shineth even unto the west', as Matthew describes the ultimate coming of Christ to reign, 'after the tribulation of those days', in chapter 24: 27-30.

'In like manner' means as the Man they knew — the One who had 'led them out as far as to Bethany', and Who had 'lifted up His hands, and blessed them'[14] before He ascended to heaven.

It was at this moment that the 'type' of the harvest was broken. Why can we say this so positively? Because the coming Day of Pentecost was not the **end**, but only the **beginning** of the great worldwide harvest of His death and resurrection.

For, since the departure of the Head in AD 33, death and disintegration have stamped this long era, now so soon to close. For this reason the 'type' has been *in abeyance* while Jesus has been absent from this earth. When will it be completed? That is the question each and all now have to face.

At the opening of this Chapter we quoted 1 Thessalonians 3: 13 and Paul's words: 'the ***parousia*** of our Lord Jesus Christ with all His saints'. This word *'parousia'* simply means 'being present' or 'being alongside'. Is it really true that Jesus, and 'all His saints' who have been in the graves for the past nineteen hundred years are to be alongside us in their immortal bodies, while we are still in our mortal flesh, prior to our translation to His 'Father's House'[15]?

Well, the implication is clear: if ever the 'type' of the resurrection harvest is to be fulfilled, *nine* more days must elapse, when the conditions of those first *forty* days at the beginning are restored. That is, **no death** in the Church, the graves emptied, and 'we which are alive and remain unto the coming of the Lord'[16] rejoicing worldwide in the knowledge that *He is in our midst,* once again in person, and has come alongside to comfort every heart and prepare, according to His promise, to receive us unto Himself (see John 14: 3).

And how shall we know that 'the Lord Himself' has actually descended, and that the dead have been 'raised incorruptible'?

---

[12] Acts 1: 3
[13] Acts 1: 10-11
[14] Luke 24: 50
[15] John 14: 2
[16] 1 Thessalonians 4: 15

Because when He comes it will be 'with a shout, with the voice of the Archangel, and with *the trump of God'* [17].

We might just as soon speak of 'a secret exodus' — with our eyes on the Exodus from Egypt — as of 'a secret Rapture' of the Church, with the saints imagining that at any odd moment of the day or night they might be called into the presence of the Lord in Heaven!

We will now look further at this most stupendous impending event.

'Two Trumpets of Silver' *(Numbers 10)*

What then is the purpose of the two trumpets — 'the trump of God' and 'the last trump'? How wonderful it is to see this expressed in Numbers 10: 2, where the first is 'for the calling of the assembly', and the other is 'for the journeying of the camps'. First, the dead in Christ are, like Lazarus, to be 'called' from their graves (the only difference being that the dead are to be 'raised incorruptible'). Then, after the little space while Jesus is with us on the earth, 'at the last trump ... we shall be changed', so as to journey with them into the heavens, 'and so shall we ever be with the Lord'. Just as the journeying of Israel was to end in Canaan, so will the journeying of the Church ('the Israel of God') end when it is carried up into the heavenly Canaan, at the sounding of 'the last trump' of 1 Corinthians 15: 52.

And as for 'silver', this metal in the Bible signifies 'redemption'*, and it is 'the redemption of our body' for which we wait (see Romans 8: 22-23).

It is of great importance to see that 'the trumpet' of Jubilee (that is, the trumpet of Redemption) was sounded at the first 'Pentecost' — on the fiftieth day after the Exodus Passover, when the Lord Himself descended from Heaven at Sinai. The whole account in Exodus 19 should be carefully considered — we read in verses 19, 20 and 18:

> 'And when the voice of the trumpet sounded long, and waxed louder and louder ... the Lord came down upon mount Sinai', and that 'the Lord descended upon it in fire: and the smoke thereof ascended as the smoke of a (smelting) furnace, and the whole mount quaked greatly'.

---

[17] 1 Thessalonians 4: 16
* See Note 4 on page 184

Whatever 'trumpet' was this that sounded the advent of the Lord of all the earth? It can have been nothing less than 'the trump of God', and in verse 13 it is called in the Hebrew, the *'jubilee* trumpet'.

What actually **was** the Exodus of Israel out of the land of Egypt? It was God celebrating *the **fiftieth jubilee** from the fall of Adam.*

The year of Jubilee, as we know, was *'the fiftieth year'* — the great year of release — when, as Leviticus 25: 10 has it, 'ye shall return every man unto his possession'. Over four hundred years earlier God has promised Abram (in Genesis 15: 13-14) that this return would take place, and that the Lord was keeping His promise. His descent on to Mount Sinai was on the 50th day after the 50th Jubilee, as a right understanding of the calendar at the Exodus will reveal. No wonder the 'trumpet of the Jubilee' sounded long, and waxed louder and louder as God drew nigh to His redeemed people!

It is interesting to note at this point that, thirty Jubilees after the Exodus from Egypt, God celebrated the *80th Jubilee* by raising up His son Jesus from the dead. (The amazing way in which God ordered the calendar, so that this would be perfectly fulfilled in AD 33 we cannot go into yet, but it stands to reason that the great '80th Jubilee' in the Redemption Calendar should be celebrated in this way, by the resurrection of Christ.) And, as all know, on the fiftieth day after our Lord's Resurrection — on the Day of Pentecost — God again descended in fire in the person of the Holy Ghost, for we read in Acts 2: 3 'there appeared unto them cloven tongues like as of fire, and it sat upon each of them'.

What then of the *hundred and twentieth Jubilee* — that which has brought in what Jesus called 'the consummation of the age'* from June 12th 1933, when the 6,000 years ended?

As we know, from the very day when the Lord God fulfilled His threat to 'cut off' the Gentile nations, as we have already shown, **there has been a standstill, or parenthesis, in the Chronology of Redemption.** God has certainly not ceased to 'forgive' repentant individuals, Jews or Gentiles, and will do so till the end — but His official relationship with the nations of Christendom, as such, has terminated and history since 1933, when Hitler rose to power, has borne strong witness to that fact, as we shall see in later pages.

The day when the Redemption Chronology is taken up again

---

* See Note 2 on page 184

will come when God officially turns to Israel — no doubt at the time when the Church of God is removed by translation, and 'caught up'[18] into the heavens.

Elijah Leaves Elisha

We may see a remarkable illustration of this in 2 Kings 2, when Elijah is taken up by a whirlwind into Heaven, accompanied by the appearance of a 'chariot of fire, and horses of fire'. He leaves Elisha to continue his witness upon earth with 'a double portion' of his spirit. In the same way, when the Church of God is called from these scenes, the 'sealed' remnant of believing Jews, referred to in Revelation 7: 4 and 12: 6, will take up their testimony in this world. They will require 'a double portion' of the Spirit of Christ, because their witness will not only be to their own nation of Israel, but also to that innumerable multitude of Gentiles who are yet to be saved out of 'the great tribulation' and brought into Christ's earthly Kingdom at His return to reign[19].

We have pointed out already that the former seven years — AD 26 to 33 — were lost to Israel when they rejected their Messiah and so, for them, *the 80th Jubilee was lost.* However, now that 'the time of the Gentiles'[20] are over, Israel must pass through another seven years, as outlined in the Book of Revelation. At the end of these, when their Messiah returns as 'King of Kings, and Lord of Lords'[21], *the year of Jubilee* will at last come in for them. Then, just as the resurrection of Jesus crowned the former seven years which Israel forfeited, these coming seven years will culminate with what Revelation 20: 5- 6 calls 'the first resurrection'. This will embrace, no doubt, all the redeemed of Old Testament times, as well as all those whose lives are laid down in what is described as 'the time of Jacob's trouble'[22] or 'great tribulation'.

Having given this brief survey of the harvest of our age, we must now return to look more closely into the long-lost secret of time during the death of Jesus as it is concealed in the gospel records. We shall not forget that 'It is the glory of God to *conceal* a thing: but the honour of kings is to search out a matter'[23].

---

[18] 1 Thessalonians 4: 17   [20] Luke 21: 24   [22] Jeremiah 30: 7
[19] Revelation 7: 9-14   [21] Revelation 19: 16   [23] Proverbs 25: 2

CHAPTER TWELVE

The Birth of Jesus

It will interest readers to know that before it became possible to establish the true dating of what has been called the 'passion week' — that which we know God regards as the central week of all time and eternity — it was necessary for those conducting this research to be able to prove the exact course of calendar and astronomical time from the first day of Genesis through to the close of the 6,000 years in 1933. This involved the accurate measurement of time by both sun and moon and also with sabbaths and weekdays in their true place throughout Biblical history. Apart from this, a calendar of 354-day* years was found to be running its course from Genesis onwards, which amazingly confirmed dated events in the Bible and brought to light their true meaning. Time designs, which could never before have been discovered, and which showed the hand of God operating behind the scenes throughout the scriptures, kept on coming to light, giving rise to praise and worship as the perfect accuracy of Bible statements was confirmed, and the 'vision' of God's works enlarged.

The purpose of God in making this revelation was plainly to show that all His works were accomplished 'according to pattern'. Moses was told that he must 'make all things according to the pattern'[1] which was shown to him on Mount Sinai.

A Week of New Creation

We therefore needed to be shown that the 'week' or seven days of the first creation was the pattern of the 'week' of the 'new

---

* See 'The Years of The Messiah'   [1] Hebrews 8: 5
on page 168 in Appendix 1

creation' in AD 33. This was why 'Jesus six days before the (Jews') passover came to Bethany'[2], and we know that in the evening (3 pm) as those six days drew to their end, Jesus cried with a loud voice. 'He said, *"It is finished"*: and ... gave up His spirit'[3]. Through His death He had brought in 'a new creation', for He had put away the old.

However, it was also necessary to see that God did not reckon the time when Jesus was in death — any more than time is ever reckoned to one who is dead! So, in this aspect of things, the glorious day of our Lord's resurrection fills the pattern of that seventh day of Genesis, which God blessed and sanctified[4].

No wonder the side of Adam was opened in the evening of a sixth day, and that taken from it which was to form his bride. For the very name *Eve* means 'living'[5], and of necessity we are carried on to the day of the resurrection to see the continuation of this pattern.

So much more than is generally understood transpired in the days surrounding our Lord's death and resurrection (and, indeed, in those days which followed) that it was absolutely necessary for God to provide in His Word the means whereby the actual dates could be fully established. It will be appreciated that, where measurement is concerned, there must be a *point* from which to measure! This is what had been lacking in those innumerable attempts men had made to fix the year and date of the Crucifixion. They had not had an *end* from which to measure back! Neither, of course, had 'the pattern' itself been revealed.

So God required a real step of faith to be taken by the group of believers He had brought together to 'watch' through the years prior to 1933, as has been described briefly in previous pages. Everything depended, when the first step was taken in November 1932, on whether God would keep to 'the pattern' (in this case, the ordered stages by which the 'seven times', or 2,520 years, of Daniel chapter 4 was being fulfilled).

As soon as the light of God had shone on His use of the 'seventy times seven' (or 490-year) cycles, and we had been shown that these were Jewish years of 354 days each, the problem was solved. For the Holy Spirit had caused it to be declared that in June 1933 the sentence of Romans 11: 22 would be carried out. This meant that, not God's 'goodness', but the absence of it,

---

2 John 12: 1
3 John 19: 30 (NKJV)

4 Genesis 2: 3
5 Genesis 3: 20

would mark the progression of things among the nations from 1933 onwards. It was clear, therefore, that 1933 was the initial ending of 'the times of the Gentiles'.

So the measurement of four times 'seventy weeks' (that is, 1,960 years) was made back to October 12th AD 33, which was found to be the first day of the Jewish seventh month. It was then seen that on October 11th the one 'year' following the 'three years' Jesus referred to in Luke 13: 7 had ended. These four years could only have commenced when 'Jesus began to be about thirty years of age'. (The Greek implies that He was *actually* thirty when He began to teach — Luke 3: 23). Measuring thirty years of 354 days further back to their beginning in October, 1 BC, disclosed the fact that the day of the Saviour's birth in Bethlehem was the 15th of Israel's seventh month in that year, as the age of the moon revealed.

The True Date of The Nativity

This confirmed what so many have instinctively known, that is, that Jesus was born at the opening of the Feast of Tabernacles. (Most investigators had realised that His birth could never have been at the end of December!) In John 1: 14 we find the statement: 'And the Word was made flesh, and *(lit.)* **tabernacled** among us', which accounts for the fact that His nativity actually took place in a 'booth' (as the Hebrew word *sukkah* should more properly be translated in Leviticus 23: 34). A 'booth', 'covering' or 'shelter' was the birthplace of the Son of God in this world — and this for a very vital reason in the sight of God, His Father, as we were presently to learn.

Jesus was God's 'firstborn, higher than the kings of the earth' (Psalm 89: 27), but away back at the Exodus from Egypt, we hear God say to Moses: 'Israel is My son, My firstborn' (Exodus 4: 22). And the day that the nation was 'born' was, of course, the day of their coming out of Egypt, following the Passover 'midnight'[6].

We alluded earlier to a calendar of 354-day years running from Genesis onwards, the measurement of which can be checked with the aid of the Appendices following the final Chapter. It began on the day after 'the seventh day' or sabbath, which God 'blessed' and 'sanctified'[7]. From this beginning, 2,513 years (of 354 days)

[6] Exodus 12: 29
[7] Genesis 2: 3

6 months and 14 days can be traced up to the day of the Passover when Israel, God's 'firstborn', was 'let go' from death at the hands of the destroying angel. On the night of the 15th the people encamped at a place called 'Succoth'[8] and sheltered in 'booths' — see Leviticus 23: 39-43, where it is plainly shown that the Exodus was in 'the seventh month'. Now we know from Exodus 12: 2 that God made that 'seventh month' to become 'the beginning of months' and said: 'it shall be the first month of the year to you'.

In order to fulfil His purposes, the original 7th month must also be the 1st month, and it was called 'Abib' which means 'sprouting'.

Those who revere God will know that He had a reason behind this change in time at the Exodus and that it must have been related also to Jesus, His firstborn Son.

So, when it was discovered that the Bible's time records proved that the Exodus took place in the year 1639 BC (see Appendices 3 & 4) a careful measurement was made through to the day of our Lord's birth in Bethlehem. In Israel's calendar (see Chapter 6) there were just 1,638 years and 6 months in the period, but in the hidden 354-day calendar, there were 1,690 years and 6 months. This meant that the month in which Jesus was born in 1 BC could be called 'the seventh month' in Israel's calendar but, in the concealed 354-day series of years, the 'first month'. (Of course, none but God Himself took account of this second aspect.)

When we sought for the reason for this, the Holy Spirit revealed that Jesus is not only God's true 'Tabernacle' — our dwelling-place upon earth in whom to abide — but He is also the Living Bread which came down from Heaven[9], and the 'Unleavened Bread' for our food and sustainment in this world[‡].

To express this fact, Christ must be born at the Feast of Booths or 'Tabernacles', which signifies our temporary abiding in Him, and at the Feast of Unleavened Bread, which signifies our feeding upon Him. This necessitated two calendars — the one a soli-lunar series which the Jews had kept from the Exodus onwards and the other a civil lunar one which could only be known to Heaven above.

But this was not all. In earlier pages it has been shown that in the Chronology of Redemption there were 1,960 years from Adam to Abram and a further span of 1,960 to the Crucifixion of Christ.

---

[8] Exodus 12: 37   [‡] See Chart 6 on page 191
[9] John 6: 33

Together with the 80 years of Jubilee which were included by God, we know that the total came to exactly 4,000 years. But reckoning only the total years in the Scripture record of this Chronology, there were, of course, only twice 1,960, or 3,920 complete, in AD 33. If we deduct the 32½ years back to the birth of Jesus in the autumn of 1 BC we find that He came into this world in the middle of the year 3888 (from Creation). This clearly appears to be by design of God for, as is widely known, the numerical value of the name *Jesus* in the Greek spelling amounts to '**888**'. The number '3' of course, signifies His deity and the number 8 signifies resurrection, seeing that eight resurrections are recorded in the Bible.

As God uses the number 888 to seal many of His time patternings (whether of days or of years) it is only right to illustrate how this total is made up. The spelling of JESUS in Greek is:

I	=	10
E	=	8
S	=	200
O	=	70
U	=	400
S	=	200
		888

888   *(which is 37 x 8 x 3)*

Before leaving the year of our Lord's birth, we feel we should draw attention to the Divine use of another number — '13' — which is eloquent of the purpose for which Christ came into the world. '13' is the number which throughout scripture signifies *sin* and *rebellion*. (An illustration of this can be seen in Genesis 14: 4 'in the *thirteenth* year they rebelled'.)

In the Redemption Chronology the number of completed years from Adam to the Birth of Jesus was 3,887. This number is 13 x 13 x 23. We found that the total in 354-day years from the Exodus was 1,690 and the factors of this are 13 x 13 x 10. However, the same period in Jewish years was 1,638, Jesus being born in the middle of the 1,639th year. 1,638 has the factors of 13 x 9 x 7 x 2.

(These multiples of '13' are in harmony with what we find in the numerical value of two of God's titles in the Old Testament, the Hebrew letters for 'Jehovah' being 26 or 13 x 2, and those for 'Adonahy' (Lord) being 65, or 13 x 5.)

Oh, how wonderful that 'God, sending His own Son in the likeness of sinful flesh, and *for sin,* condemned sin in the flesh'[10]. And how amazing that the total numerical value of the Greek spelling of *'Jesus of Nazareth'* amounts to 2,197, which has the factors of 13 x 13 x 13. God made Him, Jesus, to be *sin* for us — that is, He was identified with our sin — that we might become 'the righteousness of God in Him'[11].

Let us never forget that the Bible is *a numerical book.* Every single letter in the Hebrew and also in the Greek language, stands for a numeral. Every one of the words of God has a value of its own, so that the value of a phrase will often provide a positive clue as to its meaning, which would not otherwise appear. Not for nothing does our Lord tell us that 'the very hairs of your head are all numbered!'[12]   Let us ask, what is there that is *not* numbered in this universe?

And what is the Chronology of the Bible? It is *the Word of the living God* and it can never be separated from His Person any more than any other part of the Divine Revelation. Have we not seen that *redemption* is inseparably linked with *time* in the Scriptures?

With this in mind then, let us look once more at the date and circumstances surrounding the *Redeemer's* birth in Bethlehem, which name in Hebrew signifies 'the place of food'.

When all the facts had been brought together, it was established that the hour of the Saviour's birth was 8 am* (the opening of the hour of incense or morning sacrifice) on October 29th 1 BC. This 15th of the 7th month was the first day of the Feast of Booths, commonly called 'Tabernacles'[13]. This feast was to remind Israel that God made them dwell in booths when He brought them out of Egypt. For this reason Jesus needed to be born in an outside shelter, or booth, no doubt constructed of branches or rough wood for the beasts that fed there.

In His Father's hidden calendar‡ however, this same day was the 15th of the 1st month — the first day of 'Unleavened Bread'[14] — and there is no doubt that for this reason the babe was laid in a feeding trough or manger. In His manhood, He could say of Himself 'The bread of God is He which cometh down from heaven, and giveth life unto the world'[15].

---

[10] Romans 8: 3	[13] Leviticus 23: 33-43	* See Note 5 on page 184
[11] 2 Corinthians 5: 21	[14] Leviticus 23: 6	‡ See 'The Years of The Messiah'
[12] Matthew 10: 30	[15] John 6: 33	on page 168 in Appendix 1

And did this Feast of Tabernacles that year have a 'last day' (like that in John 7: 37, where the eighth day is called 'that great day of the feast')? Yes, it was on the 'eighth day' after His birth, when the child was circumcised, that 'His Name was called JESUS'[16]. We cannot stay to touch on the significance of this now, but trust to do so later. *(See pages 109-117 — Ed.)*

In the foregoing details we have sketched the timing of the Lord's birth in Bethlehem so that we might the better be able to appreciate the miracle of His Father's timing when, once again, He brought together the two Feasts (of Tabernacles and Unleavened Bread) that is, at the culmination of His work, when Jesus died and rose again in AD 33. *(See Charts 6 & 9 on pages 191 & 194.)*

---

[16] Luke 2: 21

CHAPTER THIRTEEN

God's Hidden Day of Atonement

*'If they hear not Moses and the prophets, neither will they
be persuaded, though one rose from the dead'
(Luke 16: 31)*

God has a very positive reason for allowing the exact timing of
the events to do with our Lord's First Advent to come to light at the
present time. That reason is that 'leaven' must now be purged out
from the houses of His redeemed people. And what is leaven?
Jesus had to explain the meaning of this to His disciples.

The Son of God had perfect foresight of conditions that would
prevail at the close of our age, and in His parable of Matthew 13: 33
He saw that 'the whole' of the pure teaching of New Testament
days would be 'leavened' by thoughts and doctrines of men. It
would commence as 'three measures of meal' (unleavened) but it
would end as a wholly-leavened mass. He made it absolutely clear
that the 'leaven' He had in mind was the liberty of teachers to think
and say exactly what they would about the truth of God (Matthew
16: 6-12). Actually it was the 'leaven' in the minds of the Pharisees
of His day which caused Him to be put to death (see John 19: 7).

Now, however, the hour has come for the Church of God
when 'leaven' is to be purged out from all our dwellings, and this is
pictured in Exodus 12: 19. It is well known that before Israel could
leave Egypt, at the time of God's great *'midnight'* intervention in
that land, His people had to eat *'unleavened bread'* ‡.

In the counterpart illustration in Genesis 19: 3, before Lot and
his daughters could be rescued from Sodom — the very night
before they left the doomed city — he, too, 'did bake unleavened
bread' and eat it. And to complete the picture on the last night

---

‡ See Chart 10 on page 195

before King Saul died at the end of his 'forty years'[1] (which are typical of our Christian dispensation of forty Jubilee years) he also had to eat 'unleavened bread'[2].

So we see that it is not sufficient for God to require that the impure teaching of men be put away, but that there is need for this to be replaced by the truth, as it is 'in Jesus'[3]. All down the ages men have tried to make God's truth palatable to the world and to explain it away (if they could not explain it), but it stands to reason that now, as we face the end of the journey, 'the true light' must once again shine out — for God is 'not willing that any should perish', and desires 'all men to be saved, and to come unto the knowledge of the truth'[4].

The Week of The New Creation

We come now to look again at the 'week' of the 'new creation' which we considered briefly in Chapters 8 and 12. When Mary anointed Jesus at Bethany in the evening of the true 10th of the 1st month, as we saw, she chose out the Lamb of God four days before the Lord's Passover and, as the Lord said, wherever the gospel should be preached throughout the earth, this action of hers must be told for a memorial of her. It was a vital part of the plan of redemption.

But Mary also anointed Jesus as King (John 12: 3 *cp* Song of Solomon 1: 12). We learn from John 12: 12 that the next morning Jesus rode into the holy city in triumph and was acclaimed as 'King' by the multitude of His disciples. Matthew's gospel tells us that 'the multitudes that went before, and that followed, cried, saying "Hosanna to the Son of David: Blessed is He that cometh in the Name of the Lord; Hosanna in the highest"'[5]. The word 'Hosanna' (Heb. *Hoshiah Nah)* has the meaning 'Save now, we pray Thee'!

The requisition of the 'young ass'[6], upon which Jesus rode, and its being covered with the disciples' garments before they set Him on it, all had specific reference to the hidden meaning of this day, as we are about to see. The account in John 12: 23-33 should be carefully studied. We read that Jesus emphasised a certain *'hour':* 'The *hour* is come, that the Son of man should be glorified ... *Now* is my soul troubled (or afflicted); and what shall I say? "Father, save me from *this hour"*: but for this cause came I unto

---

[1] Acts 13: 21
[2] 1 Samuel 28: 24
[3] Ephesians 4: 21
[4] 2 Peter 3: 9 & 1 Timothy 2: 4
[5] Matthew 21: 9
[6] John 12: 14

this hour. "Father, glorify Thy name". Then came there a voice from heaven, saying, "I have both glorified it, and will glorify it again"' (verses 23, 27-28).

Then once again Jesus emphasised the significance of that hour with the words, *'now* is the judgment of this world: *now* shall the prince of this world be cast out'. And looking on four days, He continued: 'And I, if I be lifted up from the earth, will draw all men unto Me', this signifying what death He should die (verses 31-32).

What then was the secret of this day, which Jesus viewed as the day of His burying? What was this *hour,* which Jesus looked on as the hour of His death, when 'through death' the prince of this world would be cast out and his power annulled?[7]

Let us put all incredulity away — for we are certainly about to discover something very wonderful, so deeply has it been concealed by the mighty hand of God; and scarcely in 3,600 years have the people of Israel understood the meaning of this day which, however, they have most sedulously observed at quite a different season, from year to year.

The Hidden 'Day of Atonement'

'On the tenth day of this seventh month there shall be a day of atonement: it shall be a holy convocation unto you; and ye shall afflict your souls, and offer an offering made by fire unto the Lord.' (Leviticus 23: 27)

If we acclaim Jesus as the Head of a 'new creation', we shall readily accept the fact that when He came unto the world, His Father saw *a new calendar* come into being. To prove this, we must measure our Lord's years forward from the day of His Nativity, which was October 29th 1 BC. Taking this as the first day of the new calendar, we find that the age of Jesus on April 27th AD 33 — the Jews' 10th of Nisan — was **33 years** (of 354 days each), **6 months and 10 days**. In other words, it was the Day of Atonement in His 34th year. (In terms of our solar years, this measurement was 32 years and 181 days, or a total of 11,869 days.)

The seventh month in Israel's calendar, of course, fell annually in the autumn and the last occasion when any Israelite would ever accept that a 'Day of Atonement' fell in the spring would be that day when the lambs were chosen for the Exodus Passover (see Exodus

---

[7] Hebrews 2: 14

12:3 and Leviticus 23: 41-43 where it is obvious, as we have previously stated, that God saw the Exodus take place in a 'seventh month').

So now at last we have the reason why Jesus said: *'Now is my soul troubled'*,[8] for to Him it was a reality that that day was, indeed, *the true 'Day of Atonement'* — the one day in the year when every Israelite must 'afflict his soul', according to the law. But none in Jerusalem then knew what God was accomplishing in secret. He had ceased, long before this, to take pleasure in the round of Jewish festivities. As He says in Isaiah 1: 14 'Your new moons and your appointed feasts My soul hateth' and in the previous verse, 'the new moons and sabbaths, the calling of assemblies, I cannot away with (or endure)'. Also, in Amos 5: 21 we hear Him say: 'I hate, I despise your feast days'. God knew, from the beginning, of the Calvary Passover and of Israel's scornful rejection of His beloved Son.

How wonderful it was for the eye of God to see *the true Israelite, Jesus,* perfectly fulfilling His Word and magnifying His law, according to a calendar which the Father Himself had conceived, and would ultimately make known to men.

Here on this secret Day of Atonement, as we learn from His words already quoted from John 12: 27-33, we find He was even then offering Himself as 'an offering made by fire unto the Lord'[9]. To Christ the interval of *four days* to the actual hour of His death on Calvary was as though it did not exist — to Him it was *now.*

The Day of Atonement is the day of *covering* (for the Hebrew word 'to make atonement', implies this). So we see Jesus — 'the Lamb of God' — covering the ass's colt with Himself as He sat upon it, His disciples having first covered it with their own clothes. For in Job 11: 12 we are told that 'man' is 'born like a wild (or free) ass's colt', and in Exodus 13: 13 that 'every firstling of an ass thou shalt redeem with a lamb ... and all the firstborn of man among thy children shalt thou redeem'.

The disciples had identified themselves with the ass by putting their own clothes on it. The unclean animal typified them, but the *Redeemer* had covered it, and the rejoicing of the multitude knew no bounds. How wonderful that Jesus should manifest *Atonement* (covering) personally in this way!

It was now just **four days** of a thousand years each (4,000 years

---

[8] John 12: 27
[9] Leviticus 23: 27

88

in the Redemption Chronology) from the Fall of Adam when God Himself had made atonement with His own hand by the shedding of blood, in Eden, for 'unto Adam also and to his wife did the Lord God make coats of skins, and clothed them'[10]. And at that very hour when the first blood was spilled in Eden, the Redeemer had looked ahead to Calvary. To Him each 'thousand years' was 'as one day'[11] and over that time He would bear with sinful man and blot out 'as a thick cloud' his transgressions and 'as a cloud'[12] his sin. To the Saviour the work was 'finished' as it were, 'from the foundation of the world'[13].

This appears to be the thought of God behind the Day of Atonement on the tenth of the month, while the slaying of the lambs on the fourteenth of the first month (the Passover aspect) showed that the death of the Redeemer would not take place until the 4,000 years were ended.

Much more could be said as to the anointing of Jesus, our Great High Priest, at the opening of this hidden Day of Atonement — a day which Leviticus 23: 32 carefully informs us commences 'in the ninth day of the month at even'. We mention this because of the timing of the Supper in Bethany when Mary anointed the Lord with her precious ointment. We are told that 'the house was filled with the odour of the ointment'[14] and there is no doubt that our Lord's command: 'Verily I say unto you, Wheresoever this gospel shall be preached in the whole world, there shall also this, that this woman hath done, be told for a memorial of her'[15] will be obeyed throughout the household of God, before the end comes. Even the chief apostles were ignorant and sided with Judas Iscariot in decrying Mary's act, because they failed to see the reason for this anointing — and nothing is more clear than the fact that Mary enjoyed an intimacy with the heart of God which none of the others shared. As Jesus had said on a previous occasion, she has 'chosen that good part, which shall not be taken away from her'[16].

---

[10] Genesis 3: 21
[11] 2 Peter 3: 8
[12] Isaiah 44: 22
[13] Hebrews 4: 3
[14] John 12: 3
[15] Matthew 26: 13
[16] Luke 10: 42

CHAPTER FOURTEEN

The Death and Resurrection of Jesus

'He revealeth the deep and secret things'
(Daniel 2: 22)

The Gospel of Mark enables us to trace with accuracy the events of the four days from our Lord's entry into Jerusalem on Monday, April 27th AD 33. In chapter 11, verse 12, we read of the cursing of the fig tree 'on the morrow', that is, on the Tuesday; and in verse 19 'when even was come, He went out of the city'. In verse 20 'in the morning' — Wednesday — the fig tree is seen dried up from the roots. On this day Jesus ended His ministry in the Temple and departed from it (chapter 13: 1).

Matthew 24 and 25 give our Lord's teachings on this final day, after His departure from the Temple, and in chapter 26, verse 2, He says: 'Ye know that after two days is the Passover, and the Son of Man is betrayed to be crucified'. These 'two days' were, inclusively, the Wednesday on which He spoke and the Thursday — April 30th — in the evening of which He took the Passover with the twelve and Judas betrayed Him.

Friday, May 1st, was the day of His Crucifixion. It was the 15th of the 1st month in the Divine Calendar and, as we see so clearly from the gospels, the Jews' Passover was a day later — that is, the Lord was crucified on their 14th Nisan and buried that same evening[1].

As already mentioned in Chapter 9, the days of the coming out of Egypt proved to be an exact pattern of the days between our Lord's death and resurrection in AD 33. Revelation 11: 8 likens

---

[1] John 19: 31-42, and see Chart 9 on page 194

'the great city ... where also our Lord was crucified' to 'Egypt'. That is, Jerusalem 'spiritually is called Sodom and Egypt' and, when we read Luke's account of the Transfiguration, we find Moses and Elijah speaking with Jesus about His coming 'exodus' *(lit. Greek)* which He was about to accomplish at Jerusalem[2].

It is important to note this, because we have to insist that there was a perfect antitypical fulfilment in AD 33 of which the events at the Exodus from Egypt were typical. (See Chart 7 on page 192.)

In 1639 BC the whole nation of Israel 'departed ... on the fifteenth day of the first month; on the morrow after the Passover'[3]. This was the type. In AD 33, one Man 'went out' of the 'Egypt' of this world by crucifixion and all of the redeemed went out with Him. Paul argues this way in 2 Corinthians 5: 14. The 'Passover', therefore, which God was observing for the fulfilment of His Word, was certainly not 'the Jews' Passover'[4], which John's Gospel alone mentions. Similarly, the 'first day of Unleavened Bread' or 'the Feast of Unleavened Bread', to which Matthew, Mark and Luke refer[5], and which is always the 15th of the first month (commencing in the evening of the 14th), was certainly not the Jewish Feast — which did not commence until the time of Christ's burial. The only reference made to the Jews' Feast is in John 19: 31, where the evangelist says that 'that sabbath day' after the crucifixion, 'was an high day'. That is, the Jewish weekly Sabbath (our Saturday) which commenced on the Friday evening, when the bodies of the crucified were taken down for burial, was 'a high day' because it was also the beginning of the Jews' Feast of Unleavened Bread.

Because He 'hated' the Jews' Feasts[6], God ignored the celebration on their 15th of Nisan, which was the Saturday. Was it likely, then, that He would acknowledge the Jews 'first day of the weeks', that is, the Sunday? On this day the Jews were presumably keeping the ordinance of Leviticus 23: 11-12, offering a sacrifice together with the first sheaf of their harvest 'on the morrow after the Sabbath'. One thing is perfectly clear: the Lord could hardly accept their burnt offerings and recognise their Feast of 'Firstfruits' when they had just put His own Son to the most terrible death it was possible for man or devils to devise!

It will be clearly understood that the reason we are saying this is to show plainly that 'the first day of the weeks' (or more

---

[2] Luke 9: 31
[3] Numbers 33: 3
[4] John 11: 55
[5] Matthew 26: 17, Mark 14: 1, 12 & Luke 22: 1-7
[6] Isaiah 1: 13-15

correctly, the First Day of the Sabbaths* — that is, the seven Sabbaths to Pentecost) which all the gospels declare was the day of Christ's Resurrection[7], **was not the Jewish one.** God waited until these two observances of the Jews, the 'holy convocation' of the Feast of Unleavened Bread, and the Jews' 'First Day of the Weeks' (our Sunday, May 3rd) which followed it, were past and gone before He raised up Jesus our Lord from the dead.

Therefore Monday May 4th AD 33 was the true 'first (day) of the weeks', and how perfectly our blessed Lord and Master fulfilled the Divine requirements of this day, as has already been described in our Chapter 11.

Now that we can see how Christendom has failed to understand the timing of our Lord's abode in death and in the grave, we can look afresh at the 'week' of the New Creation. We have already patterned out the *four days,* from the evening of the hidden Day of Atonement, to the evening of the 14th of the 7th month in the Calendar of the Life of Jesus. The two days of His entombment, Saturday and Sunday, May 2nd and 3rd, were thus the 15th and 16th of the 7th month, and His glorious Resurrection, therefore, took place on 'the seventeenth day' of 'the seventh month' — reminding us of the day when the Ark came to rest upon the mountains of Ararat (Genesis 8: 4).

How wonderful now to discover that this 'week' of seven days was to God a miniature, each day for a thousand years, of the whole course of man's time upon the earth!

We have seen the 4,000 years from Creation to the Cross shadowed in the *four days* Jesus looked ahead to His death; we have seen the *two days* His body lay in the sepulchre as the pattern of these past 2,000 years of Jewish dispersion, and the bloodstained history of Christendom. And we now know that we live on the borderland of that seventh day — the 'thousand years' of Christ's coming Kingdom.

The Hours of The Cross

We learn from Mark's record that our blessed Redeemer was crucified at 'the third hour'[8] of the day. Jewish daytime counting began at sunrise, so the third hour would be between 8 and 9 am. Inclusively reckoned, it was for seven hours that He suffered on

---

* See Note 3 on page 184   [8] Mark 15: 25
[7] Matthew 28: 1, Mark 16: 2, Luke 24: 1 & John 20: 1

the Tree — until 'the ninth hour' (2 - 3 pm), and His purpose was to make atonement for the sins of seven thousand years.

Of necessity, many questions will arise which must for the present remain unanswered in this brief survey of Time in the Scriptures. Those whose minds are active in this matter will quickly grasp the fact that the great intervention of God in the celestial sphere, when He caused the earth's revolution to come to a halt for 'about a whole day'[9] must have directly affected the order of the weekdays thereafter, creating a day's difference between time as reckoned in Heaven and as recorded by man on the earth. The fact was that there was only one sunset in 48 hours. This, indeed, was how God 'wrought' to preserve His 'Sabbaths', as He says in Ezekiel 20: 12-22. Heaven's calendar became one day in advance of Israel's after the 'long day'. Therefore, when Christ died, in God's sight it was already a Sabbath and, as He refused to reckon time to His Son while He was dead, the day of the resurrection (Monday May 4th) became to God 'the morrow after the Sabbath'[10].

This was not the only reason why this tremendous miracle was wrought in 1599 BC but it certainly effected this purpose, and it is also a very significant fact that the next great intervention of God with the sun, in the time of Hezekiah (712-711 BC) was, inclusively, '888' years later (see Isaiah 38: 8). This certainly confirms that both of these acts of God in the heavens were directly related to the Person of Jesus, whose number is 888.

'Three Days and Three Nights'

We can now look back and see how perfectly the one and only sign Jesus said would be given to His generation was fulfilled — 'the sign of the prophet Jonas'[11].

The Friday upon which He died, 'at the ninth hour' was clearly *the first day,* and the Friday night, *the first night.* The Saturday and Saturday night were *the second day and night* and the Sunday and Sunday night were *the third day and third night.*

'The Third Day' and 'After Three Days'

Three times in Mark's Gospel our Lord stated that He would be 'killed, and *after three days* rise again' (chapter 8: 31 and in the

---

[9] Joshua 10: 13
[10] Leviticus 23: 11
[11] Matthew 12: 39-40

Revised Version chapters 9: 31 and 10: 34). This expression includes the day of His death as the first of the three days. When however, as in Matthew 16: 21, we find the expression 'be killed and be raised again *the third day'*, we know that the two days of death commenced with the evening (3-6 pm) on the Friday, after Jesus yielded up His Spirit at 'the ninth hour' and once again 'the third day' is found to be the Monday, when God raised Him from the dead.

A Note on 'The Evening'

It has to be remembered that the Jewish period of a day in Scripture commences in 'the evening' and the very word for 'evening' in Hebrew means 'mixture' or 'mingling'. Thus, one day merges, so to speak, into the next in the evening. A proof of this may be seen in Matthew 26: 17 where 'the first day of the Feast of Unleavened Bread' clearly began in the afternoon before 'they made ready the Passover' (verse 19). The account continues in verse 20, 'Now when the even (that is, sundown, or 6 pm) was come, He sat down with the the twelve'. The Divine 15th day was thus beginning as the 14th was ending.

CHAPTER FIFTEEN

The Eighteth Jubilee
Yom Kippur 1973

Before passing on, it is only right to draw attention to a further confirmation that the day of Christ's Resurrection was a Monday and not a Sunday, as Christendom has held for so many centuries.

Between the hour of our Lord's ascension to His Father on the Monday morning, to present Himself and those raised with Him as the 'sheaf of the firstfruits'[1] and the hour of His departure, when He ascended back into the heavens on Saturday June 13th, AD 33, was a measure of exactly *forty days*. It has often puzzled students of Scripture why, as the disciples returned after the Ascension, it should have been stated in Acts 1: 12 that it was '*a Sabbath day's journey*' from 'the mount called Olivet' to Jerusalem — if, as Christendom has universally asserted, the Ascension was on a Friday.[‡] When the Holy Ghost caused Luke to write (in Acts 1: 3) that Jesus was 'seen of them *forty days*' after His Resurrection, He was measuring the period exactly to the hour, and we can thank God that we now know that Jesus did ascend on a Jewish Sabbath. We also know that 'when the day of Pentecost was fully come'[2] (nine days later) it was a Monday in our calendar; the multitude who had gathered for the Jewish festival the previous day not having yet dispersed.

'Let My people go, that they may serve Me'
(Exodus 9: 1)

We must now turn our attention to a most marvellous

---

[1] Leviticus 23: 10, *cp* John 20: 17   [‡] See Chart 8 on page 193
[2] Acts 2: 1

manifestation of the patterning of God, as His Word was fulfilled in the death and resurrection of His Son.

In earlier chapters we have seen how gloriously the God of Israel stretched forth His hand to deliver His people at the *fiftieth Jubilee* (that is, 50 times 49 years from Adam in the Redemption Chronology). And we stated that, although Israel lost their 80th *Jubilee* (in AD 33) because of their rejection of their Messiah, yet it was perfectly fulfilled for everyone, Jew or Gentile, who has believed in Jesus as risen from the dead.

God celebrated the year of Jubilee at the Exodus, by letting His people go, on the 15th of the 7th month. Then, when we come to the 490th year after Exodus in this Jubilee Chronology, we see the glory of God filling the House of the Lord again on the same day, that is, at the feast of the seventh month (Tabernacles) — see 1 Kings 8: 1-11*. Again, after Nehemiah had restored the gates and wall of Jerusalem in 458 BC, we find the same feast of the seventh month was kept with great joy, even though there had been a lapse in its observance (by not dwelling in booths) 'since the days of Joshua' — see Nehemiah 8: 14-17.

So, when we come to AD 33, we need to ask 'How did the God and Father of our Lord Jesus Christ perfectly fulfil this greatest of all Jubilees, without which none of the previous Jubilees could have had full significance?'

The Jubilee Still On Time!

Surely enough, when we come to the '10th of the 7th month' at the close of the 'seventy times seven' years (the 'seventy weeks' of Daniel 9: 24)‡ and have had our eyes opened to see the great hidden 'Day of Atonement', four days before the Crucifixion, we are thrilled at what we read in each of the gospels. When the Lord spoke to Moses in Leviticus 25: 9, He instructed that the trumpet of *(lit.)* 'joyful sound' should be heard on the 'Day of Atonement'. It was to be, indeed, the day of loud and uninhibited rejoicing. And so it was, on that 27th of April in AD 33, for we read in Luke 19: 37, that 'the whole multitude of the disciples began to rejoice and praise God with a loud voice for all the mighty works that they had seen'. And when the Pharisees wanted this outcry to cease, Jesus answered: 'I tell you that, if these should hold their peace, the

---

* See Appendix 4, pages 176-177, and see Chart 3 on page 188   ‡ See Chart 1 on page 186

stones would immediately cry out' (verse 40). So for the disciples it was, indeed, a real 'Jubilee' celebration, and the Spirit of God focused their eyes on the coming of the Messianic Kingdom which, if the Jewish leaders had not rejected Him, should have opened as from that very day.

It was not likely that the great adversary of God and man would let this occasion go unchallenged, and we know that within four days another cry had arisen from the multitude — 'Away with Him, away with Him, crucify Him'[3]. That was on Friday, May 1st; in the Lord's personal calendar, the 14th day of the 7th month.

And as it drew on to the evening of that Friday, when the 15th day was due to open, there was, indeed, 'the shout of a King'[4], but, within moments, the great Redeemer bowed His head in death.

What then of the patterning of the Almighty — had Satan triumphed and were the people who had rejected their Messiah to forfeit their Year of Jubilee for ever?

No, a million times, No! But the God of Israel would suspend their Jubilee for two thousand years. This delay had actually been spoken of in Hosea 6: 2 as *'two days'* in the words: *'after two days will He revive us: in the third day He will raise us up, and we shall live in His sight'*. How clearly God had foreseen the rejection of the Messiah by His chosen people!

Let us now take a further look at the way in which this 14th day of the 7th month (the Jews' 14th Nisan) had ended, and take account of the sign which God had given — 'a sign in the sun'. For the last three hours prior to the death of Jesus, 'there was a darkness over all the earth until the ninth hour. And the sun was darkened'[5].

What was God saying in this? We believe these last three hours had a special significance. For the previous three years, ever since Jesus made His first appearance in Jerusalem when He cleansed the Temple with 'a scourge of small cords' at the time of the Jews' Passover in AD 30[6], their animosity against Him had increased and soon, as we discover from John 5: 16-18 and 7: 1, they 'sought to slay Him'. His ministry was rejected by them and in effect what they did was to put out 'the Light of the world'[7].

Because of this enmity of the leaders of His own people, it is true to say that for three years the Son of David had walked in 'the valley of the shadow of death'[8] — and in the end had actually been

---

[3] John 19: 15
[4] Numbers 23: 21
[5] Luke 23: 44-45
[6] John 2: 13-17
[7] John 8: 12
[8] Psalm 23: 4

put to death by them. As a result, 'that which was spoken by the prophet Joel'[9] was fulfilled, and 'the sun' was 'turned into darkness'. This however, was not all and a further sign was to follow for, as Peter testified on the Day of Pentecost, 'the moon' was turned 'into blood'[10].

The Two Days of the Lunar Sign

The significance of this 'sign in the moon' is vastly greater than is generally assumed, but for the present we will take the simple surface meaning of the expression: *'the moon (shall be turned) into blood'*.

When an understanding was granted as to the exact time and duration of the death and burial of Jesus, it came to light that the moon was turned into blood over the two 'feast' days — the Jews feast of Unleavened Bread and the Jews 'first day of the weeks', when they waved the Sheaf of the Firstfruits of their harvest before the Lord, together with a lamb for a burnt offering[11]. These Jewish 'feasts' God refused to recognise but they formed a type, as already shown, each 'day' as 'a thousand years'[12], representing 'the times of the Gentiles'[13] during which the Jews would be in dispersion after being cast out of the land.

This was clearly prophesied in Amos 8: 9-10 where we read: 'I will cause the sun to go down (*lit.* 'in') at noon, and I will darken the earth in the clear day: and I will turn your feasts into mourning ... and I will make it as the mourning of an only son'.

So by turning the moon 'into blood' over those two days, while the body of His only Son was lying in the sepulchre, God was really giving a 'sign' as to the nature of the 2,000 lunar years which would follow the death of Israel's Messiah. He would certainly 'turn the feasts' of the Jews 'into mourning' and who can begin to measure the sufferings of that outcast people, as history has recorded them, from the fall of Jerusalem in AD 70 to the present day? It would, indeed, be a history of bloodshed, and the supreme effort of Satan to destroy the Jews in the days of Adolf Hitler resulted in the removal of an entire third part of their whole world population from the earth.

---

[9] Acts 2: 16, Joel 2: 31   [11] Leviticus 23: 10-14   [13] Luke 21: 24
[10] Acts 2: 20   [12] 2 Peter 3: 8

The Eightieth Jubilee

Jesus was raised from the dead at midnight on May 3rd (that is, at the opening of the Roman day of May 4th) AD 33, which the gospel writers call *'the first (day) of the weeks'*[14]*. In the sight of His Father, (**who did not reckon the time of His death and entombment**) this day can have been no other than the **15th of the 7th month**. It was certainly this date in the calendar of *His life in this world,* that is, if the whole of the day on which Jesus was born — October 29th 1 BC — is taken as the beginning of His 33 years, 6 months and 14 days to His death. (This calendar reckoning has to begin at 6 pm on October 28th 1 BC.)

Hallelujah! 'And ye shall hallow the fiftieth year, and proclaim liberty throughout all the land unto all the inhabitants thereof: it shall be a Jubilee unto you; and ye shall return every man unto his possession, and ye shall return every man unto his family' (Leviticus 25: 10).

What could be more wonderful than to discover that this great 'year of release' — this year which followed immediately on 'the Day of Atonement' at the end of 49 years — had really looked on to the resurrection of Jesus our Lord from the dead! And this at the close of the last great era of 'seventy weeks' (or 10 x 49 years) which God had sent Gabriel to reveal to the prophet Daniel. In His death our glorious Lord and Saviour had, indeed, made an 'end of sins' and made 'reconciliation (*lit.* atonement) for iniquity' and, in His own person, brought in everlasting righteousness[15]. And the very next *day of His life* — and, praise God, it was now *life* **beyond the grave** — was the opening of that mysterious year, 'the fiftieth year' which (as shown in Chapter 7) could never be reckoned as an addition to *time,* because it spoke of eternal **life**, and all that Redemption really implies. *Oh, hallelujah!*

We will not now enlarge further on the meaning and vast significance of the Year of Jubilee, as our purpose is to reveal what we believe is an aspect of our Lord's personal calendar in which He can be seen to have perfectly and gloriously fulfilled 'the feasts of the Lord' pertaining to the 'first' and 'seventh' months (as outlined for us in Leviticus 23: 4-8 and 34-36). But, before doing so, we must again make special reference to the great *Day of Atonement* which God secretly designed to fall on April 27th AD 33, as already shown.

---

[14] Matthew 28: 1, Mark 16: 2
Luke 24: 1 & John 20: 1

[15] Daniel 9: 24
* See Note 3 on page 184

The Day of Atonement and the Two Thousand Years

Towards the end of Chapter 13, it was shown how simply and wonderfully the Redeemer figuratively enacted the *covering* of His people. He had 'need' of the ass's colt (see Exodus 13: 13) and then, when His disciples had covered it with their own garments, we read that 'they set Him thereon'[16]. He covered the ass, which represented them (see Job 11: 12) and with which they had identified themselves by clothing it with their own raiment. We believe it is clear that when Jesus arrived at *'the hour'*, so strongly emphasised in John 12: 23-33, from which He could look ahead exactly four days to the actual hour of His death, then He uttered the words: 'The hour is come, that the Son of Man should be glorified'.

Let us ask what hour it was which called forth the words, 'Now is my soul troubled (or afflicted); and what shall I say? "Father, save me from this hour": but for this cause came I unto this hour. "Father, glorify Thy name"'. It was then that a voice came from heaven saying, *"I have both glorified it, and will glorify it again"*. It was after this that Jesus declared: *"Now is the judgment of this world"*.

'The hour' of His death, four days later on May 1st, was 'the ninth hour', as Mark's Gospel tells us, and that was between two and three in the afternoon (Mark 15: 33-34).

'The hour is come'
Yom Kippur — October 6th 1973 at 2 pm

Those who had watched every phase of world history since 1914, with their eyes on the Bible's amazingly timed chronology, were not surprised to be alerted several days before October 6th 1973 by the knowledge that the God of Israel could by no means pass the end of 2,000 years from the Cross of Jesus without showing His hand in some dramatic way.

These 2,000 lunar years contain 708,734 days, or 1,940 solar years and 162 days in our calendar, and if they are measured from the 'hour' of 2 pm on April 27th AD 33 they will be found to end at 2 pm on October 6th, which was Israel's Day of Atonement in 1973; that is, they spanned the exact time between two Days of Atonement — the one known only to God, and the other the

---

[16] Luke 19: 34-35

accepted date observed by modern Israel, the tenth day of Tishri, which is their seventh month.

Although it was kept a complete secret beforehand by the Arab leaders involved, exactly at that hour the terrific artillery barrage simultaneously burst out on both the Syrian and Egyptian fronts; and, as many will remember, Israelis had to rush from their Yom Kippur services in their synagogues and make a dash for their tanks, planes or trucks. It is reported that among the last words they heard from the Hebrew Prayer Book, before the alarm was given, were these:

> 'On the Fast Day of Atonement it is sealed ... who is to perish by fire, who by water, who by the sword...'*

That war was amazing in every respect and the Jews call it, so we are told, 'The War of the Day of Judgment'. The events of it are too well known to rehearse here but those who take an interest in the exact timing of world affairs will be asking, 'did the God of Israel take account of the end of these 2,000 lunar years when they spanned the distance between the day of our Lord's Resurrection and the equivalent point in the Middle East War?'

Let us put this question more clearly. The greatest 'offence' Israel ever perpetrated against their God (which appears to be referred to in Hosea 5: 15) was the putting to death of their Messiah, and John 12: 10-11 shows that their religious leaders finally plotted this on April 27th AD 33. As this was with God His true, though hidden, Day of Atonement, He at once measured forward the great span of **'two days'**[17] or 2,000 exact lunar years, to end on the Jews' Day of Atonement at the precise moment when the firing broke out in all its fury, on October 6th 1973.

Then, just as there had been six days between April 27th and the midnight of May 3rd AD 33 when, as 'the resurrection and the life'[18], Jesus had turned the tables upon death, so God allowed the fearful conflict of the Yom Kippur War to continue until Friday 12th October, when the Israelis had become desperate for arms, ammunition and supplies. Their opposition to being forced to accept a ceasefire was furious, but they had to be ready to agree in the end. By this Friday, in consultation with the superpowers of Russia and America and with Egypt, Henry Kissinger was sure that he could force a ceasefire *in situ*. But at midnight the British Foreign Office realised that Egypt was not really ready to accept.

---

[17] Hosea 6: 2   * See Note 6 on page 185
[18] John 11: 25

Indeed, on the morning of October 13th President Sadat confirmed this. Egypt wanted to fight on to attain a still better position, before any ceasefire, and to bring Israel to her knees.

It was this continuation of hostilities that compelled America to decide at once to send Israel an immense airlift of supplies and ammunition, replacing what she had lost in this first week of fighting, and this they did. The result, as is well known, was that by midweek the Israelis managed to cross the Suez Canal and a week later, by the 23rd October, they had cut off supplies and water to the Egyptian Third Army.

What we have seen then is the most amazing spectacle — the same God who had operated in 1948 to bring Israel to nationhood exactly 4,000 years from His covenant of Genesis 15, made in 2053 BC — the God who had fought for Israel in the Six Day War of 1967*, when Jerusalem ceased to be 'trodden down by the Gentiles'[19] — this God in 1973 had now literally timed the appalling blow suddenly struck without warning by Egypt and Syria which, to put it mildly, would have knocked Israel right out if their enemies had been given a free hand to fight on, and if further supplies and arms had been delayed in coming from the USA.

Why then did the Lord God allow this affliction to fall upon His ancient people? ('Ancient' because of the covenant relationship God established with Israel 4,000 years ago.) I read these words from Leviticus 23: 29 relating to the law of the Day of Atonement:

> 'For whatsoever soul it be that shall not be afflicted in that same
> day, he shall be cut off from among his people.'

'But', a million Jewish voices will at once exclaim, 'Israel **was** fasting and keeping their Day of Atonement, and afflicting their souls on October 6th 1973, at the very hour when the war broke out.' We would agree, but how many among them remembered the fact that for 2,000 years *Jesus* had been abhorred and despised by their nation whose rulers had delivered Him to be crucified by the Romans in AD 33? They certainly were not 'afflicting their souls' in repentance because of what they had done to Him!

Yes, everything depends upon whether or not *Jesus was,* and is, *the Son of the Living God, and Israel's promised Redeemer.* The Gentiles have said that 'God is dead' but Israel should know better, and the facts presented in this book relating the two Days of Atonement — the hidden one in AD 33 and the one the nation

---

* See Note 7 on page 185
[19] Luke 21: 24 (RSV)

102

kept in 1973 — should, if proved to be true, provide sufficient answer. God would have His Jewish people to consider — the Messiah is not dead, He is alive for evermore!

We must not attempt to deal with the question of responsibility for the death of Jesus; but all should remember one vital point. Luke (in his Gospel chapter 22, verse 6) informs us that the Messiah was betrayed and taken to Israel's chief priests and scribes 'in the absence of the multitude'. It seems clear that the time has now come for the people (the multitude) of Israel to study their Scriptures and to pray, not only for themselves, but for their leaders that enlightenment as to the actual truth of God's Word may be granted to every sincere and seeking heart. For it has been no small matter for the nation to lose nearly 2,500 precious lives in the Yom Kippur War with Syria and Egypt and to find themselves in their present position of economic and geo-political precariousness.

It may be easy for man to say, 'no more war' and this, indeed, is the universal desire of the peoples of the world and will ultimately find fulfillment at the return of the 'Prince of Peace'[20] — following what is called 'the Supper of the Great God' in Revelation 19 (verse 17). But before all this, as we know from 1 Thessalonians 5: 1-10, there is to be a last great effort of man after 'peace and safety', prior to an outbreak of judgment from which there will be no escape, and of which the Second World War was but a shadow.

However, as the world knows, there is no hope of either peace or safety in the present hour, unless the continuous strife over the boundaries of Israel can be calmed and healed by a solution which is satisfactory to both Jew and Arab. Perhaps we are about to see that calm Figure, hitherto 'asleep on a pillow, in the hinder part of the ship' rise up and utter His rebuke to the treatening wind and waves, saying to the sea (of the nations), 'Peace, be still' (see Mark 4: 37-41).

We shall make no further comment on the Divine reasons for allowing the Yom Kippur War, as far as Israel is concerned, but must turn at once to watch its effect upon the civilised world. Over that very weekend, which was 2,000 years from the resurrection of Christ, a new situation developed in the Middle East, and already Egyptian and Saudi Arabian Oil experts were

[20] Isaiah 9: 6

commencing to discuss ways in which their 'Oil Weapon' might be used against Israel.

How little did the nations dream that (after the *'two days'* of a thousand years) a *'third day'* had been reached in world history.

'As a thief in the night'
(2 Peter 3: 10)

No one needs to be reminded of the economic difficulties into which the so-called Christian nations have been plunged as a result of the Arab oil embargo of 1973. One thing is clear (or should be clear to all who pay the least attention to the strong exhortation of 2 Peter 3: 8, that we should 'not be ignorant of this one thing, that one day is with the Lord as a thousand years ... ') and that is this, that measured from the death of Christ, *'two days'* had passed and therefore that a *'third day'* had come in October 1973. And for the civilised world that 'day' came *'as a thief in the night*[21]. Have any attempted to estimate the financial loss to the western nations which has been occasioned since the Yom Kippur War?

The Church of God, practically as a whole, has no knowledge of these things because they have not understood how to 'watch' for the coming of the 'day of the Lord'. In the foreknowledge of God, all Christendom is depicted in Matthew 25: 1-13 as 'ten virgins' or bridesmaids who are well-equipped with 'lamps', but only half of whom have taken 'oil' (signifying the Holy Spirit) with them, as they settle down to wait for the Bridegroom's arrival. Before long, however, all are overcome with sleep. But the parable shows that at the hour of 'midnight' they were awakened by a cry, and one and all became aware of the need to 'trim their lamps', i.e. to get their profession and their testimony in line with the Holy Spirit's requirements in relation to the Lord's appearing.

Who can doubt that this end-time awakening has already begun with a multitude of individuals the world over. These, indeed, are busy with the trimming of their lamps and delight in the ever brighter burning of their 'oil'.

However, we must now return to consider 'the hidden things' in AD 33.

---

[21] 1 Thessalonians 5: 2-6

CHAPTER SIXTEEN

Jesus Keeps the Feasts of the First and Seventh Months

'In His temple doth every one speak of His glory'
(Psalm 29: 9)

When we study God's ways in nature we are accustomed to look for absolute perfection in His designing — take the marvellous patterning of a butterfly's wing, for instance! And once we have begun to appreciate that His time designs are, like all His works, wrought for His glory — 'for the whole earth is full of His glory'[1] — then we look for perfection in all that He does and, when we seek it, we find it. For 'the works of the Lord are great, sought out of all them that have pleasure therein'[2].

The question before us now is this: 'How much of the Law relating to the 'Feasts of the Lord' did Jesus and His disciples fulfil at the time of His all-atoning Sacrifice in AD 33? That He fulfilled it *in part,* every Bible expositor would agree, for it is clear that at the time of a Passover He certainly laid down His life for us. And that God accepted His sacrifice is also clear, because He raised Him from the dead.

But we hear Isaiah say (chapter 42: 21) 'The Lord is well pleased for His righteousness' sake; *He will magnify the law, and make it honourable'.*

To make quite plain what we are really saying, we must ask a further question. Where do we find Jesus and His disciples keeping the two 'holy convocations', one at the beginning and the other at the end of the 'seven days' of 'unleavened bread'?[3]

Never have we heard a suggestion from any writer that any

---

[1] Isaiah 6: 3
[2] Psalm 111: 2
[3] Leviticus 23: 6-8

such thing happened, or could have happened, in the year of the Crucifixion. We all know, without dispute, that the first 'holy convocation' at the beginning of the seven days — that is, in the evening of the true 14th day of the first month — was the scene of 'the Passover' and 'the Lord's Supper' when, reckoning Himself as having laid down His life already, Jesus gave His body (symbolically in the bread) and His blood (symbolically in the wine) to His disciples to eat and drink.

But as for keeping a second 'holy convocation' seven days later, in view of the New Testament's apparent complete silence on the matter, who would dare to suggest that any such gathering took place?

However, when we were reminded that on two previous occasions — at the Exodus and at the Birth of Christ, as we have already seen — God's design had been to bring together the two 'feasts' of Unleavened Bread and Tabernacles so that they ran concurrently, we had to ask why this should have been, unless the same design was destined to recur in AD 33?

Revelation on this matter came slowly, and over many years; but in the end the whole glorious pattern of what had been accomplished before, at, and after Calvary stood out in bold relief.

For the moment we must ask the reader to accept by faith a fact which later it will be possible to prove — and that is that the actual hour of the Birth of Jesus was **8 am*** on October 29th 1 BC.

If we then measure the calendar *of His life* **from the hour of His birth**, we shall find that Jesus was put to death, that is crucified, at 8 am on May 1st AD 33 after 33 years (of 354 days) 6 months and 13 days. His sufferings, and being 'made a curse for us'[4] as He hung upon the Tree, lasted from 8 am to around 3 pm when He actually died.

God then suspended the reckoning of the calendar of His Son's *life* in this world until midnight on Sunday May 3rd, when He raised Him from the dead. (See Chart 9 on page 194.)

So the fact stands out that the major part of Monday May 4th, as measured from the Sunday midnight, was still the 14th day of the 7th month.

---

* See Note 5 on page 184
[4] Galatians 3: 13

The 15th Day — 'A Holy Convocation'
'As for God, His way is perfect'
(Psalm 18: 30)

We shall now see how perfectly (that is, completely) the Word of God was fulfilled by our Lord and His apostles on the day of His Resurrection.

Many have wondered why it was that Jesus left it so late on 'the first (day) of the weeks'* before meeting with the gathered disciples in the Upper Room in Jerusalem. This was some time after the two, with whom He had 'broken bread' about sun-down at Emmaus, had returned to their brethren in the holy city — a distance, we are told, of 'sixty furlongs' which would be a journey of at least two hours, and probably more (Luke 24: 13).

We now need to consider this 'holy convocation', late on Monday May 4th, which doubtless went on far into the night, for it could not have commenced before about 9 pm when Jesus came and 'stood in the midst'[5]. In John's account (chapter 20: 19-23) we see how, at long last, the God of Israel was able to come and dwell among His people, as represented by these apostles. A thousand years before this, in the time of Solomon, the cloud had 'filled the house of God' on the opening day of the 'feast' of 'the seventh month'[6]. This was the 60th Jubilee from Creation. But now the Great Redeemer made it possible for His disciples to **continue to abide in Him**, for 'He breathed on them, and saith unto them, "Receive ye the Holy Ghost"' (verse 22).

For the next seven days these disciples were 'dwelling together in unity', indwelt by the Spirit of Christ. Hallelujah! Was this the first time the Heavens had actually witnessed the real 'Feast of Abiding in Christ?' Had such a thing ever been possible before in the history of Israel? These questions will answer themselves in due course.

We must turn at once to another aspect of these same seven days, as given in Luke's account (chapter 24). Here we see Jesus feeding His disciples on the true 'unleavened bread'. If He had previously explained to them that 'leaven' was the doctrine and teaching of men (such as the Pharisees and Sadducees)[7] then it should not have been difficult to discover the meaning of **unleavened** bread. We believe it is true to say that on the night of May 4th AD 33, for the first time in history, the Son of God opened

---

[5] Luke 24: 36
[6] 2 Chronicles 5: 3-14

[7] Matthew 16: 6-12
* See Note 3 on page 184

the understanding of His disciples 'that they might understand the Scriptures'. He expatiated to them on all the things 'which were written in the law of Moses, and in the prophets, and in the psalms' which concerned Himself. And what He showed them was *the truth* which man had never known before. Was this not the real 'Feast of Unleavened Bread?'

It could only be so if it took place at the opening of the 15th day of the first month. But what 'first month' could it be?

We have to look back again to the Exodus[8] and consider the 'type' and pattern of the first Passover and see what God did then. If we read the final verses of Leviticus 23, we find that Israelites were to 'dwell in booths' in the feast of the 'seventh month' — 'that your generations may know that I made the children of Israel to dwell in booths, when I brought them out of the land of Egypt'. So spake the Lord. And the very first night after their departure from Rameses on the 15th day of the **first** month, we are told in Numbers 33: 3-5, the children of Israel 'pitched in Succoth'. As Succoth means 'booths' it is perfectly clear that 'the first month of the year' referred to in Exodus 12: 2 had originally been 'the seventh month'. (Most interpreters have accepted this and the Bible's chronology fully substantiates the fact.)

So, after the Exodus from Egypt, we discover that God still thinks of Israel keeping in remembrance *'the seventh month'*, although He had made it *'the first month of the year'* to them.[‡]

It was the same month, but it had two aspects and, once this is accepted, it can be appreciated how needful it was for God to call this 'seventh month' in the 34th year of our Lord's personal chronology — *'the first month of the year'* — for it was the inaugural month of an entirely 'New Creation'. The 'old things' had 'passed away' and 'behold', says Paul in 2 Corinthians 5: 17, *'all things* are become new'. At the Exodus, truly, the birth of the nation of Israel took place when they were separated from Egypt; but it was not until AD 33 when the real loosing of Israel, God's *'firstborn'*[9], could be effected because it was then that Jesus became 'the first begotten from the dead'[10]. How, let us ask, could *He* be born in Bethlehem on the 15th of the 7th month in 1 BC and not be 'the firstborn from the dead' on *the same date,* that is, in a calendar known to God before the foundation of the world?

---

[8] Exodus 12, and see Chart 7 on page 192
[‡] See Chart 6 on page 191
[9] Exodus 4: 22
[10] Revelation 1: 5 *(literal trans)*

So Jesus and His disciples did keep the first 'holy convocation' of each of the two 'feasts' **simultaneously**, in the evening of May 4th AD 33.

Now we know that a question will at once arise with all who have treated this matter of time seriously in the foregoing pages — what about the Lord's Passover Supper on Thursday April 30th — was this not the true 'holy convocation' opening 'the Feast of Unleavened Bread'?

No doubt all reading this will know that Jesus, in the most wonderful revelation of His personal love relationship with His own at, and after, that Last Supper (as John so fully recounts in chapters 13-17), had to say: 'I have yet many things to say unto you, *but ye cannot bear them now*[11]. Yet, four days later, on the Monday evening, He was to be found pouring out from the Scriptures all those things which concerned Himself. This, of course, was because the time had at last come when He could also impart to His hearers the Spirit of God, without whose indwelling they would never have been able to benefit by the unfolding of these wondrous things.

Could anyone, even in eternity, gauge how much had transpired in those intervening four days, or how great a change had been wrought in those disciples?

An expression in Exodus 12: 6 in the Hebrew has often been a puzzle to expositors, for the word says:

'Ye shall keep it (the lamb) up until the fourteenth day of the same month: and the whole assembly of the congregation of Israel shall kill it (lit.) *between the two evenings'*.

Which 'two evenings'?

How deep is the Word of the Living God — how unsearchable are His judgments and His ways past searching out!

Any normal commentator would refer us to Leviticus 23: 32 and say that the day of the Passover would commence the previous evening and run 'from even unto even' like the Day of Atonement. We need not debate the correctness of this assumption but have to remember this fact: the death of Jesus Christ brought the four periods of 490 Redemption Years from Abram's birth (which we call 'the times of Israel') to an end and in Divine reckoning they ended with the hour of the Lord's Passover Supper.

Imagine if God had not raised up Jesus from the dead —

---

[11] John 16: 12

would there have been any Feast of Unleavened Bread, or Feast of Tabernacles? But because Christ was raised up, there was a new beginning — this time in the power of His resurrection!

What was necessary, however, was that it should be **the same date** so that the Scripture might be fulfilled. In Exodus 12: 18 the word was given to Israel: 'In the first month, on the fourteenth day of the month at even, ye shall eat unleavened bread, until the one and twentieth day of the month at even'[‡].

Oh, praise God — 'praise ye the Lord from the heavens: praise Him in the heights ... praise ye Him, sun and moon ... praise Him, ye heavens of heavens' (Psalm 148: 1-4) it was, indeed, *between the two evenings* of April 30th and May 4th AD 33 that everything pertaining to *the Great Passover* was accomplished, so that the true Feast of Unleavened Bread could open for those disciples who represented Israel. And it was in the night of May 4th, no doubt around midnight, that the real 'letting go' of these disciples took place. At the previous midnight Jesus — 'the Firstborn' of God — had been 'let go' from death; but on the Monday night it was His people that were 'let go' (see Exodus 5: 1, etc.) as He breathed on them His Holy Spirit.

And then the disciples kept the Feast for seven days, until Jesus rejoined them and there was a second 'holy convocation' as we read in John 20: 26.

His Second Appearing

The expression 'after eight days', of course, included the whole of 'the first (day) of the weeks' in the late evening of which Jesus first met with the apostles, as described above. So these eight days ran on to the evening and midnight of May 11th. This was the solar anniversary of the midnight of the Exodus Passover, which took place on May 11th 1639 BC. (1,671 solar years had passed but, as shown previously, a total of 201 years — 131 years of the Servitudes in the time of the Judges and the 70 years of the Babylonian Captivity — had been viewed by God as *lost* to Israel in this long era. This meant that exactly three times 'seventy times seven' or 1,470 **solar** years had now elapsed, in the sight of God, from the start of Israel's national history at the Exodus midnight deliverance, when 'the firstborn' were 'let go' from death in Egypt.)

‡ See Charts 7 & 10 on pages 192 & 195

Before dealing with the significance of this second 'holy convocation' kept by Jesus and the disciples at the end of the 21st day of the seventh month in the calendar of His *life,* we have to point out that with God this is viewed as taking place 'on the eighth day' (Leviticus 23: 34-36). Let it be said that where the eighth day is spoken of in Scripture, the emphasis is on the **beginning** and not the end of the day. Both Tabernacles and Unleavened Bread were feasts of 'seven days' but the close of the seventh day could be viewed as the opening of the eighth. Space does not allow us to go into the finer points of this difference here but the reason will become clearer when we go on to see the dispensational meaning of these feasts in the next Chapter. We shall also see the significance of Thomas's absence during the seven days and his recovery when He saw the Lord at their end.

CHAPTER SEVENTEEN

The Meanings of The Feasts for The Church Dispensation

*Jesus saith unto them, 'Have ye understood
all these things?'   (Matthew 13: 51)*

There is no way in which we can actually 'understand' anything in the Bible unless we are 'taught of God'. And when we come to figures and numbers in the Scriptures, especially in regard to *time,* it is absolutely necessary that we have a clear vision of 'the pattern' of God's works. In Ezekiel 43: 10 the prophet is told: 'Thou son of man, show the house to the house of Israel, that they may be ashamed of their iniquities: *and let them measure the pattern'.*

The previous three chapters of Ezekiel had been filled with detail, measurements and description of the coming great Millennial Temple; but until a clear diagram and plan could be drawn up to show the *'pattern'* of it all, those measurements remained meaningless. It is exactly so with the Bible's Chronology and we can apply this illustration to 'the feasts of the Lord' — for we need to see and measure the pattern of them and know what they actually signify. (See Chart 9 on page 194.)

'Let us keep the feast'   *(1 Corinthians 5: 8)*

When Paul wrote 'Christ our passover is sacrificed for us: therefore let us keep the feast ... with the unleavened bread of sincerity and truth' (verses 7-8), he was making a Jewish feast apply to the Christian Church. He was showing that it had a spiritual meaning which would obviously be applicable to the whole dispensation, which we have seen measures 1,960 lunar years in the Redemption Chronology. We have also seen that 'the feast' was one of **seven days**.

Therefore, viewing the 1,960 lunar years as representing the *seven days,* we find that each 'day' would be of 280 years' duration. Without stopping to establish the reason why God views 280 years as one 'day'*, we will now ask how many such 'days' there had been from Adam to the great Passover of AD 33 in this Chronology. The answer is, of course, *fourteen days,* for 14 times 280 amounts to 3,920 — the year of the Crucifixion, as we have already seen.

So 'the pattern' of the Passover and Feast of Unleavened Bread can now be discerned in its simplicity — the *fourteen days and seven days* representing the whole course of the 6,000 Years of Redemption (5,880 or 21 x 280 in actual time) from Adam to the present day. And, of course, the feast of the seventh month, with its 14 and 7 days, shows the same period in another aspect, that of *abiding in Christ,* which 'Tabernacles' or 'Booths' signifies, as we have already seen.

The Two Divisions of Six Months

At last we are beginning to see why it was that the eye of God saw each year divided into *two periods of six months.* This continuous alternation showed every six months picturing the whole course of the six thousand years from Adam to the Kingdom. For this reason, each six-month period began with the marked 21 days (14 + 7) to show the two aspects of Redemption — Feeding upon the Truth of God, and Abiding in Christ.‡

We can now take a further look at the seven days from May 4th to 11th in AD 33 and, comparing with the other Gospels, we shall at once ask why it is that John alone makes any mention of this week, spent quietly in Jerusalem, before Jesus and His apostles made their departure for Galilee. For both Matthew[1] and Mark[2] emphasise that the angel's message, given to the women at the open tomb, was 'Go your way, tell His disciples and Peter that He goeth before you into Galilee: *there shall ye see Him,* as He said unto you'.

Why was there a delay of seven days? We know, of course,

---

[1] Matthew 28: 7
[2] Mark 16: 7

* See Note 8 on page 185
‡ See Chart 6 on page 191

that Jesus waited until that same night before appearing to the whole company in the Upper Room but why, after that, was there a delay of **a whole week** and then a second appearance in Jerusalem before the journey into Galilee was commenced?

We shall see the answer to this very clearly when the meaning of Thomas's stubborn unbelief opens up to our vision (see John 20: 24-29). Thomas is a type of unbelieving Israel down the past age, and of a remnant of the Jews who now, as the Christian dispensation closes, are about to turn from their unbelief in Jesus and, as Paul indicates in Romans 11: 23-32, be delivered from the blindness which has characterised them from the beginning. This is why Jesus revealed Himself so specifically to Thomas when He made His second appearance around the midnight of May 11th; and this is a major reason why God requires the full truth concerning His Son's earthly pathway to be made available for the benefit of Israel today.

'The Dispensation of the Mystery'
(Ephesians 3: 9 RV)

This hidden week between our Lord's first and second appearances after His Resurrection is clearly typical of the Church dispensation, and is pictured in other parts of the Scriptures as the 'seven days' of a Marriage Feast (see Genesis 29: 27 and Judges 14: 12). It is typical of what has been an *interval* in God's relationship with Israel, while He has been showing grace to the Gentiles, and so it has been 'hid in God', as Paul says, 'from the beginning of the world' (Ephesians 3: 9).

The expression 'after eight days' in the Greek implies 'with the completion of eight days' and these, measured from the opening of the 'first (day) of the weeks'* when Jesus was raised up, bring us to the midnight of May 11th, and it is then that we see the Lord restoring Thomas as He appears for the second time to 'the twelve'[3].

How wonderful it is to discover after this that the disciples' journey to Galilee, with the Lord 'going before'[4] them, was the exact chronological counterpart of the original journey Israel's twelve tribes made out of Egypt, the Lord 'going before' in a pillar of cloud and of fire[5] — that is, the solar dates were identical. For,

---

[3] John 20: 24-29
[4] See Matthew 28: 7
[5] See Exodus 13: 21
* See Note 3 on page 184 and Chart 9 on page 194

after the midnight recovery of Thomas, the apostles must have made their 'exodus' from Jerusalem ('which is spiritually called ... Egypt, where also our Lord was crucified' — Revelation 11: 8) on May 12th AD 33, the solar anniversary of the Exodus in 1639 BC[‡].

After the Exodus, Israel's journey to Marah had taken seven days, at the end of which they were able to halt and encamp at Elim, 'where there were twelve wells of water, and seventy palm trees'[6]. (Both 'seventy' and 'palm trees' are always associated with the Gentiles in Scripture, just as the number 'twelve' is with Israel; and so Elim is a beautiful type of the coming Kingdom of Christ where the Gentile world — originally seventy nations[*] — will be blessed through Israel, as so much prophecy foretells.)

---

[6] Exodus 15: 27 and
   see Numbers 33: 1-9

[‡] See Chart 10 on page 195
[*] See Note 9 on page 185

CHAPTER EIGHTEEN

The Sign Miracle of John 21

*'This is now the third time that Jesus showed Himself to
His disciples after that He was risen from the dead'
(John 21: 14)*

Before touching on the actual date of our Lord's appearing in
John 21, it will be best to set the three main accounts of this
manifestation of the risen Christ in Galilee in order — as given by
John, Matthew and Paul.

The first of these (John's) specifically states that in the early
morning the appearing of Jesus to the seven brethren was 'the
third' occasion that He showed Himself to His apostles after His
resurrection. And we note that, instead of vanishing out of their
sight, the account ends with His leading them away from the sea
shore. We see them 'following' Him.

Matthew's version tells us that 'the eleven disciples went away
into Galilee, into a mountain where Jesus had appointed them'[1],
and from the remainder of his statement it is clear that this must
also have been at the time of His 'third' appearing. In other words,
Jesus and the seven went on to join the other four disciples
after the breakfast on the sea shore. This brought 'the eleven'
together.

Paul, in 1 Corinthians 15: 5-7, mentions first the private
appearing to Cephas (Peter) after his return from the sepulchre on
the resurrection morning; then His appearing to 'the twelve'
(which must have included when Thomas was recovered, before
they left Jerusalem). Then, 'after that' says Paul, 'He was seen of
above five hundred brethren at once ... '. (After that, He
interviewed His brother, James, privately, and then finally

---

[1] Matthew 28: 16

appeared to 'all the apostles' when He led them out to Bethany and then ascended to Heaven.)

Now it appears clear from this that when Jesus showed Himself to the 'five hundred' at once, it was at the time of His third appearing, after the breakfast on the sea shore and when all were gathered later in the day.

What was the significance of this gathering together unto Him? It was a wonderful resurrection reunion — a real 'Kingdom' scene and so the setting was 'in a mountain'. In Matthew's account it was here that Jesus declared: 'All power (authority) is given unto Me in Heaven *and on earth'* — words that are redolent of that kingdom which Nebuchadnezzar had seen as 'a great mountain' which 'filled the whole earth'[2]. It is here that Jesus gives instructions for the making disciples of all nations and baptising them with the baptism of the Kingdom (see Matthew 28: 18-20).

Now for the date, which was May 18th AD 33, fourteen days after the Resurrection on May 4th. For this we must probe what has always been a mystery in Leviticus 23, which speaks of two feasts in the seventh month. In verses 34 to 44 many have been amazed to see what at first appears to be a duplication of instructions containing an absolute anomaly. First we have a feast of 'seven days', beginning with 'the fifteenth day of this seventh month', and with 'the eighth day' as 'an holy convocation'. Then in verse 39 we are again told that 'in the fifteenth day of the seventh month ... ye shall keep a feast unto the Lord seven days: on the first day shall be *a sabbath,* and on the eighth day shall be a *sabbath'!* [‡]

When we hold to the verbal inspiration of the Holy Scriptures, we have to be careful how we dismiss what we might call 'difficulties' — especially when men have wrested the Word in every conceivable way in their attempts to make sense of it to their natural minds.

We have seen that there is a difference made by the Holy Ghost between a 'holy convocation' and a 'sabbath'. These are not synonymous terms, and we may best contrast these two seven-day 'feasts' by taking a further look at the fourteen days after our Lord's resurrection.

The first week — May 4th to the 11th — with its two 'holy convocations', or gatherings of Jesus with His disciples, has been

---

[2] Daniel 2: 35
[‡] See Chart 6 on page 191

shown to be, in the Calendar of His *life,* the 15th to the 21st of the 7th month, inclusively. But this 'week' really foreshadowed the Church dispensation or 'dispensation of the mystery' which had previously been 'hid in God'[3]. It certainly could not have been looked at as having any place in Israel's time, for it represented what has proved to be the period of their dispersion to the ends of the earth. It was the Feast of Tabernacles for the (mainly) Gentile Church, which is the 'Body of Christ'. (The 'week' which Jacob was told to 'fulfil' for Leah, before he served a second seven years for Rachel in Genesis 29: 27, is an Old Testament picture of the same era — Rachel representing the Jews whom Jesus came to win and Leah the Gentile bride whom He was given in their place.)

But as we know, after the 'midnight cry' of Matthew 25 and the departure of the true Church (like Enoch) by translation from the earth, then another 'week' — that 'one week' of Daniel 9: 27 — is to intervene before our Lord returns to set up His Kingdom. It is these last seven years, we believe, that are typified by the original seven days of Unleavened Bread (or, in the other aspect, 'Booths') which followed the 'midnight cry' in Egypt. And it is clear from Leviticus 23: 39-43 that the second seven day 'feast' looks back to those days of the coming out of Egypt.

So in this second 'feast', which positively relates to Israel (for 'all that are Israelites born' were to keep it), we find the first and eighth days are to be kept as 'sabbaths' and we know that the seven years they typify will lead to the start of the Messianic Kingdom which is the Earth's great *Sabbath* of a thousand years of rest (see Revelation 20: 2-6).

When these facts are appreciated, it will be seen that Israel could not possibly have kept *two* concurrent seven day 'feasts' in the same seventh month, observing the first and eighth days as both 'holy convocations' *and* 'sabbaths'!

Our object, therefore, in calling attention to this particular part of God's instructions to Moses (Leviticus 23: 33-43) is to show that from the beginning He had His eye on this *one month* in all human history when there would be a fulfilment of both of these 'feasts' — and that He would regard each of them as commencing with 'the 15th day of the 7th month'. That month can only have been in May AD 33.

Our God is presented to us, in Romans 4: 17, as the One 'Who

---

[3] Ephesians 3: 9 (RV)

quickeneth the dead, and calleth those things which be not as though they were'. And after He had quickened His own Son and brought Him again from the dead, this is precisely what we find He had to do in the fulfilment of His unbreakable Word.

God foresaw the Church dispensation stretching ahead — a long age to us, yet to Him just one 'week' — and in it the Body of Christ would be fully formed. (Another aspect of the same period, as we know, is the 'two days' or 2,000 lunar years between Christ's death and the resurrection of His body.) **And as God does not reckon this interval to Israel, it can only be regarded as a standstill in their chronology.**

As far as Israel is concerned, God really sees the Resurrection of Christ completed when all the members of His body have at last shared in His physical resurrection, as explained in 1 Thessalonians 4: 14-17 and 1 Corinthians 15: 50-57; see also our Chapter 11. We know that this takes place at our Lord's Second Appearing, for 'unto them that look for Him shall He appear the second time *(lit.)* apart from sin' — that is, apart from the question of sin, which has been fully dealt with at the Cross — 'unto salvation' (Hebrews 9: 28).

So, when this interval of Church history is over, God will have a 'sealed' minority of believing Jews in Israel (see Revelation 7: 4-8) who will be called to pass through the seven years, so clearly shown in Revelation 12: 5-14, where they are pictured as the 'woman' or mother of the 'child' which has been 'caught up unto God, and to His throne'. They are then seen fleeing into the wilderness, which depicts the essence of keeping the 'feast of booths' — that is, abiding temporarily as in a journey, with 'no certain dwellingplace'4 — and they are 'nourished' or fed. This will, of necessity, be on 'unleavened bread', or the pure truth of God, and this in a world wholly given over to evil.

Summing up this brief outline of the events following the Lord's Resurrection on May 4th, we have attempted to show the significance of the two weeks which led to His third appearing on the shores of the sea of Tiberias. There is vastly more to add, when the time comes for a full investigation of the facts, but space does not allow for this now. Much more can be drawn from the fathomless depths of the chronology of God's Holy Word in support of the date of May 18th AD 33 but we must now go on to

---

4 1 Corinthians 4: 11

examine *the eighth 'sign'* of John's Gospel, which took place on this day.

The One Great Resurrection 'Sign'
(See John 21: 1-14)

Many of God's greatest works have appeared insignificant to men, and certainly this one Resurrection miracle recorded in the Gospels appears to have been written off as of minor importance by the teachers and preachers of the Church of God today. This is, of course, due to the fact that its significance has never been unfolded.

John only records eight of all the Lord's miracles in his Gospel and each of these was for a 'sign' (see John 2: 11 RV). We may therefore expect to find that the *eighth* 'sign' has a 'resurrection' significance and the fact that Peter's net was not broken, but contained the complete catch of '153 great fishes', suggests this (John 21: 11).

The first key to the understanding of this miracle came with the revelation to one of our company in 1932 that the distance of 'two hundred cubits' from the shore, in verse 8, had a *time* signification. (This fact was mentioned briefly in our Chapter 2). Those who use one of the modern paraphrase versions of the Bible would require a King James or Revised Version to check this.

We first of all saw these '200 cubits' as typifying the closing **200 days** of the age — not realising, of course, that there was a long 'consummation of the age'[5*] to follow. This latter would be separate from the main Christian dispensation which ended, as described in our opening chapters, with the official representative coming-together of all the nations of the world on June 12th 1933.

Only years later were we able to demonstrate that these actual 200 days were also the last days of the *'2,000 years'* in the Chronology of Redemption (that is, 1,960 civil lunar years and 40 Jubilees, as previously shown). So the 'sign' of John 21 really covers the whole of the Christian dispensation during which 'fishes' — Jesus had said to Peter and Andrew: 'I will make you fishers of men'[6] — were to be gathered out of the 'sea' of the Gentiles. It should be remembered that the 'tenth' part is often taken in Scripture to represent the whole — 'the tithe' is an

---

[5] From Matthew 13: 39
– see page 33

[6] Matthew 4: 18-19
* See Note 2 on page 184

example of this — so the '200' is actually a miniature of the '2,000' (see Joshua 3: 4, where the full '2,000 cubits' are mentioned and 1 Kings 7: 23-26, where a 'sea' containing '2,000 baths' is part of the Temple furniture and gives the same thought of the measurement of the Church dispensation).

'A Hundred and Fifty and Three'
(John 21: 11)

This number has intrigued all who have an interest in the 'things of God' and many have remembered that Solomon hired '153,600' non-Jews, that is, 'strangers' or Gentiles from Tyre for the building of the House of God at Jerusalem[7].

153 is 9 x 17 and it has been noted that if all the numbers from 1 to 17 are added together, the sum of them is 153. '17' is a number related to the resurrection of Christ. That is, May 4th was the 17th day of the 7th month in His 34th year (34 being twice 17). Many will also remember that the Ark, in Genesis 8: 4, 'rested' on the 17th of the 7th month, on the mountains of Ararat.

153 times 17 days (2,601) will be found to be the full length of the ministries of John the Baptist and Jesus — from April 25th AD 26 to June 13th AD 33, inclusively — if the six days of Redemption (the four days prior to the cross and the two days of the tomb) are viewed as outside of this measurement. A fresh glance at what is said about the *hidden* Day of Atonement in Chapter 13 will suffice to show the serious reader why these six days would be held apart in the eye of God from the rest of the total, for Jesus accepted that the hour of His death had come on that dreadful April 27th (see John 12).

We constantly find that the thoughts of God (which 'are not our thoughts'[8]) are revealed as we meditate on the true chronology of His Word, and we shall now see a yet deeper significance in the '153' of this final 'sign' of the Lord Jesus before He ascended to where He was before.

By design of God the words 'the net' (Gr. *to diktuon*) have the numerical value of 1,224, which is 8 x 153. The significance of this is really wonderful. We were shown to measure the exact length of the Lord's Ministry, from when He was 'thirty years old' (November 25th-26th AD 29) to the day of His Resurrection (May

[7] 2 Chronicles 2: 17
[8] See Isaiah 55: 8

3rd-4th AD 33), and found it was 1,255 days. We were then reminded that in the Chronology of Redemption God never takes account of intercalary months, or anything above an exact 354 days in the year. In AD 32 there was an intercalation amounting to 31 days which would therefore have been ignored in Divine reckoning. (See Chapter 6 for an explanation of intercalation.) So, with God, the duration of His Son's Ministry would have been 1,224 or 8 x 153 days.

So we see that 'the net' which could not be broken actually expressed *the testimony of Jesus,* and every member of the Church, Gentile or Jew, who has been enclosed in that testimony will be drawn in safety to the resurrection shore.

Another feature in this eighth 'sign' was the way Peter — 'the son of Jonas' — traversed the distance of the '200 cubits' by going down into the sea, as Jonah had done. Jesus had first addressed him as 'Simon Bar-jona' on March 23rd, when the Father made the original revelation to him that Christ was 'the Son of the living God' (Matthew 16: 16-17). That day, which we may later be able to show was just forty days inclusively before the Crucifixion, was when Jesus had first openly spoken of His death to the disciples.

But now, on May 18th, some 57 days inclusively had passed from that first revelation, and again Jesus addresses Peter as 'Simon, son of Jonas' in John 21: 15-17. There had been *57 hours* between the death and resurrection of Jesus which, as we have seen in earlier pages, was in the Bible's inclusive reckoning 'three days and three nights'.

Can anyone ever imagine the agony of soul which Peter passed through in the horror and darkness of his Master's death? For the prophet Jonah it had been, indeed, a *baptism* of 'three days and three nights'[9] in the likeness of the death of Jesus but for the Lord Himself it had been the dark waters of death itself in which He had been immersed. Yet He had spoken of it as His own 'baptism' and declared that others would share it with Him (Matthew 20: 23).

So Peter reached the shore, wearing his 'fisher's coat' and the other disciples 'came in the little boat ... dragging the net with fishes'[10].

We must now consider a most important side of this 'sign' on the Lake of Tiberias.

---

[9] Jonah 1: 17
[10] John 21: 7-8 (partly RV)

Why 'The Right Side of The Ship'?

(John 21: 6)

The normal side for the casting of nets being the left side, why did Jesus command this significant change to be made? In the Bible, as we know, the right hand is the side of power and authority and the left the side of weakness. And in demonstration of this, for some three years after the Cross the Jewish apostles continued to 'preach the word to none, but unto the Jews only' (Acts 11: 19) — that is, to fish on the left side of the ship. The idea of going to the people in power — the Romans — was not in their minds, until in Acts 10 we find God Himself taking a hand in directing Peter to go to the house of Cornelius.

And where did Peter get this instruction? We read in Acts 9: 36-43 that this 'son of Jonas' had experienced the power of God in resurrection at *Joppa,* when Dorcas was raised up at His Word! Jonah and Joppa in conjunction are suggestive! (See Jonah 1: 3.)

And to complete the 'Jonah' picture, there had also been a 'storm' for, after Stephen's death in October AD 33, a 'great persecution' had arisen against the Jewish church in Judæa[11] and Galilee which did not die down, as we learn from Acts 9: 31, until after the conversion of Saul of Tarsus. No 'fishes' (men and women out of the great 'sea' of the Gentiles) had been caught — they hadn't even been fished for — until the Gospel net was cast 'on the right side of the ship' in the house of the Roman, Cornelius, in AD 36.

So it was that our Gentile dispensation commenced — a minute speck in the great Roman Empire — just a 'church' in the house of a converted Roman Centurion in Caesarea, but the power of the Holy Ghost was there. And from this small beginning, the size of a grain of mustard seed, the Gospel of the grace of God commenced to spread among the nations for the space of *two thousand years,* during which 'the net' would remain submerged in the great Gentile 'sea'. And why 2,000 years? Because for two full days the Body of Christ had lain motionless in the tomb, until that 'third day' came when He who had been 'sown in weakness' was 'raised in power'[12].

Before we proceed to reveal some of the multiplicity of ways in which the Most High God has chosen to portray these *two 'days'* of a thousand (lunar) years each in the calendars of time, we must

---

[11] Acts 8: 1
[12] 1 Corinthians 15: 43

boldly state, from our observations over fifty years, that God will do nothing in this world, except He does it for the glory of His only begotten Son. *The Bible's time-patterning makes this manifest.*

How has He measured time from Creation? We have seen it in these pages — He has reckoned it on the principle of *forgiveness,* and all other periods of time outside the 'seventy-times-seven'-year cycles have been found to be eras of punishment or rejection by God. He forgives 'until seventy times seven'[13], or multiples of 70 times 7 years, and then He pronounces judgment.

Why is our civilisation rapidly plunging morally into the state of Sodom and Gomorrah? Why are 'violence and corruption'[14] on the rapid increase all over Christendom? Simply because God has actually fulfilled His warning that if the nations did not 'continue in His goodness', He would 'cut them off'[15].

Did He take steps to warn the world that He would do so? Most certainly, and the facts are found to be stated simply in our earlier chapters.

But God is a God of great mercy and His principle is to begin and end His 'dispensations', not by a sudden termination but over stages which would be recognised by all who revere and understand His Word. There are many Christians who have no use for the word 'dispensation' as applying to a limited period of time. The Greek word *oikonomia* means 'the law or arrangement of a house'. Has anyone ever seen a *house* devoid of 'arrangement' or measurement? And when we read in 1 Kings 6:17, for instance, that 'the house, that is, the temple before it, was forty cubits long', can we not perceive the analogy to the forty Jubilees of the Church dispensation? Or the 'twenty cubits' of 'the oracle' or 'holy place'[16] — are not these analagous to the twenty Jubilees, or thousand years of the coming Kingdom? We have often asked the question: what is the significance of the Bible's measurements of length and breadth if they have no relation to the duration of time?

[13] Matthew 18: 21-22
[14] See Genesis 6: 11-13
[15] See Romans 11: 22
[16] 1 Kings 6: 16, 20

CHAPTER NINETEEN

Biblical Signs in the Heavens

'I will show wonders in heaven above'
(Acts 2: 19)

'Your faith should not stand in the wisdom of men, but in the power of God. Howbeit we speak ... the wisdom of God in a mystery, even the hidden wisdom, which God ordained before the world unto our glory ... for the Spirit searcheth all things, yea, the deep things of God' (1 Corinthians 2: 5-10).

No one will question that we are having to deal with 'the deep things of God' when we touch the mysteries of time in the Bible, and these things have certainly been hidden — deeply hidden — right down the course of this age. We accept that it has been 'the glory of God to conceal a thing', as Solomon declares in Proverbs 25: 2, but if he says 'it is the honour of kings to search out a matter' does this not also imply that it is for the glory of God to do so? And if 'the Spirit' does the searching, will not the truth inevitably be recovered?

We are saying this for a reason. Before the truth can be fully revealed concerning time at the Cross of Jesus, much has to be appreciated about the significance of the two occasions recorded in the Bible when God interfered with the ordered course of time; firstly by bringing the earth's revolution to a standstill for 'about a whole day' (Joshua 10: 13) and then by causing the sun's shadow to return 'ten steps backward' on the 'steps' of Ahaz (Isaiah 38: 8).‡ These steps — they were not degrees — recorded **an hour each** on this ancient kind of sundial which was formed, it would appear, by a curved stairway; and that miracle, or *'sign'*, incidentally had a most vital meaning in relation to Israel's chronological history, as

‡ Further details on page 143

well as to the actual ten hours of the sufferings and crucifixion of Christ and the blotting out of sin. (It is most significant to note that the space between these two great celestial signs in the Old Testament was, inclusively, 888 years — the number of the name of Jesus — that is, from 1600-1599 BC to 712-711 BC.)

Before this, however, we must consider the 'wonder' to which Peter referred on the day of Pentecost and which took place while the body of Jesus lay in the grave. This was when, following the darkening of the sun at Calvary, the moon was 'turned into blood'[1] for two whole days. The prophet Joel had predicted these signs, for the three hours of darkness spoke eloquently of the Jews putting out 'the Light of the world' by rejecting their Messiah's three years of ministry, between the Passovers of AD 30 and 33 — and the following two days looked on to the bloodstained history of the dispersion over the 2,000 years that lay ahead.

God's Great Change in Time

Over six centuries before, when the Most High God had wrested the Kingdom from Judah and handed it to the Gentiles under Nebuchadnezzar, the prophet Daniel had addressed God in these terms:

> 'Blessed be the Name of God for ever and ever: for wisdom and might are His: and He changeth the times and seasons: He removeth kings, and setteth up kings: He giveth wisdom unto the wise, and knowledge to them that know understanding: He revealeth the deep and secret things' (Daniel 2: 20-22).

But now at last the King of Kings had come and laid down His life to accomplish the atonement, and the sun was darkened. The crime of all the ages had been perpetrated and the centuries ahead would be stained with the blood, not alone of the dispersed of Israel, but also of countless millions of the true children of God who would be done to death on account of their faith since the beginning of our era. Due consideration of these facts will prepare us to learn that during the two whole days (May 2nd and 3rd AD 33) while the Son of God was absent from His body, as it lay swathed in grave-clothes in the tomb, the moon was, in fact, 'turned into blood' — that is, it became 'dead' and ceased to record time for those 48 hours. In other words, although it was

---

[1] See Joel 2: 31

still to be seen as a full moon in the heavens, it did not begin to wane until the day of the resurrection opened. It was also almost certainly observed to be blood-red in aspect.

This is a fact which the absolute accuracy of the Bible's chronology has established and with God it was a necessity for this cessation to take place in the recording of lunar time, in order to make possible the perfect fulfilment of the law to do with the 'feasts' of the Lord and also the great release of 'the year of Jubilee' which must needs have its primary fulfilment at the resurrection of Christ.

It is with reverence that we must approach the examination of these matters, so vital to our redemption, which God has allowed to remain concealed down the whole course of our age but which now, as it closes, He would have His children to look into. Before doing this, however, all will be interested to consider a proof that the moon has actually 'lost' two days in its recording since the beginning of the Christian era.

The Inception of The Calendar of Julius Caesar at a Visible New Moon

Smith's Dictionary of Greek and Roman Antiquities (Art. Calendarium) confirms that Julius Caesar caused the first day of his reformed calendar to begin on the day of the new moon, following the winter solstice in December 46 BC. It says:

'Accordingly, it is found that the mean new moon occurred at Rome on the 1st of January 45 BC at 6h 16m pm.'

In this way alone can be explained the phrase used by Macrobius:

Annum civilem Caesar, habitis ad lunam dimensionibus constitutum, edicto palam proposito publicavit.

This could be translated:

'After the edict had been publicly proposed, Caesar proclaimed the State year which had been established after calculations had been taken according to the moon.'

The essence of this quotation was that the new solar year Caesar was inaugurating was advertised to commence 'at the new moon' *(ad lunam)* and this was because the Romans had become accustomed for centuries to commence their years at the moon's phasis, that is, the **first appearance** of the crescent in the sky.

It will be seen at once that if the actual conjunction of the moon did not occur until late on January 1st 45 BC, the new moon could not possibly have been observed at the earliest until the evening of January 2nd, which would have entirely defeated Caesar's object in planning that the people should see the crescent on the day his great new calendar was to commence.

The author of the above article, in common with others who consult lunar astronomical tables, of course had no knowledge of the action of the Almighty in arresting the moon's revolution for the two days of Christ's entombment in AD 33. Consequently, he could only assess the moon's age **as it would have been** in 45 BC, if the 'wonder' we are speaking of had not occurred in AD 33. But as we know from the Bible's chronology that the moon was new on December 30th, and would have first appeared as a thin crescent in the night of the 31st or, at the latest, in the evening of January 1st, we can see that Caesar's objective was attained, and that a visible new moon did mark the opening day of this great new solar calendar before the watching eyes of all the Roman populace.

It seemed necessary to give this supporting evidence as, until the massive array of chronological facts relating to the death and resurrection of Christ can be more fully apprehended, natural incredulity with many might weigh too heavily in the balance when we have to speak of such a 'wonder' as this, to which the Bible only refers in veiled terms in Joel 2: 31 and Acts 2: 20.

The Reason for the Veiling of this 'Wonder in Heaven Above'

There is a reason for everything God does, and it is not difficult to understand why the Bible had to shroud the truth about this lunar phenomenon, so that we have had to wait until the end of the age before it could even be discerned. This is because, as already mentioned, these two complete days of Christ's death themselves provided the pattern of the 2,000 lunar years to follow — during which the divine calendar of Israel (which is governed by the moon) would be at a standstill. As we know, God did not 'cast off'[2] His ancient people (the Jews) for ever, but only for the *'two days'* or 2,000 years of Hosea 6: 2 — so that He might 'visit the

---

[2] Romans 11: 1 (RV)

Gentiles, to take out of them a people for His name'[3]. Now, as we have seen in earlier pages, 'the times of the Gentiles' are over, Jerusalem is not 'trodden down by the Gentiles'[4], as it was during the Dispersion, and the Holy Ghost is bearing a mighty witness through the earth that 'the coming of the Lord draweth nigh'[5].

Why then was the moon turned 'into blood' — which signifies *death?* It was to reveal that after 'the sun' had been 'turned into darkness', when the Jews by rejecting their Messiah had put out the 'Light of the World', there would be a lapse of a full 2,000 years of 'death' for the people of Israel, '*before the great and terrible day of the Lord*'[6] would come, with its desolating judgments, to usher in the Kingdom for which both Israel and the world have waited. And because the intervening Church age is called 'the dispensation of the mystery'[7], which was veiled, or 'hid in God', in previous ages, God saw to it that the duration of this age also was veiled until such time as it pleased Him to bring this to light.

But there were even more wonderful reasons why God should hold *time* at a standstill between the death and resurrection of His Son, and these will appear as the plan of our redemption is studied and unfolded.

It will be realised that the Bible is concerned with just one aspect of world affairs, and this is related to the history of the 'Seed' of the Woman (Genesis 3: 15). That history can now be seen to be the perfectly-timed record of the struggle between Light and Darkness — actually, between Life and Death — and as the days become rapidly darker in the world, so is God allowing the light of His Word to be increased and to beam more fully than ever before upon the Person and the Work of His beloved Son, 'Whom He hath appointed heir of all things, through Whom He also did make the ages' (Hebrews 1: 2 Young's Literal).

---

[3] Acts 15: 14
[4] Luke 21: 24 (RSV)
[5] James 5: 8
[6] Joel 2: 31
[7] Ephesians 3: 9 (RV)

CHAPTER TWENTY

The Pattern of Events 1933-1948

The significance of June 11th 1938
and the seven years to 1945

It is outside the range of this writing to give more than the bare outline of the five years from June 12th 1933 to June 11th 1938, which was when 1,960 lunar years ended from October 23rd in AD 36.

During these years a concentrated study of the whole of the Bible's chronological structure was called for. Six brethren were involved in this, and by the spring of 1937 we were satisfied that every major difficulty in unravelling the whole time scheme of the Scriptures had been overcome, through prayerful waiting upon God, and through the amazing confirmation which is found in the Word itself when the actual truth is known.

The chronology of the Acts of the Apostles had been largely unveiled and it was seen that the opening of the Feast of Tabernacles (October 23rd) in AD 36 was an occasion of major importance with God. For it was then, following the Acts Pentecost of that year (in chapter 10), that the Lord's Jewish apostles in Jerusalem learned from Peter, and his 'six brethren', that 'God also to the Gentiles (had) granted repentance unto life'. We read also in Acts 11: 18 that 'when they heard' about this dramatic event which had taken place at Caesarea, 'they held their peace, and glorified God'. Until that time, of course, the Gospel had been preached 'to none but unto the Jews only'[1].

We realised that just as Jesus had been born at the Feast of Tabernacles in 1 BC, so now the Church (Jew and Gentile) could be viewed as coming to the birth at the same 'Feast' in AD 36.

[1] Acts 11: 19

It had already been noted that the God Who had measured off the four periods of 490 years of 354 days each, from the death of Stephen in AD 33 to the day of the World Economic Conference on June 12th 1933, had also marked the end of 1,960 lunar years from the same starting-point. These terminated with the great earthquake on May 31st 1935 at Quetta, British Baluchistan, in which some 44,000 people lost their lives. So it was anticipated that the end of 1,960 true lunar years from October 22nd-23rd AD 36 would also receive some marking from God.

By November 25th 1937 it had become possible to put into print in brief the whole of the Bible's chronology (with full astronomical data) to the end of the 6,000 years, and also to give the facts relating to the 'three days and three nights' of the death of Jesus, which He had referred to as 'the sign of the prophet Jonas'[2]. On December 3rd 1937 this literature was sent to all the Bishops in the British Isles (at that time there were exactly '153' of them). Only five troubled to acknowledge these documents, and none showed any inclination to look more closely into the matter.

Those of us engaged in the research had by that time, of course, learnt that we were proceeding into 'the consummation of the age'[3]*, and that the words of Jesus concerning 'watching' for His return were daily becoming more and more pertinent, especially for those who held high office in the churches of Christendom. It was an interesting fact that the evening of December 3rd 1937, when the above literature was sent to the 153 Bishops and many others (about 200 in all) was the true solar anniversary of our Lord's 'beginning of signs' in Cana of Galilee, in AD 29, when 'He made the water wine' (John 2: 1-11). We noticed that December 4th, when the documents were received, was just 12 times '153' days from the Meeting in London on November 25th 1932, at which '153' persons had been present, when we had taken the original step of faith in naming 'June 12th 1933' — then 200 days distant.

This turned our attention again to the Lord's last 'sign' — recorded in John 21 — where it was found that the numerical value of the Greek words for 'the net' *(to diktuon)* was 8 times 153, as mentioned in Chapter 18.

This discovery concerning the duration of the ministry of Jesus being 8 x 153 days began to elucidate the meaning of *'the net'* in

---

[2] Matthew 12: 39-40   * See Note 2 on page 184
[3] From Matthew 13: 39 - see page 33

John 21.

The *net* which He would use at the end of this age was His own testimony to His Church as He unveiled 'the things concerning Himself'[4]. It was a *net* which would not be broken (see John 21: 11). It was God who had 'made the ages' (that is, time measurements) according to the literal translation of Hebrews 1: 2, revealing Himself and His Son through them.

It would be difficult now to attempt to describe the forebodings and fears of Europe in the year 1938, preceding the betrayal of Czechoslovakia to Hitler by France and Great Britain in September of that year, but it was clear to many that a renewal of hostilities which might again involve all the powers was becoming imminent. We noted that June 11th was marked by an earthquake in England which seemed to be a token one, as coming at the close of 1,960 years + 40 Jubilee years, making the '2,000' from AD 36. We remembered the tragedy of Quetta in 1935 (referred to above) when we knew the hand of God had been stretched out in providential judgment, because 'the third day' had come in this aspect of time.

June 11th 1938, then, was the close of another stage when, 'two days' of 'a thousand years' each being over, the 'third day' had arrived. But instead of the 'judgment' being a sudden one as at Quetta there lay ahead for Europe and the world a terrible era of seven years to 1945 which would see the break-up of the existing order in Europe and leave the nations as a whole divided into two great halves, commonly described as 'the Free World' and the world which lay behind 'the Iron Curtain'. During this period God would take in hand to perform His 'strange work' with the people of Israel to prepare them for the fulfilment of His covenant with Abraham when He should raise them up to nationhood in 1948.

As these seven years were to be patterned upon the same framework as the seven years of the Book of Revelation, it will be good to have this all clearly in mind before we proceed. In Revelation 11: 3 we find a mention of '1,260 days'. (It will be seen by careful reading that the '42 months' of verse 2 are actually to follow the first 3½ years which are spoken of as '1,260 days'.) When these days are completed, in the middle of the seven years, we find 'three days and a half' spoken of in verse 9.

Then in chapter 12: 6 we again come upon the first '1,260 days'

---

[4] Luke 24: 27

which follow the vision of the 'child' being 'caught up to God and to His throne' in verse 5. Later in this chapter, in verse 14, we see 'a time (360 days), and times (2 x 360 days) and half a time' (180 days) bringing the seven years to an end. Adding these days together, we find we again have a total of 1,260. (We find a further mention of '42 months' as the latter half of the 7 years in chapter 13: 5.) The pattern, then, is simply 1,260 days, 3½ days and another 1,260 days. *(See Chart 11 on page 196.)*

The Timing of The Second World War Fixed by The Bible

As we have said, it is only possible to deal with the bare outlines of the War years and our starting point must be, in the first place, June 11th 1938.

From the morning of June 11th to the evening of November 25th, three and a half years later, in 1941 will be found to be '1,263½ days'. In the evening of this November 25th, 'the greatest recorded earthquake' until then occurred, at 6.08 pm (GMT) mercifully beneath the Atlantic Ocean. This was the first of a series of quakes which would belt the earth in the course of the next few days and seemed to herald the Japanese attack on 'Pearl Harbour' on December 7th, which brought the Western hemisphere into the War.

We will now take a fresh view of the above '1,263½ days' and date them from noon on June 11th 1938 which, as we said, was marked by an earthquake in Britain, and measure them to midnight on November 25th 1941. A further '1,260 days' will be found to reach exactly to midnight on May 8th 1945, when the War in Europe actually ended, with hostilities ceasing at 12.01 am, and the act of surrender being signed in Berlin.

What we have seen in the above facts, therefore, is '2,000 years' (or, 1,960 true lunar years, with the addition of 40 Jubilee years) followed immediately by an exact patterning of the seven years of the Book of Revelation (that is, '1,263½ days' and '1,260 days') to VE Day in 1945. All who remember how the third part of the Jewish race (6 million people) perished under the Nazi regime, mainly in the last three and a half years of the War, will know that this second half of the seven years must have been allowed by God to foreshadow the days of the coming 'great tribulation' which,

Jesus warned in Matthew 24: 21-30, will lead up to His actual return 'with power and great glory' (see also Revelation 19). In that final judgment era which impends over this world we read, in the symbolic language of Revelation 9: 18, that 'the third part of men' will perish, as the Most High God turns His hand to purge this world of a Christendom which has become like 'the cities of the plain' (see Genesis 19: 29).

In other words, when the time design of the Second World War is analysed, it can be seen to have been a grim foreshadowing of a Third World War which is destined to erase our present corrupt civilisation from the earth, when its iniquity has come to the full.

But this is only the beginning of that which has to be told.

Preceding the above 1,960 lunar years to June 11th 1938, which commenced with the day of October 23rd AD 36, lay another exact time-pattern of '1,263½ days' and '1,260 days' which we will now briefly examine.

The first named day in the Gospel of John (1: 29) was *November 25th AD 29,* when the Baptist 'seeth Jesus coming unto him, and saith, "Behold the Lamb of God, which taketh away the sin of the world"'. From noon of this day a span of exactly '1,263½ days' will be found to run to the midnight of May 11th AD 33, that is, 'after eight days' from the midnight of the Resurrection of Jesus on May 3rd-4th (see John 20: 26-29). In this late evening our Lord's Second Appearing took place after His Resurrection and it was then that He restored His unbelieving disciple Thomas, which was needful before the journey into Galilee could begin.

It is significant that the hour of midnight on May 11th in 1639 BC had seen the 'firstborn' let go from death in Egypt (Exodus 12: 29-51), the day of their actual Exodus being May 12th. There is no doubt that Jesus and His disciples (unseen, of course) made their exodus from Jerusalem on this same date in the solar calendar in AD 33, and He 'went before them into Galilee'[5].

We can now measure the further '1,260 days' from the midnight of May 11th AD 33 to the close of October 22nd in AD 36, when the 1,960 lunar years began. It was at the opening of this 'Feast of Tabernacles', as we have to remind ourselves, that the Lord, through Peter, was able to bring the other apostles in Jerusalem into fellowship with Himself, by revealing to them that 'God also to

---

[5] See Matthew 28: 7 and Mark 14: 28

the Gentiles (had) granted repentance unto life'[6]. Obviously, not until this vital rapport had been established between our Lord Jesus Christ in heaven and His twelve apostles on the earth could the Gospel be preached freely to the Gentiles, for we read in Acts 11: 19 that until AD 36 they had been 'preaching the word to none but unto the Jews only'.

The Challenge of These Figures — 'The Net' in Action

When we held our original November 25th meeting for Christians in 1932 we had no knowledge at all of the Bible's chronological framework, except for a very limited understanding of the 'seven times' of Daniel 4. We therefore, at that time, had no 'net'.

But in the winter of 1937 the position was entirely different. By then the Holy Spirit of God had brought to light and fashioned 'the net' which He was about to use. God knew that in 'as it were two hundred cubits' or days from November 25th 1937, He would be going into action, so a 'time-net' must be cast into 'the sea' of the Gentiles at the beginning of this period. The six brethren involved in this procedure therefore called a Press Conference in London and a paper was read giving details of the Bible's Chronology from Creation to the end of the 6,000 years in 1933, and also expounding the truth about 'the sign of the prophet Jonas'[7] (that is, the 'three days and three nights' of the death of Christ). Through the Associated Press, some 300 newsmen could have been present at this gathering at a London hotel on November 25th 1937 but, in the ordering of God, not one reporter turned up! The paper was, however, read and the facts put into print forthwith.

The ways of God are often comic to a degree, especially when He is dealing with a world which really holds His Word in contempt!

As already mentioned, on December 3rd some 200 copies of the literature unveiling the whole course of time were sent out to scholars and prominent people, including the '153' Bishops of the British Isles — this significant number being discovered **after**, and not before, the copies were despatched. So it was that, 200 days prior to the solar anniversary of Pentecost in 1938, the religious world, through its leaders, was apprised of the true facts to do with the 'sign of the prophet Jonas'.

---

[6] Acts 11: 18
[7] Matthew 12: 39-40

I his was a necessary part of the counsels of God, because He was about to perform a 'strange work' with the people of Jonah, the Jews of Europe. We need only remind ourselves of the exactitude of the '1,263½ days' and the further '1,260 days' — from the earthquake at noon on June 11th 1938, to the cessation of hostilities at midnight (12.01 am) on May 8th-9th 1945, to see the mighty God of Jacob performing 'all things after the counsel of His own will'[8] and, as ever, performing them precisely on time.

The invasion of the Continent on June 6th 1944 ('D–Day') cost the allies many lives, but it resulted in the salvation of a remnant of European Jewry. Much could be said about the importance of every such major movement during the War; as events unfolded before us we usually saw that the dates had a chronological significance.

In the spring of 1945, as the War ended, exactly *three 'days'* of 888 solar years were completed from 720 BC, when the ten tribes of Israel (whose kingdom was in Samaria) were swept away into captivity by Shalmaneser, King of Assyria, as we read in 2 Kings 17: 5-18. How wonderful to see *Jesus,* Whose number is '888', stretching forth His hand to save His ancient people — the people of the prophet *Jonah* — after they had been swallowed up in *'the sea'* of the nations for a full 'three days' (3 x 888 = 2,664 years).

The Four Thousand Years from Abram End in 1945

Abram left Haran on August 6th 2056 BC on the first stage of his journey to enter the Land of Canaan. The date of this can be ascertained from Genesis 12: 4 where we are told that at this point 'Abram was seventy and five years old'. Those who are old enough to remember how the Second World War was brought to an end will not have forgotten the date of August 6th 1945 (exactly 4,000 solar years later, if we exclude from measurement the two whole days that Christ was in the tomb).

'Blood, and fire, and pillars *(lit.* palm trees) of smoke' were surely the sign which riveted the attention of the whole world as these great *four days of a thousand years* ended; for few could ignore the enormity of the effect on the world of the first use of the atomic bomb in warfare on August 6th and 9th 1945 as a means of bringing the war in the East to a speedy termination (see Joel 2: 30).

---

[8] Ephesians 1: 11

And, when *4,000 Julian years* of 365¼ days were ended from that far-off initial step of obedience to the call of God on the part of the father of the Jewish race, Abram, when he set out from Haran after his father had died (Acts 7: 4), we arrive at the date of September 2nd 1945. This was when the *Six Years' War* finally ended from September 1939 with the signing of the surrender document by Japan on board the USS Missouri anchored in Tokyo Bay.

'Israel shall be thy name'
(Genesis 35: 10)

At midnight on May 14th 1948, President Truman granted *de facto* recognition to the new-born State of Israel simultaneously with its proclamation and, three days later, Soviet Russia granted Israel *de jure* recognition, on May 17th, from which date those watching the course of events with the aid of the Bible's chronology were able to trace back an exact *4,000 Julian years* to the day when God confirmed to Abram by a solemn covenant that his seed should inherit that land. That was in 2053 BC when the prophecy of the *'four hundred years'* to the Exodus from Egypt was given in Genesis chapter 15.

It was interesting to see America and Soviet Russia in agreement upon such a step as the recognition of the new State of Israel.

We must now mention briefly a time-patterning of God from the Birth of Jesus to the Birth of Israel in 1948, with which is connected a remarkable prophecy:

'Behold, this Child is set for the fall and rising again of many in Israel; and for a sign which shall be spoken against'.

These words are found in Luke 2: 34 and were uttered when Mary and Joseph had brought the Child Jesus to present Him to God, just forty days after His Nativity in Bethlehem, according to the Law. The date was December 8th 1 BC.

If we measure forward a full 2,000 years of 354 days, we shall find these reach to May 17th 1939 which was the day when Britain abrogated the Palestine Mandate and presented to Parliament a White Paper forbidding the return of Jews to Palestine after 1944. (This White Paper shocked Sir Winston Churchill and many others

— who saw that Britain would ultimately have to pay dearly for such a flagrant betrayal of trust.) However, God was then about to move and, nine years later to the day, the rise of the State of Israel was officially recognised by Russia (as stated above) — Russia being within the sphere of ancient 'Assyria' which power God had used to bring about the carrying away of Israel (the ten tribes) in the days of Hezekiah[9].

These *'two days'* (2,000 years) and *'nine hours'* (as expressed by the 9 solar years) were among several perfect time-designs of God showing the year 1948 as the *'midnight'* of the resurrection, for between 3 pm on Friday and the midnight of Sunday when Jesus was raised from the dead, we have the actual *'two days and nine hours'* of death which have been the pattern of so many of God's wonderful works since the foundation of the world. (We shall mention the significance of the year 1948-9 as that in which the 'resurrection' of the new State was consummated, in our next Chapter.)

'I Am Alpha and Omega, The Beginning and The Ending, saith The Lord, Which is ... The Almighty'
(Revelation 1: 8)

Some years ago the Spirit of God revealed the significance of the number of days between Simeon's great prophecy of Luke 2: 34 to do with the 'rising again of many in Israel' and the fulfilment of his words in 1948.

When the error of two days in our Gregorian Solar Calendar is remembered, it should not be difficult to check the measurement of the 711,288 days between December 8th 1 BC and May 15th 1948.

Two most significant numbers make up these 711,288 days. '888' — the numerical value of the Name of *Jesus* — is multiplied by '801', which is simply '1' = *Alpha* and '800' which is *Omega* the last letter of the alphabet.

So this total shows *Jesus* — *Alpha and Omega* — in resurrection power restoring Israel to the land of Promise, following the all-out effort of Satan, through Hitler, to blot out God's ancient people.

---

[9] See 2 Kings 17

The word for 'dove' *(peristera),* the well-known symbol of the Holy Spirit, also has the numerical value of 801.

Many have spent their lives discovering the unending marvels of Divine design in the Hebrew and Greek wording of Scripture; but it is only now, when it has been made possible to measure Time in the Bible, that the same 'watermark' (so to speak) can be seen in the pages of history. Let those beware who would think to turn back the pages of history by attempting to undo what the Lord God Almighty has been doing since 1948 when He commenced to fulfil His sworn promises to Abraham. The Arab Muslim world, as we know it, is unable to relinquish its objective which is to regain possession of the Jews' homeland.

The Bible's miraculous timing seals the stages of Israel's restoration to their land with the seal of 'the King's ring', for it shows the fulfilment of the Word of God (see Esther 8: 8).

CHAPTER TWENTY-ONE

Biblical Signposts Which Signify The Divine Establishment of the Modern State of Israel

How Did The 'Seven Times' of The Exile End?

The 2,520 Years From 583 BC

We cannot bring these pages to a close without revealing how the 2,520 years of the Gentile overlordship of the Holy Land, from the Babylonian Captivity era, were brought to an end at the time of Israel's rise to nationhood in 1948. The last stage of these 2,520 years commence with the 23rd year of Nebuchadnezzar, which was 583-582 BC, and we read in Jeremiah 52: 27-30 about this final de-population of Jerusalem and of how 'Judah was carried away captive out of his own land'.

In the spring of 1938, when 2,520 years were ending from 583 BC, the European scene was growing darker and the small group of 'watchers', who had published the Bible's chronology and sent copies of the literature to all the Bishops in the previous December, became impressed with the fact that if man had disregarded the printed warning that trouble lay ahead for the world then **God Himself must give a sign**.

We saw from Luke 21: 24-25 that 'there shall be signs in the sun, and in the moon' after 'the times of the Gentiles' were 'fulfilled'. It was made clear to us by the Holy Spirit that a warning of some such 'sign' should be given on March 31st, to take effect at noon on April 1st. (As already remarked, God's ways of dealing with a world that has persistently mocked at the thought of the verbal inspiration of the Holy Scriptures are at times bordering on the comic! However, there was nothing 'comic' about the long-term fulfilment of the warning we had to give relating to April 1st 1938.) As British people know, April 1st is 'All Fools' Day' — that is, until noon.

There had been sunspot activity earlier in the year and the impression was strong that we must not hold back from giving this warning. Accordingly, on March 31st, brief but carefully worded letters were sent to the Editor of 'The Times' newspaper in London, the Archbishop of Canterbury (both of whom had had knowledge of our previous expectations) and the Astronomer Royal. It was not said what the exact nature of the 'sign' would be but those who gave the warning believed that a darkening of the sun, similar to that on the day of the Crucifixion, might be expected.

The day of April 1st passed uneventfully — and, as the following comments on Hezekiah's 'ten hours' will show, it was not until some ten years had passed that it fully dawned upon us that God had perfectly fulfilled His counsel in relation to the matter. We were then able to look back upon a most amazing sequence of events which revealed precisely the purpose and significance of this warning. God *had* 'darkened the sun' but in such a way which had never begun to dawn upon our minds or hearts in the spring of 1938.

The 3,700 Days of Testimony 'To The Jews Only' (AD 26-36)

We must first consider the 'seven times' or 2,520 days during which Nebuchadnezzar lost his reason, as described in Daniel 4. These days were typical, 'each day for a year', of 2,520 years in which the Gentile powers, holding dominance on earth in place of the Kingdom of Judah, would remain in their moral darkness, until their reason was restored to them. The 'seven times' of years had their commencement over an era in the time of the Kingdom of Babylon and were coming to their end over well-defined stages in the present day. God used the measurement to mark the phases of the going into captivity of the people of Judah during Nebuchadnezzar's reign and the world today has witnessed the corresponding ending stages of these 2,520 years.

We had seen many in the Church of God awaken, all over the

world, to the fact that the coming of the Lord was drawing nigh, because for over thirty years students of the prophetic word had been in expectation that 1917 would see movement on God's part to begin to restore the Land of Israel to the Jews — and they were not disappointed.

Then we know that 1923 — the year when the Palestine Mandate had at last begun to operate — had also been clearly forecast by Dr. Grattan Guinness in the 1880's. And those who have read these pages will know how plainly God marked the end of 2,520 years from 588 BC to 1933, when the 6,000 years also ended.

Christians, however, had failed to take account of the most obvious sign of all, and that was that in 1914 — just 'seven times' from when God began to break up the Kingdom of Judah in 607 BC (see Daniel 1: 1) — He had commenced to bring about the downfall of our present civilisation by the outbreak of the First World War. Such things as these were too big to discern at the time, needless to say, but now that the world as a whole has a stockpile of infinitely superior weaponry, in readiness for a third outbreak, few can remain ignorant of the words of Jesus, when He said (in Luke 21: 31) 'When ye see these things come to pass, know ye that the Kingdom of God is nigh at hand'. But He had to add, 'Take heed to yourselves, lest ... that day come upon you unawares. For as a snare shall it come on all them that dwell on the face of the whole earth'[1].

So it was that, as things quietened after the First World War, a drowsiness appeared to settle down upon the Church as a whole, and one feels that this end-time 'slumber' is what our Lord had in mind in the first parable of Matthew 25: 'while the Bridegroom tarried' (verse 5).

In the above heading we referred to the *3,700 days'* during which, first John the Baptist testified to 'Messiah the Prince'[2] between AD 26 and AD 29, and then Jesus Himself ministered for 3½ years until His Ascension in AD 33. After this, from Pentecost in AD 33 to the salvation of the first Gentile household in Caesarea at Pentecost in AD 36, there were three further years during which the preaching of 'the word' was 'unto the Jews only'[3]. The whole period amounted to exactly 3,700 days — the two days of Christ's entombment and the nine days between His Ascension and

---

[1] Luke 21: 34-35
[2] Daniel 9: 25
[3] Acts 11: 19

Pentecost being omitted from reckoning (for the reason that no Divine Person was then ministering on the earth).

We have had to go into this detail for an essential reason. Apart from many other significant measurements which had *April 1st 1938* as their starting point, was one which ended with May 17th 1948 — the day the newborn State of Israel received *de jure* recognition from the Soviet Union, on the third day after its proclamation on May 14th-15th. This period was exactly 3,700 days.

We must attempt to uncover the tremendous significance of this fact.

When the exact patterning of the seven years from 1938 to 1945 was examined and compared with that of the years AD 26 to AD 33, we were amazed to see that the one was a chronological shadow of the other. (Attention has been drawn already to the 1,263½ days' and '1,260 days' which spanned the time from June 11th 1938 to May 8th 1945, when the War in Europe ended and the remnant of the Jews was saved from Nazi genocide.) The 3 years and 9 days from May 8th 1945 to May 17th 1948 can be seen to compensate chronologically for the 3 years and 9 days between the Ascension of Christ in AD 33 and the Day of Pentecost on June 22nd in AD 36.

These facts spoke loudly to us, as the facts of history will speak if we consider them, but what were they actually saying?

AD 26 to 33 compared with AD 1938 to 1945

During the three years of His public ministry to the Jews, between the Passover of AD 30 and that of AD 33, John's Gospel reveals that, in the main, Jesus ministered in Galilee because, in Judea, 'the Jews sought to kill him' (see John 7: 1 & 5: 16-18). And, when He eventually came back to Jerusalem in AD 33, He knew full well that they would have their way. The shadow of the Cross hung over His whole pathway in those years and, in a very real sense, with perfect foreknowledge of all that lay before Him, Jesus walked in 'the valley of the shadow of death'[4] until, in the end, for seven hours, forsaken of God and afflicted, He was to be seen hanging upon a tree. These seven hours were also divided, like the seven years, into four hours and three.

---

[4] Psalm 23: 4

The Hours of the Cross

Mark's Gospel (15: 25) tells us that 'it was the third hour, and they crucified Him'. This third hour of the day, from 8 to 9 am, was the hour of the morning sacrifice and we can be sure that it was close to the beginning of this hour that our blessed Redeemer, already 'so marred more than any man'[5] through the scourging and the buffeting He had received, was nailed by His hands and feet to the stake (Greek *'stauros',* pole or stake), which was then erected and dropped into the hole dug for it.

From that hour until noon the sun shone pitilessly down upon His suffering body, but after that the darkness came 'until the ninth hour' when Jesus died. For three more hours His body hung there lifeless upon the tree before, 'when the even was come', Joseph of Arimathæa went to Pilate and obtained permission to take it down for burial in his own new tomb (Mark 15: 33, 42-46).

So for *ten hours* on that day of May 1st AD 33 *the curse of God* had rested upon the body of His Beloved Son, 'for it is written, *"cursed is everyone that hangeth on a tree"'* (Galatians 3: 13, Deuteronomy 21: 23).

We each one know that He bore that curse for us.

The Ten Years and the Ten Hours

A sizeable book could be written about the significance of the *'sign'* given to Hezekiah (as recorded in Isaiah 38, etc.) when 'the sun returned ten *(lit.)* steps, by which steps it was gone down' but, of necessity, the fact can only be alluded to here in brief. The purpose of this great interposition of God, at the time of what was probably the supreme crisis in the history of the Kingdom of Judah, as the context of Isaiah chapters 36 and 37 shows, was to provide *'a sign'* that He would deliver and defend His people and city from the King of Assyria.

The Divine promise was, 'Behold, I will bring again the shadow of the degrees (*lit.* steps), which is gone down in the sun dial (*lit.* steps) of Ahaz, ten degrees backward'. The Encyclopædia Britannica of 1949 comments that 'a more correct translation of Isaiah 38: 8 may be: "Behold, I will bring again the shadow of the steps down the steps of Ahaz, ten steps backwards"'. (*Editors' note:* Jay P Green's *Literal Translation of the*

---

[5] Isaiah 52: 14

144

Bible, 1985, (in his Interlinear Hebrew/Greek Bible) also says for verse 8: 'Behold, I will bring back the shadow of the steps which has gone down in the steps of Ahaz with the sun, backward ten steps. And the sun went back ten steps by the steps which it had gone down!')

These 'steps' registered **hours**, and the hour is the smallest unit of time of which the Bible takes account.

It is one thing for the child of God to believe in 'the wondrous works of God'[6] and to know that the Bible is true when it records the amazing miracle of the sun standing still 'for about a whole day' in Joshua 10, or that 'the sun returned ten steps' — the great sign we are now considering in Isaiah 38 — but it is another thing to receive what the Spirit of Truth reveals as to *why* these things occurred in history so long ago. What *was* the significance of the *cancelling of ten hours* out of time in the days of Hezekiah?

Without giving this the massive support which can be drawn from the Bible's chronology as applied to Israel's history, let us say in all simplicity that it has to do with the putting away of *sin.* We can remember the words of Hezekiah in Isaiah 38: 17: 'Thou hast in love to my soul delivered it from the pit of corruption: for Thou has cast all my sins behind Thy back'.

God on that occasion turned 'the shadow of death into the morning'[7] by causing that at sundown the fiery orb should return and register but the third hour of the day (8-9 am). That is, what was still the hour of 6 pm in Heaven's time had now become 8 am on earth so that the day might run its course again.

Leaving all other reasons for this 'sign' aside, why do we think of this great miracle in the time of Hezekiah as having any bearing upon the history of our modern civilisation? For one pre-eminent reason. We have seen the ten years from AD 26 to AD 36, when 'the word was preached to none but unto the Jews only' (Acts 11: 19), chronologically repeated between 1938 and 1948, when the national resurrection of Israel took place. Between AD 36 and 1938 we have measured a great *'two days'* (2,000 lunar years or 1,960 years with the addition of 40 years of Jubilee) — the era of waiting to which Hosea refers in chapter 6: 2.

And, looking back at the Gospel records, we see the sufferings of Christ at the hands of the Romans were for *ten hours* until the time of His death — from the opening of 'the sixth hour' (5-6 am)

[6] Job 37: 14
[7] Amos 5: 8

when Pilate had Him scourged[8], to the Jewish 'ninth hour' (2-3 pm) when He yielded up His spirit[9]. And, after this, *'two days'* until the afternoon of Sunday May 3rd.

The Ten Hours to Resurrection

It was not until the midnight hour of 12-1 am on Monday May 4th that God raised Jesus from the dead. We must briefly digress and consider this important aspect of the death and rising again of Jesus our Lord.

Jesus is God's *'firstborn,* higher than the kings of the earth' (Psalm 89: 27) and, as such, He was 'let go' from death at the hour of *midnight,* like the 'firstborn' in Egypt, at the time of the Exodus. But Jesus had also been the sin-bearer — 'reckoned among the transgressors[10] — and suffering judgment, like the 'firstborn of Pharaoh' (see Exodus 4: 22-23 & 12: 29). How then was He to **die at midnight**, and thus, as a substitute, fulfil this rôle in the mighty plan of Redemption?

We believe the answer is to be found in the following facts. When God interfered with the ordered course of time in Hezekiah's day (712-711 BC) He never changed the calendars of Heaven. When '8 am' might be the time on earth, '6 pm' (the opening hour of the next day) still registered with God. Hence, if we travel onward to the Cross of Calvary, we find that the hour when Christ was crucified was the opening of a new day, in terms of 24-hour days as reckoned from Creation. It was in fact '6 pm' when, like a lamb, Jesus was put to death by crucifixion — and 'midnight' (our 2-3 pm) when He died. No wonder darkness covered the earth as this dread hour approached!

It was then, at the time of the death of Jesus, that God 'changed the times and the seasons'[11]. The 1,960 years of Israel's Redemption Calendar had ended, so now the Father would wait until the true solar midnight was reached on May 3rd before commencing the new Calendar of the Resurrection.

What has been shown in these past pages is the simple pattern of the death and resurrection of Christ which is, inclusively, *'two days and ten hours',* following the preceding *'ten hours'* of His great sufferings, when He 'put away sin by the sacrifice of Himself' (Hebrews 9: 26). And this is the pattern of the years which we have outlined — the *ten years* from AD 26 to AD 36, followed by the *two*

---

[8] John 19: 1, 14
[9] Matthew 27: 45-50
[10] Luke 22: 37
[11] Daniel 2: 21

days (2,000 years) and then the *ten years* from 1938 to 1948 which saw the Nation of Israel 'raised from the dead'.

The Sign of Darkness

It is only because of the importance of these facts for Israel and the world in the days which are to come, that it has been necessary to go so carefully into all this detail, which we well know could be burdensome to the normal reader. We must, however, draw attention to the 'horror of great darkness' which Abram experienced, before dealing directly with the question of the 'sign' forecast in 1938.

When the Most High God gave Abram the prophecy and vision of the *four hundred years* to the Exodus, in Genesis 15: 12-13, He gave to the patriarch a foretaste of the 'horror of great darkness' which would eventually come in Egypt, when that land experienced 'a thick darkness in all the land' for 'three days' (Exodus 10: 22). We also know that at the end of the 4,000 years in the Chronology of Redemption from Adam to Calvary, there was the darkening of the sun for three hours, as Matthew, Mark and Luke each testify.

What then of the great *four thousand years* from the Covenant of Genesis 15, which ended in 1948?

Let the fact dawn upon all, both Jews and Gentiles, that the *three years (1942 to 1945) stood out in those final ten years to 1948* as the **three hours of darkness in the ten hours of the Cross of Jesus**.

This was the 'sign in the sun' of which a warning needed to be given at the opening of those last 3,700 days, and it was mainly in **these three years** that the third part of the whole Jewish race was taken from the earth.

Upwards of twenty-four million souls perished in the Second World War (both civilians and military personnel) but the *'horror of great darkness'* (Genesis 15: 12) fell mainly upon the people of Israel, and no one conversant with the history of those last three years of the war should think of challenging that fact.

'The Sign of Resurrection' in Isaiah 38

'What is the sign that I shall go up to the house of the Lord?'
(Isaiah 38:22)

If we read the account in 2 Kings 20: 8-11, we shall see the picture drawn even more clearly. 'Hezekiah said unto Isaiah, "What shall be the sign that the Lord will heal me, and that I shall go up into the house of the Lord *the third day?"'*

What was the 'sign'? It was the sign of the sun's returning to run its course again for *ten hours.* And what was the means used for the recovery of King Hezekiah from his sickness? If we read in Isaiah 38: 21, we find that it was *'a lump of figs'.*

If scattered 'figs' portray the dispersion of the Jews from their land, of what does a *'lump of figs'* speak, if not the regathering of the Nation again, as the whole world witnessed in 1948? (Figs are symbolic of Jews carried away captive, and later restored to their land — see Jeremiah 24.)

'3,700' Civil Lunar Years From the Exodus End in 1948

God is a God of absolute perfection when it comes to the designing of the chronology of His Word. Not only must He cause that the opening of the last *3,700 days* from 1938 to the rise of the State of Israel in 1948 should be clearly marked by the warning of a sign, but in planning the ages He had foreseen and, indeed, actually designed, that a span of *3,700 years* (of 354 days each) should terminate at this great resurrection hour in the history of the Jewish people. For we shall find, if we measure this period from the very day of the Exodus, which was May 12th 1639 BC (and leaving unreckoned the two days of the death of Jesus in AD 33), that it ended on the solar anniversary of Pentecost — June 22nd — in 1948, and that it was on this same day that the first U.S. Ambassador to Israel accepted his appointment, thus sealing America's relationship with the new State.

This was most clearly a design of God, because the original *3,700 days* from the beginning of the John the Baptist's ministry in AD 26 had been timed to end at **Pentecost** — June 22nd — in AD 36, as previously explained.

What was God really saying in all this? The Jews — apart from the small minority in Israel who had received Jesus — had as a nation rejected and *lost* the Divine testimony of John the Baptist and of the Messiah Himself, and lastly (between AD 33 and AD 36) that of the Holy Ghost, during those former *ten years.* **Therefore God had caused the period to run its course again at this end of the age.** This, indeed, was what we had seen with our own eyes and we had seen it end with the rise of the State of Israel!

Was not this chronological repetition of the *ten years,* like the sun's shadow retracing its course on 'the steps of Ahaz'[12], the appointed *'sign'* to the people of Israel that *'the third day'* had now come — the day of their deliverance from an enemy worse than Sennacherib — because the 'two days' or '2,000 years' of the Gentiles had ended?

What of the 'Seven Times'?
'How great are His signs! and how mighty are His wonders!'
(Daniel 4: 3)

This chapter was headed with the question *'How Did The Seven Times of The Exile End?'* The period in question was the 2,520 years* which started over the 23rd year of Nebuchadnezzar, 583-2 BC, and ended over the year 1938-9. Instead of ending with a literal sign in the sun, they had merely ushered in the darkest era in the entire history of the Jewish people — at least, as far as the Jews of Europe were concerned. 'The shadow of death' was, indeed, to pass over Israel but praise be to God — to the God of Abraham, Isaac and of Jacob — that shadow in the end would be turned 'into the morning' (Amos 5: 8).

The history of the returning of the exiles of Israel over the year 1948-9 is too well known to all who love the God of Israel to need repeating here, for countless books were published on the subject. The story of the Yemenite Jews, borne back to their homeland 'on eagles' wings'[13] — in the airlift from Aden — is, indeed, a tale of wonder to all who read it. But the *sign* of Daniel 4: 16-17 is in essence *a chronological one* — it must be exactly measured. So the question still remained, how could this great span of 2,520 years relating to the Gentiles ever become a *sign* to all the peoples of the world?

The fourth chapter of Daniel is the one and only chapter in the Bible which is written by a *Gentile* and it is, of course, the testimony of *'the head'* of the succession of powers spoken of in Daniel 2. It is to be noted that in Daniel 4: 1, this King addresses himself to *'all people, nations, and languages, that dwell in all the earth'.* And the purpose of the seven times measurement is clearly stated in the chapter by 'a holy one ... from heaven' (v 13), to be:

---

[12] Isaiah 38: 8
[13] Exodus 19: 4

* See Note 1 on page 184

'That the living may know that the Most High ruleth in the kingdom of men, ... and setteth up over it the basest of men' (v 17)
that is Jesus, whom men slew and hanged upon a tree.

The 2,520 Years + 10 Years or 2,530 Years
Revealed in the Holy Scriptures

It is only while writing these pages that the perfect pattern of
the 2,520 and 10 years has come to light, and it lies upon the
surface of the Bible's chronological structure.

According to the genealogical tables of Genesis 5 and the data
given in Genesis 6 to 8, it was 1,657 years (of 354 days) from Adam
to the end of the year of the Flood (2469 BC). From this new
beginning, after which the sons of Noah began to repopulate the
earth, there were precisely *2,520 years* in the Bible's chronology to
AD 26, when John the Baptist began to bear testimony to 'Messiah
the Prince'; that was when 4,177 years had been completed
(4,177 − 1,657 = 2,520).

Seven times had passed over the Gentile world, since the
Flood of Noah, before those final *ten years,* which we have been
so long considering, came into view. But the word was preached
'to none but unto the Jews *only*'[14] right through until Pentecost
AD 36, and **then** it was that the Gentiles first began to hear how
God had exalted Him who had, at His Crucifixion, truly been *'the
basest of men'.* The whole *ten years* had been for a *sign.*

The numerical value of the Hebrew word for sign, or ensign or
pole — such as the pole upon which Moses 'lifted up the serpent
in the wilderness'[15] — is 110 and the word is *nes,* spelt with the
Hebrew letters *nun* (50) and *samech* (60).

We find that 2,530 is 23 times 110 and from this fact we begin to
see the design of God concerning the 'seven times'. Apart from
the addition of those *ten years* from AD 26 (containing the
testimonies of John the Baptist, of Jesus Himself and of the Holy
Spirit until Pentecost, AD 36) the 2,520 years could have been no
sign to the Gentile world. But when the three-fold testimony to
Israel was completed, then in AD 36 it could begin to be unfolded
to the Gentiles, as recorded in Acts 10.

God's ways are perfect and many illustrations could be given
to show the Divine use of the number 110 in connection with the

---

[14] Acts 11: 19
[15] John 3: 14

Cross of Jesus, if space were to permit, but the spiritual mind will readily grasp the thought of God in causing the 2,520 years from 583 BC to end with the whole *ten years* from 1938 to 1948 — making 23 times 110 years in all.

Actually, we believe God may have looked upon AD 26 to 36 as a *lost* period in the seven times, so that its *repetition* over the years 1938 to 1948 would but bring the 2,520 years to fulness. But, whichever way we may look at it, it is certain that the God of Israel now requires both Jew and Gentile to receive an understanding of what He has done and of what He intends to do in relation to the people of Israel and their land.

The Year of Israel's Rise Among the Nations

It is of importance to note that the United Nations Organisation recognised Israel as a member State a year after its inception in May 1948. The day and hour when their vote was cast is of great significance, for it was exactly 360 days after May 16-17th in 1948, when the 2,520 years + 3,700 days were complete from the opening of the 23rd year of Nebuchadnezzar in 583 BC. (The Babylonian year, or 'time' was 360 days.)*

The day and hour was *'May 11th, at midnight'* in 1949, when by a majority of '37' votes the State of Israel was granted recognition by the world. This was of course, to the hour, the solar anniversary of the Exodus 'midnight' deliverance from Egypt in 1639 BC.

It was exactly *ten years* of 354 days each from September 1st 1939 when Germany invaded Poland (the country where the greatest number of Jews in Europe were congregated) at the beginning of the Second World War.

Let all who have pondered Israel's long history of suffering at the hands of the Gentile nations, and who consider their present position of crisis in the world, remember the closing words of the great king Nebuchadnezzar in Daniel 4: 37:

> 'Now I Nebuchadnezzar praise and extol and honour the King
> of heaven, all whose works are truth, and His ways judgment:
> and those that walk in pride He is able to abase.'

And let us also remember that these words of Nebuchadnezzar are addressed to us, for they were to 'all people, nations, and

---

* See Note 1 on page 184

languages, that dwell in all the earth'. And we remember that he went on, 'I thought it good to show the *signs and wonders* that the high God hath wrought towards me. *How great are His signs! and how mighty are His wonders!*'[16]

It is with the object of beginning to uncover these *'signs and wonders'* that these pages have been written. This perfectly-timed overruling of world history by the Almighty God is manifestly proceeding to a conclusion in these days of increasing darkness and strife among the nations. 'Men's hearts' are indeed 'failing them for fear, and for looking after those things which are coming on the earth'[17]. But what of us, who are 'children of the light'? We are promised the shining 'day star'[18] and the gift of the 'morning star' — yes, indeed, the light of Jesus Who is 'the bright and morning star'[19].

Has it ever occurred to the saints of God that this might be an *astronomical* light?! A light we can see with our eyes, just as we actually see the morning star?

How many millions have blindly accepted that '4,004 BC' or thereabouts was the date of Genesis 1, simply because a few scholars had agreed that there probably would have been about four thousand solar years between the creation of Adam and the birth of Christ?

God in His wisdom and in His mercy has brought the figures of His Word (that is, in the Hebrew Masoretic text — upon which our King James Version is based) to the rescue, so that we may discern the *pattern* and the bold *outline,* as well as the fine detail, of *His works* over the past six thousand years. Praise His Holy Name!

Yes, we are at the 'resurrection' end of a long and darkened age, and, just as it was at the beginning, Jesus is now, in a multitude of hearts and minds, presenting Himself *'alive ... by many infallible proofs'* (see Acts 1: 3). Let us no longer ignore this marvellous side of His Holy Word.

Before proceeding to consider certain *'signs in the moon'* in the next Chapter, let us ask soberly what probability is there that the network of facts and figures we have summed up in these preceding 21 Chapters could have come about by accident?!

It is the prevailing state of blindness in the world and in the Church, as it gropes its way along the edge of an appalling abyss (well beyond the point of no return) that causes us to go into print,

[16] Daniel 4: 1-3
[17] Luke 21: 26
[18] 2 Peter 1: 19
[19] Revelation 2: 28, 22: 16

however poorly or inadequately our case may have been presented.

And our case is simply that God has given light to shine on the Person of His Son Jesus, Jesus Who is still *the light of the world,* the only light it needs, or will ever have.

Nineteen centuries ago fear and prejudice put out that light for the people of Israel at large, and a small persecuted minority of Gentiles commenced to bear it aloft — which were destined to become the Church of God. Now, it would seem, it is the turn of Israelis and Jews generally to look again upon the Person of their Redeemer, and to get know the true facts concerning His coming down to earth, to take His place among them and to become, as the Samaritan woman said, *'the Christ, the Saviour of the world*[20].

If we look for a brief moment in this fourth chapter of John's Gospel, we shall see that 'after two days' (verse 43) spent in Samaria, Jesus 'departed thence, and went into Galilee' where, we read, 'the Galilæans received Him, having seen all the things that He did at Jerusalem at the feast ... so Jesus came again into Cana of Galilee, where He made the water wine'. This return to Cana, *'after two days'* (which had actually been spent in a Gentile sphere — for the Samaritans were not Jews) prefigured Jesus, after the two thousand years of the Christian dispensation, returning to reveal Himself in Israel, so that the people who have been 'in darkness' might see 'a great light' (see Isaiah 9: 1-2).

---

[20] John 4: 42 (then 43-46)

CHAPTER TWENTY-TWO

The Chronological Significance of The Apollo Missions to The Moon

'A faithful witness in the sky'   (Psalm 89: 37 RV)

*The Word of God Spoken from The Moon
on December 24th-25th 1968*

The 'light' which God appointed to 'rule the night'[1] was *the moon,* and most Christians have agreed that, because its light is reflected, the moon is a type of the Church (see Song of Solomon 6: 10). For this reason it seems right to add this Chapter relating to the achievements of the American astronauts in actually reaching the moon successfully on seven occasions, and the significance of the timing of these events, which held the attention of the whole world.

In Revelation 3: 14, our Lord Jesus Christ addresses His Church as 'the Faithful and True Witness, the beginning of the creation of God' — but when we find this expression used in the Psalms, it is *'the moon'* that is described as a *'faithful witness'*[2].

In previous Chapters we summarised the total years and days which have been traced in the Bible's chronology. These have been presented in outline, rather than in detail, but in the final Appendix it will be found possible to check time in the various sections to the day and hour from the beginning in Genesis 1. It is important to remember that the whole course of time has been accounted for and recorded by the *moon,* which is the celestial timepiece of the people of Israel.

In the winter of 1968 the Christian world made much of the

---

[1] Genesis 1: 16
[2] Psalm 89: 37

fact that the first ten verses of Genesis were read by the three astronauts on the eve of their return from the moon, late on the 24th or in the early morning of December 25th 1968, while still in orbit around it.

As that Christmas approached, the writer had the thought that, while the world was celebrating the *birth* of Christ in Bethlehem, the intention of God was to cause men to know the truth concerning Christ's *rising again as 'the firstborn' or 'first begotten of the dead'*[3] — in other words, to have the real facts to do with His Resurrection. We then looked into the timing of the incident more closely. The first fact discovered was that the Creator had allowed man to reach the moon early in a lunation which was:

The 74,740th Lunation from Creation

Measuring from the first new moon at the opening of 'the first day' of Genesis 1 (March 3rd 4075 BC at 6 pm), we found that on December 19th 1968 the span of 74,739 lunations had been completed, and so it was on the sixth day of the 74,740th moon (December 24th-25th) that the three Americans read out from the heavens the account of God's handiwork on the first three days of Genesis.

The Significance of '74'

'74' is twice '37', and all who know the meaning of numbers in the Scriptures will realise the significance of this figure. But for the benefit of others, we will quote R T Naish, the author of *'Spiritual Arithmetic'*. Writing of '37' he says:

'Of all the numbers, this is perhaps the most sublime, setting forth the wonders of the written Word, and revealing through its pages Him, Who is the living Word of God!

'My attention was first directed to it by a remark of that gifted writer, Ivan Panin, that there were no less than six different combinations of this number (37) *in the very first verse of the Bible.* This set me thinking, and the Lord graciously opened up the wonders of this glorious number, till my heart was filled with praise!'

---

[3] Colossians 1: 18 and Revelation 1: 5

As previously explained, all Greek and Hebrew letters of the alphabet possess a numerical value (having been used instead of figures) and it has already been shown that the number of the name of 'JESUS' in the Greek is '888', which is 12 times '74'. Following the same pattern:

The numerical value of 'CHRIST' is 1,480, or 20 times '74'
The word for 'GODHEAD' amounts to 592, or 8 times '74'
The numerical value of the Greek for 'BEHOLD, THE BRIDEGROOM COMETH; GO YE OUT TO MEET HIM'[4] is 5,920, or 80 times '74'.

These few examples must suffice as a clue to the significance of the number 74, as space forbids further elaboration here. Those who have checked and verified the accuracy of the Bible's chronology will realise that there was no accident about the timing of the Apollo 8 venture when, for the first time, men set out from the shores of earth to explore and survey that dead celestial sphere. For the moon, as God's 'faithful witness in the sky'[5], will, by its exact recording of the whole Divine Plan of the Ages, play a vital part in the heralding of 'the Bridegroom's' approach.

No wonder that the Most High required the opening words of the Scriptures to be read out to the whole civilised world on this first occasion when He allowed men within orbitting reach of the moon. The reason for this will become more apparent as we go on to examine the hidden significance of the 'Christmas 1968' date in relation to the Church dispensation which commenced at the Pentecost of Acts 10, that is when the first Gentiles received the gift of the Holy Ghost in the house of Cornelius on June 22nd AD 36, just three solar years after the Jerusalem Pentecost of Acts 2.

This dispensation had proved to be exactly 1,900 solar years but, owing to the error made by Pope Gregory when he adjusted the solar calendar in 1582, *this period ended on June 20th 1936,* by which time it had pleased God to allow the Bible's Chronology of *Redemption* to come to light in all its perfection. There have been several occasions when we have had to take note of this dual ending of the dispensation over the three years 1933 to 1936 — on account of its commencement over the three years between Pentecost, AD 33, and its solar anniversary when the Holy Ghost descended upon the Gentiles in AD 36.

[4] Matthew 25: 6
[5] Psalm 89: 37 (RV)

A Chronological Repetition of The Life of Jesus

From 'Pentecost' 1936 (June 20th) we may measure the exact span of 32 years and 187 days to December 24th-25th 1968. This, *to the day,* was the length of the life of Jesus from His Birth in Bethlehem, on October 29th (Tishri 15th) in 1 BC to the day when He became *'the firstborn from the dead'*[6] on May 4th AD 33.

So, while the civilised world was remembering His Birth in Bethlehem, God had designed that this era of 'the consummation' should total the precise age of Jesus *at His birth from 'among the dead'*[7].

Praise God, those who love our Lord Jesus Christ will rejoice that the Almighty should take man's highest achievement in the realm of science (to reach the moon and orbit it ten times) and make it the occasion of proclaiming His Creatorship to the whole earth — and at the same time set His seal on the true age of His Beloved Son when He was raised from the dead! For *His Resurrection* was the point at which the Most High brought in His *'new creation'.*

(There are other time-patterns of the period of the Lord's death which reach to December 24th-25th 1968 as the 'resurrection' point. Space does not permit full explanation here, but one of these starts at the time of His Baptism and the opening of the temptation in the wilderness.)

The Two Moon Landings in 1969

The first occasion when man set foot on the moon's surface was July 21st 1969, and this date also appears to confirm the length of the whole course of time from Creation to June 12th 1933. God has shown that He has wondrous ways of *manipulating time* for the glory of His Son, Jesus. In this case we have to remember the number of days in the whole era to the end of the 6,000 years in 1933 but take no account of the two full days in AD 33 when *the moon was turned 'into blood'*[8] — that is, while the body of Jesus lay in the grave. The total number of days in this case was 2,194,112.

We had found the Chronology of Redemption to have commenced on the day following the Fall of Adam and Eve, after their probationary period of 40 days in the Garden of Eden, which

---

[6] Colossians 1: 18
[7] Luke 24: 5
[8] Joel 2: 31

ended on April 19th 4075 BC. This was the point where Adam's first '130 years' of Genesis 5: 3 began to be measured; that is, *it was the starting date of the Chronology of Redemption,* the first day of which being April 20th.

Measuring time from this beginning, *but omitting the whole era from Christ's Nativity in Bethlehem (October 29th 1 BC) through to the Feast of Tabernacles in AD 36 (October 23rd)* for reasons we are about to give, the close of the 2,194,112 days (the total shown above) will be found to be July 21st 1969, when man first set foot upon the moon. (This date was July 20th in Eastern Daylight Time (USA), but the 21st in Middle East Time.)

It should be remembered that October 23rd (Tishri 15th) AD 36 was the date of the conference of Acts 11, when 'the apostles and brethren' met in Jerusalem, to whom the apostle Peter related all that had occurred the previous Pentecost when he had opened the door of the Kingdom to the Gentiles in the house of Cornelius. Not until this point in the history of Acts were the Lord's Jewish apostles given to see that 'God also to the Gentiles' had 'granted repentance unto life'. It was then that 'they glorified God', being at last brought into communion with Him concerning His purposes to do with the new age then starting (see verses 1-18). It was this 'Tabernacles' date in AD 36 from which many main measurements relating to our Gentile dispensation have had their beginning (see Chapter 20).

After considering the matter, we were shown that in this aspect of time God was looking at the period from the Birth of Jesus at the Feast of Tabernacles in 1 BC to the Feast of Tabernacles in AD 36 as being *an interval* in the whole course of time, *specially related to His First Advent,* when He came to Israel. It was time lost to the nation, because they rejected the Messiah. Therefore, the end of the period (which we can view as the close of the last two thousand years) is extended to July 21st 1969.

When the 2,194,112 days had run their course in 1933, on June 12th, the whole world had its eye upon the World Economic Conference — 'the World's Second Tower of Babel' — *but on July 21st 1969* the world's attention was fixed upon the moon. Man, indeed, *had climbed up to heaven* and the feeling was, as at the Tower of Babel, that 'now nothing will be restrained from them, which they have imagined to do' (see Genesis 11: 6).

There was, however, another side to the picture, which only later came to the writer's attention.

It had been impressed upon Col. E E ('Buzz') Aldrin (the second man to set foot upon the moon on that day), and many others in the programme with him, that what they were doing was part of God's eternal plan. He determined, with the agreement of His pastor, that he should take communion on the moon, in the Eagle, before stepping down onto its surface. This he did, with the comment: 'It was interesting to think that *the very first liquid ever poured on the moon, and the first food eaten there, were communion elements'*. And, before partaking of these, he read the 5th verse of the 15th chapter of John's Gospel, which concludes with these words: *'without Me ye can do nothing'*. (We are indebted to 'Guideposts' of October 1970 for this information.)

It is certainly significant to read of this remembrance of God and of the Sacrifice of His Son, Jesus, taking place as man's first act before treading upon the surface of the moon, which is God's 'faithful witness in Heaven'[9]. And especially so, as we recall the last act of the whole human race (through its governments on June 12th 1933) which was to *ignore the very existence of the Creator of heaven and earth!*

Before proceeding, we feel it right to state that it was not until we had watched and noted the Divine time-patternings of the whole series of Apollo Moon Missions that it pleased God to show us why He had chosen to overrule these exploits. These reasons we will attempt to explain fully below.

The second occasion when astronauts set foot upon the moon was on November 19th 1969. In this further aspect of time we shall see God taking account of the exact 280 days of our Lord's Incarnation in the womb of the virgin. For if the 13,301 days between January 23rd 1 BC, the day when the Angel Gabriel came to Mary with the Annunciation of His First Advent, and the Day of Pentecost in AD 36 (June 22nd), when the Holy Ghost came down upon the Gentiles, be viewed as *an interval* (similar to the one described above) *related to our Lord's First Advent to Israel,* we shall find the total of 2,194,122 days was reached on November 19th 1969. This is the full total of days from Creation to Pentecost (June 20th) in 1933, when these run their course without a break.

We are fully conscious that the above are time-designs which

---

[9] Psalm 89: 37

can only carry weight with those who have personally measured every detail of the Bible's chronological chain of time and become assured of the accuracy of the figures — but, at least, they can hardly be seen to be coincidental or fortuitous!

The next occasion when American astronauts set out to make a further landing on the moon had no significance whatsoever in relation to the Bible's plan of the ages. The abortive attempt of Apollo 13, in mid-April 1970, will be remembered by the 600 million viewers all over the world who watched their perilous journey through to the end, after an accident to their oxygen supply and two minor engine failures after take-off. No doubt, millions of prayers went up for the safety of the astronauts in Apollo '13', and God showed mercy, but He also withheld that full support which had been the mark of the previous journeys into space.

As Col. Aldrin quoted from the Psalms, before returning to earth in Apollo 11 in July 1969, 'When I consider Thy heavens, the work of Thy fingers, the moon and the stars, which Thou hast ordained; what is man, that Thou art mindful of him'?[10]

But God *is* mindful of man, and millions over the earth today are praising the wonderful Name of Jesus, as they experience His loving-kindness in the pathway of their individual lives. But the day of grace is rapidly drawing to an end, and God in His great mercy would use every means to warn His creatures of the approaching doom of this apostate civilisation. We can praise Him that He has kept in reserve a *final* means — the same for the Gentile world now as He reserved for Israel: *'last of all He sent unto them His Son'*[11]. **This is the reason the Bible's perfect record of time has been restored to the human race:** it is **to reveal the truth** concerning the Birth, the Life, the Death and the Resurrection of Jesus of Nazareth, the Son of God.

The Moon Landing of February 5th 1971

The third landing of man on the moon, from Apollo 14, once again marked the ending of a time-pattern relating to the First Advent of Christ, the interval in this case being the exact time between His Nativity on October 29th 1 BC and the Day of Pentecost which was June 22nd in AD 33. The 1,960 years of the Gentile age, however, were measured in terms of true lunar years

---

[10] Psalm 8: 3-4
[11] Matthew 21: 37

from October 23rd AD 36. These terminated on June 11th 1938, a day which was marked by an earthquake in Britain, and also felt in other parts of the Continent of Europe.

The date of June 11th 1938 was 2,195,939 days inclusively from March 4th 4075 BC (the first day of Genesis 1). But, when the *interval relating to the First Advent of Christ* — from His Birth to Pentecost AD 33 — is omitted, then we shall find that the total of 2,195,939 days was reached on February 3rd 1971. This interval was 11,925 days, so that the total days from Creation amounted to 2,207,864. Why was this figure apparently two days short of the required number needed to reach February 5th?

The simple answer to this enigma came when we realised that the above 2,207,864 days contain 74,765 lunations and 10 days (apart from odd minutes) in Mean Time, *but the moon does not show this recording until two days later, that is, February 5th,* the day when this third lunar landing was made. (The moon was in conjunction at 5.55 pm Eastern Standard Time (USA) on January 26th, and several hours later than this in Middle East Time, so that the following 10 days extended to February 5th.)

It would seem that God's purpose in thus overruling the timing of this fourth successful Apollo Mission to the moon was to specifically call attention to the fact that its revolution has, indeed, been arrested for two whole days since the Creation in 4075 BC. As we have shown, each of the preceding arrivals of man (either to orbit around the moon, as with Apollo 8, or actually to land on its surface, as with Apollo 11 and 12) has been to confirm various aspects of the Bible's exact chronology, and in **each** case it can be shown by calculation that the moon fails by two days to accord with the total of days given.

(Quite apart from this, as we know, is a fact positively stated in Joshua 10: 12-13 that both sun and moon were together caused not to record time for 'about a whole day', soon after Israel's entry into Canaan in 1599 BC.)

This revelation concerning the cessation of the recording of *time* for *two whole days*, while the body of Jesus Christ, the Son of God, lay lifeless in the Sepulchre after He had suffered death on the Cross to take 'away the sin of the world'[12], is not only basic to the entire structure of the Bible's chronology, but without it no one can fully 'see' and appreciate the whole Plan of Redemption.

---

[12] John 1: 29

The Three Further 'Signs' in The Moon

It will be no surprise to anyone who has carefully considered the chronological significance of the preceding four successful moon missions of Apollo 8, 11, 12 and 14, to learn that the dates when the American astronauts landed on the lunar surface from Apollo 15, 16 and 17 were also overruled by Almighty God so as to provide *'signs'* which perfectly confirm the Bible's amazing time structure.

Apollo 15 — July 30th 1971

As in the case of Apollo 14, the timing of this arrival on the moon was designed to mark the end of the 2,195,939 days which, when recorded in unbroken sequence, terminated on June 11th 1938 — see Chapter 20.

If we compare this Apollo 15 Mission with that of Apollo 11 in July 1969 we shall find that the time-pattern again commences with April 20th 4075 BC, which was the first day of the Redemption Chronology and the beginning of the years of Adam's life, which were timed to start immediately after the Fall, 47 days from the new moon of Creation. Leaving these first 47 days unmeasured, we may trace time through to the day when the silence of God was broken concerning the Coming of the Messiah.

We discovered from Luke 1: 59-79 that this was through the testimony of the Holy Ghost which was *'noised abroad throughout all the hill country of Judæa'* (verse 65) after, at the circumcision of John the Baptist, the tongue of his father Zacharias was loosed. It was then that he uttered his great prophecy concerning Jesus which ends with these words: 'the dayspring from on high hath visited us, to give light to them that sit in darkness and in the shadow of death, to guide our feet into the way of peace' (verses 78-79). Prior to this moment, the events recorded by Luke had been of an entirely private nature which had not reached the outside world, and Zacharias' utterance broke an age-long silence when it was 'noised abroad'.

The date of the circumcision of John was June 11th 1 BC, and it is from this date that we can trace an exact 33 solar years (extended only by the two days of Christ's entombment which, in this aspect, God ignores) as yet another expression of an *interval related to the*

First Advent of Christ through to the day of His Ascension — June 13th AD 33 — which His Father designed should stand out as a period set apart from the rest of time. We then found that the end of the above 2,195,939 days extended to the close of July 30th 1971, when Apollo 15 landed its astronauts on the surface of the moon. We shall later be able to reveal the significance of man's being allowed by God to reach, and then to stand up and walk about upon, the 'dead' planet but will first record the patterning of time relating to the landings from Apollo 16 and 17.

Apollo 16 — April 21st 1972

Underlying this date there was found to be an exact expression of the three periods of 1,960 years (of 354 days) extended into **true lunar time.** These three eras of 4 x 490 years had constituted the whole of the Bible's *Chronology of Redemption, which ended with June 11th-12th 1933.* As we know, in this Chronology all other time is viewed by God as lost, and is therefore unreckoned.

But in this time pattern we find an interval of exactly 34 years (of 354 days) which dates from Jesus' Birth on October 29th 1 BC through to the Martyrdom of Stephen on October 11th AD 33. This was at the end of the one 'year' of Luke 13: 8, after which the 'fig tree' of Israel was 'cut down' (see verses 6-9). These 34 years formed an *interval relating to our Lord's First Advent* which God designed to stand apart from the rest of time by this sign. (It must not be forgotten that the last era of 1,960 years referred to above commenced from Israel's official rejection of Jesus when they put Stephen to death, and ran exactly to the date of the World Economic Conference in June 1933.)

In order to measure this time-pattern accurately we had to take the total days from Creation to June 11th 1933 (2,194,113 days) — when the three periods of 1,960 years ended. To this we had to add 2,158 days, which is the excess when these 5,880 years are expressed as *true lunar years* of 354 days, 8 hours, 48 minutes and 33.6 seconds. This extended the total to 2,196,271 days, and to this the interval of 34 x 354 days (or 12,036 days) had to be added. This made the full number of days from Creation to be 2,208,307, and the last day was be found to be April 21st 1972, in the evening of which the two Apollo astronauts clambered down onto the moon's surface from Orion.

After this, one more 'sign' remained.

Apollo 17 — December 11th 1972

It is a most significant fact that this *seventh* and last arrival on the moon was timed to take place exactly *seven times seven* (49) lunations from the first orbit of Apollo 8 on December 24th-25th 1968, and it is clear that God had designed that there should be a *sevenfold* period set apart for the fulfilment of these seven 'signs in the moon'.

To see this last sign clearly we again had to take the total days from Creation to June 11th 1933, that is 2,194,113 days, and add to these an excess of 2,273 days. This was the difference between the total number of 354-day years contained in the 6,000 solar years — that is 6,191 years — and, when this whole period was given its *true lunar* expression of 354 days, 8 hours, 48 minutes and 33.6 seconds per year, this extended the period to September 1st 1939, when the Second World War opened with the invasion of Poland by Germany.

Lastly, we had to discover what the interval was, relating to the First Advent of Christ, that God had designed to stand out as a period set apart from the rest of time by this sign. We found that it was the whole of His earthly pathway as Man in the flesh — from His Incarnation in the virgin's womb, on January 23rd 1 BC, to the moment when Jesus became 'the Firstborn from the dead' in the night of May 3rd AD 33 — a period of 12,155 days. Adding this number of days to September 1st 1939, we were brought to December 11th 1972, when the final landing of American astronauts on the moon took place.

Without further comment on the above 'signs', we must proceed at once to provide the answer to those who are asking: "How much can we say that these 'signs' 'in the moon' are actually related to those of which Jesus Himself spoke in Luke 21: 24-25, as immediately following the fulfilling of 'the times of the Gentiles' — are they really intended to be 'signs'?"

The answer to this question, significantly enough, was given to the writer on May 4th 1972, and we dare not withhold it from those who are honestly seeking to know the truth in this matter.

The **two days** during which the 'moon' was 'turned into blood'[13] (and became 'dead' in its recording in AD 33) **were May 2nd and 3rd**, while the Body of God's Son lay in the Tomb. These two days are symbolic of our past age or dispensation, during which the Jews have been in dispersion, but at the end of which Israel has come again to nationhood in her land and the bloodstained history of Christendom has come near to its close.

We have noted that each of the seven time-designs of the Apollo missions has registered the end of the 6,000 years (in one or other aspects) and that this has therefore also been the close of the last 2,000 lunar years — of the *'two days'* of Hosea 6: 2, of which the two literal days in the Sepulchre were typical.

During those two literal days the 'moon was turned into blood' which speaks of *death*. We asked then, 'what *sign* could be given at their close to herald the opening of *'the third day'* — the day of the Lord's *Resurrection?*

What Sign Could be Given but The Sign of LIFE?

What! *Life on the moon! Living men on that dead planet?* None but the novelist could have imagined it forty years before but it happened under our own eyes and the eyes of all the world. *Men* have stood up and walked upon the moon and, of course, spoken to the whole world from it.

I remember thinking, as I watched the astronauts making their return journey to earth for the last time this century, how, needless to say, we never had a doubt as to their safe return, knowing that their mission had been in the plan of the Almighty.

Once again we were reminded of Col. Aldrin's words, read from John 15: 5 just before that first landing on the moon in July 1969 ... 'Without Me ye can do nothing'.

---

[13] See Joel 2: 31

List of Appendices, Notes and Charts

APPENDIX 1

An Overview of Biblical Chronology

The Calendar

No one could possibly arrive at a true computation of time by simply adding together the years on the surface of Scripture unless they have been initiated into the ways of God. For one thing, they would never know from what point of time in history they could measure back to Creation. Too many have tried by various methods over the centuries, but it has been like attempting to unlock the door of a safe with numberless keys — none will work, except the one specially cut to fit the lock.

The key which, it was revealed, would actually turn in the lock and open up the storehouse of knowledge to do with time in the Bible was what we call the *civil lunar year, or calendar lunar year,* of 354 days.

Every lunar year is 354 days long, being composed of twelve 'moons', for a single lunation has been found to be, in Mean Time, 29 days, 12 hours, 44 minutes and 2.8 seconds. As the calendar month must be either 29 or 30 days, the Divine order was found from the Scriptures as follows: the first month of the year was always of 30 days, and the second of 29 days (that is, all 'odd' months contain 30 and all 'even' months 29 days). This order never varies.

Prior to the Exodus, that is, between 4075 BC and 1639 BC, time in the Bible was found to be reckoned in a succession of 354-day years, God having designed that these should 'fit' the age of the moon at given times, such as at the Flood of Noah and at the Exodus, but run their course between the occasions dated in Scripture independently of a true (astronomical) lunar calendar.

Every date in the Bible is, of course, a lunar one, for the Hebrew word for 'month' *(chodesh)* literally means 'new moon'; and twelve lunations — that is, the astronomical lunar year — amount to 354 days, 8 hours, 48 minutes and 33.6 seconds, as stated in Chapter 22.

This odd excess of hours and minutes would apparently make the keeping of a perfect calendar a matter of extreme difficulty; that is, with man, as the Jews discovered when their present calendar came into being during their dispersion. With God, however, everything is simple, provided His people walk in dependence upon Him!

After the Exodus, the Jews found they had to keep a 'luni-solar' calendar. This meant that, while each single year was of 354 days, it was necessary to insert 'intercalary' months or lunations after, generally, the third, sixth and eighth years in order to keep their Passovers and Feasts of Firstfruits in the Spring season. In order to know when to commence their new years after an intercalation, they simply had to 'see' the new moon. Their first month was called 'Abib', or month of 'green-ears' (Exodus 13: 4-10). They had to wait for their barley harvest.

But in the Bible there is no mention of any 'thirteenth' months, nor is there any provision for them, for God saw only twelve months in the year and ignored all intercalation.

After the apostolic era and until the end of 'the times of the Gentiles' — while the Jews have been in dispersion — God again secretly reckoned a succession of 354-day years, although Gentile believers have used the Roman solar calendar, and there is evidence in the New Testament that solar anniversaries of the Resurrection and Pentecost were kept in apostolic times.

On certain occasions God has marked the close of the same era, measured first in *civil lunar years,* and later in *true lunar years.* An instance of this was seen in the 1,960 civil lunar years which ended on June 12th 1933, with the World Economic Conference. In 1935, however, the close of 1,960 true lunar years was marked by the terrible Quetta earthquake on May 31st. (Quetta was then on British territory — British Baluchistan. It is now in Pakistan.)

Similarly, the full total of 6,198 civil lunar years and 21 days from Creation to June 11th-12th 1933, when given their *true lunar* expression, were found to have ended on September 3rd 1939, with the outbreak of the Second World War. This all indicates that God has kept time in the Bible in a measure of secrecy, and not as man has recorded it (except between the Exodus and the Cross, when the Jews kept their calendar in luni-solar time, very much as they do today). No doubt the object of this secrecy was so that 'the Father' should keep 'the times' and 'the seasons ... in His own power' (Acts 1: 7) until such time as it suited His purpose to reveal them. After all, has man *ever* been able to understand the deep things of God unaided with his own mind?

The Years of The Messiah

The existence of a hidden series of 354-day years was disclosed during research. These began on the day following the first Sabbath of Genesis. They appear only infrequently on the surface of the Bible's chronology — the most notable occasion being the '430 years' to the day of the Exodus from Egypt (Exodus 12: 40-41). In this series the Passover was the 14th day of the 7th month of the 2,514th year. This was the seventh month which the Lord instructed Moses was to become 'the beginning of months: it shall be the first month of the year to you'[1]. This series was named the 'Years of the Messiah' as they ran their course without a break, and in their recording have thrown light on many Old Testament events and incidents in the Gospels.

---

[1] Exodus 12:2

The Jubilee Cycles of 49 Years

Leviticus 25 reveals that the hidden measuring rod of the Almighty is the cycle of 49 years which ushers in the 'fiftieth year', or year of Jubilee. It is hidden in the sense that it ceases to record where the hand of God is stretched out in judgment, as during the seven servitudes recorded in the books of Judges and 1 Samuel, and during the seventy years of the Babylonian Captivity.

After the Exodus, Israel was instructed to proclaim the year of *Jubilee* at the end of 48 years and 6 months, that is, on the Day of Atonement in the 7th month of the 49th year. This was at the close of 48 x 12 months and 6 months, or 582 months in all. To these have to be added the necessary 18 intercalary months, which make a total of 600 lunations.

600 Lunations are 50 Lunar Years

So when 'the fiftieth year' was being 'hallowed' with rejoicing throughout Israel, halfway through their 49th year (which had to be kept on the soli-lunar basis), God had already seen *50 lunar years completed*.

Israel, however, could never look upon their 'fiftieth' year as being an addition to time — which they reckoned as **a succession of 49-year cycles**; each year beginning with the Passover. Their 'year of Jubilee' simply ran from the Autumn of their 49th year through to the beginning of the following Autumn in the middle of the first of their next series of 49 years. **God alone was able to reckon each period as being 50 years**. *

We shall have more to say about the miraculous design of the Jubilee when we see why to God a year, in the Chronology of Redemption, is always 354 days — no more and no less.

The Great 'Year' of Redemption — 3,540 Years

With God everything has been wrought according to a pattern, and so we naturally look for the basic pattern upon which *time* is framed.

Clearly the Exodus Passover saw the beginning of the national history of Israel, and we have traced the 1,500 years of Redemption through to the Crucifixion in AD 33, after which a further 2,000 Redemption years lead up to 'the consummation of the age' in our own day. So we can measure a simple design of **3,500 years**.

But prior to the Exodus we find Moses keeping sheep in 'the backside of the desert' (Exodus 3: 1), and doing so over the space of forty years (see Acts 7: 23 & 30). So the pattern is a complete 3,540 years, beginning with those lost forty years of Moses' life spent keeping sheep. God takes a tenth of the period, with the forty years analogous to the four days the Passover lambs were kept waiting for death before they were sacrificed at the Exodus. We know that God also saw those four

---

* See Chart 5 on page 190

days — each 'day ... as a thousand years'[2] — as the time reaching back from the Crucifixion to the Fall of Adam when 'sin entered into the world, and death by sin; and so death passed upon all men'[3].

The 'Six Years' and 'The Sabbath' of Leviticus 25

It has been necessary to establish that the pattern of the Bible year is 354 days before we come to examine time in Leviticus 25 — where God clearly has in view the whole 6,000 years and the Millennium (total 7,000 years) in every seven years that pass.

Let us now measure the days leading up to the opening of 'the Day of Atonement' at the close of the ninth day of the seventh month in the 49th year, seeing that 'the trumpet of the Jubilee' is 'to sound on the tenth of the seventh month'[4].

The 48 years (of 354 days each) contain	16,992 days
and the six months and nine days	186 days
Total	17,178 days

Now it is at this point that God requires 'the fiftieth year' to be proclaimed (as a year of Jubilee), when to man only a bare 48½ years have reached their close. What is the explanation, and why has the hour been reached when the Most High God can rightly celebrate the opening of a 'fiftieth year'?

We believe the explanation is simple, once we accustom our minds to think as God thinks, and to see each 7-year period as 7 x 350 days. But, as these are each a miniature of the 7,000 years, He must also see one break of 4 days in the pattern, to express the blotting out of the 4,000 years from Adam to the Cross. So each 7-year period in this secret reckoning is 7 x 350 days (or 2,450 days) with a gap of 4 days, making 2,454 days in actual time. These 7 x 2,454 days will be found to be 17,178 days — the exact equivalent of the forty-eight 354-day years, six months and nine days, as shown above!

Praise God: 'His way is perfect'[5], and in these days we need to know His way when, in increasing measure, His judgments are already in the earth.

The Great War of 1914-1918 opens after Four Times 'Seventy Times Seven' Years from April 27th AD 33
'Now is the judgment of this world'   (John 12: 31)

From the very evening of that great hidden Day of Atonement (April 27th) in AD 33 can be measured exactly 40 times 17,178 days or, as shown above, 40 Jubilee periods containing God's secret reckoning of 49 years of 350 days. This total of 687,120 days is the shortest expression of the

---

[2] 2 Peter 3: 8　　　　　　　　　　[4] Leviticus 25: 9
[3] Romans 5: 12　　　　　　　　　　[5] Psalm 18: 30

fourfold period of 'seventy times seven'[6] (or 1,960) **Years of Forgiveness** which we have shown from the Scriptures is God's 'way' of controlling history in relation to a sinful world. This measurement ends with the evening of August 3rd 1914, and from that moment *peace* departed from the earth as *the First World War commenced.*

It must also be remembered that all time from Creation to the end of the *6,000 years of man,* on June 12th 1933, (when shown in years of 354 days) totals 6,198 years and 21 days, as already mentioned. But, when every 354-day year has been extended to its true lunar measurement of 354 days, 8 hours, 48 minutes and 33.6 seconds, the whole period reaches to the opening of *the Second World War on September 3rd 1939.*

How to Measure Back to The Cross
In Our Present Solar Years

People who have never really studied the calendar or time-measurement into the past often make statements about the length of the year — both solar and lunar — having varied over the ages. Invariably these people also think of time in terms of 'millions' rather than thousands of years!

However, in Psalm 89: 37 God said that 'the moon' was 'established for ever' as 'a faithful witness in heaven' and this we have amply proved from the Scriptures to the glory and praise of God. When we come to the solar year, we have the strongest evidence that this has remained constant over the last 6,000 years — apart from what is called 'the precession of the equinoxes', an acceleration which has changed the length of the year from around 365 days, 5 hours, 49 minutes and 12 seconds at the time of Creation to its present length of 365 days, 5 hours, 48 minutes and 46 seconds. We have found that the mean length of 365 days, 5 hours and 49 minutes is sufficient for all practical purposes.

We must, however, explain a discrepancy in our present Gregorian Calendar, which any calendar expert will be able to confirm.

What Happened in 1582?

We found that, in measuring 1,900 years back from AD 1933 to AD 33, the succession of weekdays showed that our calendar was out by two days. We soon discovered that in 1582 Pope Gregory, when adjusting the inexact Julian calendar (based on exactly 365¼ days), only dropped ten days instead of twelve. When Great Britain adopted this 'New Style' calendar in 1752, we accordingly only dropped eleven days from the month of September when, actually, thirteen would have been the correct figure. The Nautical Almanac Office has confirmed that, in comparison with the beginning of the Christian era, our calendar is in

---

[6] Matthew 18: 21-22

error by two days, as the vernal equinox in Caesar's time was March 23rd, but it is now March 21st.

The Divine object in allowing this error clearly seems to have been so that our present calendar would show time as though the two days of the death of Christ had been ignored, because God Himself had not reckoned them in the calendar of His Son.

APPENDIX 2

The 2,000 years from Adam to Abram

Solar Year BC	Years of Scripture	Event	Age	Scripture Reference
4075		Creation and Fall of Adam		Gen. 1–3
4028	49	Abel born at 1st Jubilee		Gen. 4: 2
3995	82	Abel's death	Adam 82 yrs	Gen. 4: 8
3949	130	Seth born	Adam 130 yrs	Gen. 5: 3
3847	235	Enos born	Seth 105 yrs	Gen. 5: 6
3760	325	Cainan born	Enos 90 yrs	Gen. 5: 9
3692	395	Mahalaleel born	Cainan 70 yrs	Gen. 5: 12
3629	460	Jared born	Mahalaleel 65 yrs	Gen. 5: 15
3472	622	Enoch born	Jared 162 yrs	Gen. 5: 18
3409	687	Methuselah born	Enoch 65 yrs	Gen. 5: 21
3228	874	Lamech born	Methuselah 187 yrs	Gen. 5: 25
3052	1056	Noah born	Lamech 182 yrs	Gen. 5: 28
2565	1558	Shem born	Noah 502 yrs	Gen. 11: 10
2470	1656	The Flood	Noah 600 yrs	Gen. 7: 11
2468	1658	Arphaxad born	Shem 100 yrs	Gen. 11: 10
2434	1693	Salah born	Arphaxad 35 yrs	Gen. 11: 12
2405	1723	Eber born	Salah 30 yrs	Gen. 11: 14
2372	1757	Peleg born	Eber 34 yrs	Gen. 11: 16
2343	1787	Reu born	Peleg 30 yrs	Gen. 11: 18
2312	1819	Serug born	Reu 32 yrs	Gen. 11: 20
2283	1849	Nahor born	Serug 30 yrs	Gen. 11: 22
2255	1878	Terah born	Nahor 29 yrs	Gen. 11: 24
2129	2008	Abram born	Terah 130 yrs	Gen. 11: 32 & 12: 4

Notes and Comments

1. The new moon of Genesis 1 was at 6 pm on March 3rd 4075 BC. Then followed the six days to the Creation of Adam and Eve on March 9th, after which they entered 'the sabbath', or seventh day. The period of this 'sabbath' rest in Eden continued for 40 days until the Temptation and Fall, which was in the evening of April 19th. The *Chronology of Redemption*, commencing with the years of Adam, began the next day, April 20th.

2. The **Chronology of Redemption** registers exactly **40 Jubilee Cycles** of 49 years to the day of Abram's birth. It ignores the 48 years of 354 days between the murder of Abel and the birth of Seth, whom Eve called 'another seed instead of Abel'[7] and it also ignores the five months of the Flood between the 17th of the 2nd, and the 17th of the 7th month[8] — a period of 147 days.

---

[7] Genesis 4: 25
[8] Genesis 7: 11 & 8: 4

The birth of Abel was found to be at the end of 49 x 354 days from the Fall of Adam and Eve — October 16th 4028 BC. Like our Lord Jesus Christ — 'the Good Shepherd' — Abel lived for 33 x 354 days, 6 months and 14 days, and was slain on April 19th 3995 BC — the 80th solar anniversary of the Fall.

The break in the Redemption Chronology is 48 x 354 days between the murder of Abel and the birth of Seth, which took place on the 15th day of the 7th month, October 27th 3949 BC.

Time from Creation to the birth of Abram on November 23rd 2129 BC

Days	711,026
Solar Years	1,946 years, 264 days
Lunations	24,077 lunations, 18 days,
	49 minutes *(to 6 pm November 22nd)*

APPENDIX 3

The 500 years from Abram to the Exodus

Solar Year BC	Years of Scripture	Event	Age/Comment	Scripture Reference
2129	2008	Abram born	*Terah 130 yrs*	Gen. 11: 32, 12: 4
2056	2083	Abram leaves Haran	*Abram 75 yrs*	Gen. 12: 1-4
2047	2093	Abram marries Hagar	*Ishmael conceived*	Gen. 16: 3
2046	2094	Ishmael born	*Abram 86 yrs*	Gen. 16: 16
2032	2108	Isaac born	*Abram 100 yrs*	Gen. 21: 5, 17: 17
2027	2113	Isaac weaned	*Ishmael cast out*	Gen. 21: 8 & 14
1996	2145	Sarah's death	*Sarah 127 yrs*	Gen. 23: 1
1993	2148	Marriage of Isaac	*Isaac 40 yrs*	Gen. 25: 20
1974	2168	Birth of Esau and Jacob	*Isaac 60 yrs*	Gen. 25: 26
1848	2298	Jacob & sons enter Egypt	*Jacob 130 yrs*	Gen. 47: 9
1639	2513	Exodus of Israel from Egypt		Exodus 12: 41

Notes and Comments

1. The **Chronology of Redemption** records **10 Jubilee Cycles** from the birth of Abram to the day of the Exodus. It ignores the 15 x 354 days between the marriage of Abram with Hagar and the birth of Isaac. The *seed* through whom the Redeemer was to come could not be Ishmael, and Redemption Time was therefore suspended until Isaac was born, because Abram's marriage with Hagar was an expedient contrary to the purpose of God, and a departure from the path of faith and obedience[‡].

2. To establish the chronology to the Exodus it is necessary to use the 430 years of Exodus 12: 40-41. These 430 x 354 days commenced 4 days after Abram was 75 years old (August 6th 2056 BC) and ended on the day of the Passover, which was May 11th 1639 BC. During research into this period, it was revealed that the *four days* between the 10th and 14th of the first month at the Exodus (while the lambs were shut up awaiting sacrifice at the Passover) were *unreckoned* by God because they were typical of the *four thousand years* 'the Lamb of God' would await death — from the Fall of Adam to the great Passover in AD 33.

Time from Creation to the Exodus on May 12th 1639 BC

Days	889,800
Solar Years	2,436 years, 69 days
Lunations	30,131 lunations, 13 days, 20 hours, 30 minutes *(to 6 pm May 11th)*

Note The calendar now becomes 'luni-solar' until AD 33[*].

[‡] See Chart 2 on page 187
[*] See Chart 4 on page 189

APPENDIX 4

The 500 years from the Exodus to Solomon's Temple

Solar Year BC	Years of Scripture	Event	Comment	Scripture Reference
1639	2513	Exodus of Israel from Egypt		Exodus 12: 41
1599	2553	Israel enters Canaan	*40 years end*	Exodus 16: 35
1592	2560	Division of Canaan	*Caleb 85 yrs*	Joshua 14: 6-10
1572	2580	Time of Joshua to first Servitude – 20 years		
1564	2588	8 years' Servitude	*Mesopotamia*	Judges 3: 8
1524	2628	40 years' Rest under Othniel		Judges 3: 11
1506	2646	18 years' Servitude	*Moab*	Judges 3: 14
1426	2726	80 years' Rest under Ehud & Shamgar		Judges 3: 30
1406	2746	20 years' Servitude	*Canaan*	Judges 4: 3
1366	2786	40 years' Rest under Deborah & Barak		Judges 5: 31
1359	2793	7 years' Servitude	*Midian*	Judges 6: 1
1271	2881	88 years' Rest under Gideon, Abimelech, Tola & Jair		Judges 8: 28, 9: 22 & 10: 2-3
1253	2899	18 years' Servitude	*Philistines, etc.*	Judges 10: 8
1222	2930	31 years' Rest under Jephthah, Ibzan, Elon, Abdon		Judges 12: 7-14
1182	2970	40 years' Servitude	*Philistines (Samson judged 10 years)*	Judges 13: 1 & 15: 20
1142	3010	Eli judges Israel 40 Years		1 Sam. 4: 18
1122	3030	20 years' Servitude	*Philistines (in time of Samuel)*	1 Sam. 7: 2-3 & Acts 13: 19-20
1112	3040	Victory at Mizpeh to Saul's reign – 10 years		1 Sam. 7: 11-13
1111	3041	'Saul reigned one year'		1 Sam. 13: 1
1110	3042	390 years of sin begin	*Saul's 2nd year*	Ezekiel 4: 5
1072	3080	Reign of David begins	*Saul's 40 years end*	Acts 13: 21
1032	3120	Reign of David ends	*40 years*	1 Kings 2: 11
1029*	3124	Temple begun	*Solomon's 4th year*	1 Kings 6: 1
1022*	3131	Temple built	*Solomon's 11th year*	1 Kings 6: 38
1019*	3134	Dedication of Temple	*at 'Tabernacles'*	1 Kings 8: 1
1018*	3134	15th year opens	*490 years end at Passover*	

* The apparent discrepancies between the columns *'Solar Year BC'* and *'Years of Scripture'* are mainly because events are at different times of the year, some being only six months apart – the Jewish and Gentile calendars starting at different points in the year.

Notes and Comments

1. The **Chronology of Redemption** records **10 Jubilee Cycles** of 49 years (with intercalation) from the Exodus to the end of Solomon's 14th year, in the 7th month of which 'the glory of God' filled the Temple at its Dedication,[9] and Israel became a theocracy. It ignores the seven periods of **Servitude**, enumerated above, which amount to 131 years. *(See Chart 3 on page 188.)*

2. The time of Joshua to the first Servitude (which followed the division of the land) is not stated to be '20 years' but must have been so to make up the '450 years' which Paul mentions in Acts 13: 20.

3. The '10 years' between 1122 and 1112 BC are a second unstated period which was necessary to complete the '480 years' of 1 Kings 6: 1. (There is a wonderful reason why these ten years preceding the Kingdom of Israel should exist but not be mentioned, but space precludes going into this here.)

Time from Creation to end of Solomon's 14th year on April 22nd 1018 BC

Days	1,116,596
Solar Years	3,057 years, 50 days
Lunations	37,811 lunations, 14 days, 22 hours, 30 minutes

---

[9] 1 Kings 8: 1-11 & 2 Chronicles 7: 1-3

APPENDIX 5

The 500 years from Solomon's Temple to Nehemiah

Solar Year BC	Years of Scripture	Event	Time/Comment	Scripture Reference
1018	3134	490 years begin	*Solomon's 15th year*	
992	3160	Reign of Solomon ends	*40 years*	1 Kings 11: 42
975	3177	Reign of Rehoboam ends	*17 years*	2 Chr. 12: 13
972	3180	Reign of Abijah ends	*3 years*	2 Chr. 13: 2
931	3221	Reign of Asa ends	*41 years*	2 Chr. 16: 13
906	3246	Reign of Jehoshaphat ends	*25 years*	2 Chr. 20: 31
902	3250	Reign of Jehoram ends	*4 years*	2 Kings 8: 16-17
		(8 years including joint kingship)		
901	3251	Reign of Ahaziah ends	*1 year*	2 Chr. 22: 2
895	3257	Reign of Athaliah ends	*6 years*	2 Chr. 22: 12
855	3297	Reign of Jehoash ends	*40 years*	2 Chr. 24: 1
826	3326	Reign of Amaziah ends	*29 years*	2 Chr. 25: 1
814	3338	Interregnum of 12 years		*cp* 2 Kings 14: 17 and 15: 1-2
762	3390	Reign of Uzziah ends	*52 years*	2 Chr. 26: 3
742	3410	Jotham's 20 years (4 as Judge, 16 as King)		2 Kings 15: 30-33
726	3426	Reign of Ahaz ends	*16 years*	2 Chr. 28: 1
720	3432	Captivity of Israel – End of 390 years of iniquity of Israel	*Hezekiah's 6th year*	2 Kings 18: 10-11 Ezekiel 4: 4-5
697	3455	Reign of Hezekiah ends	*29 years*	2 Chr. 29: 1
642	3510	Reign of Manasseh ends	*55 years*	2 Chr. 33: 1
640	3512	Reign of Amon ends	*2 years*	2 Chr. 33: 21
609	3543	Reign of Josiah ends	*31 years*	2 Chr. 34: 1
609	3543	Reign of Jehoahaz ends	*3 months*	2 Chr. 36: 2
606	3546	70 years in Babylon begin	*Jehoiakim's 4th year*	Jer. 25: 1, 11
598	3554	Reign of Jehoiakim ends	*11 years*	2 Chr. 36: 5
597	3555	Reign of Jehoiachin ends	*3 months, 10 days*	2 Chr. 36: 9
588	3564	Jerusalem besieged	*Zedekiah's 9th year*	2 Kings 25: 1
586	3566	Fall of Jerusalem	*Zedekiah's 11th year*	Jer. 52: 5, 12
582	3570	40 years of sin end – Nebuchadnezzar's 23rd year		Jer. 52: 30
536	3616	Decree of Cyrus – 70 years in Babylon end		Ezra 1: 1
458	3694	Commandment to restore and rebuild Jerusalem		Neh. 2: 1-8

Notes and Comments

1. The **Chronology of Redemption** records **10 Jubilee Cycles** of 49 years (with intercalation) from Solomon's 14th year to the Commandment given to Nehemiah to restore and rebuild Jerusalem in 458 BC. It ignores the 70 years of the Captivity in Babylon.

2. The '390 years' of Ezekiel 4: 5, which commenced in 1110 BC and ran to 720 BC, confirm the length of the above reigns to the beginning of Israel's Captivity in 720 BC.

3. From the Fall of the Kingdom of Judah and the stages of the Captivity to Babylon (from 607 BC to 582 BC) we find the great 'seven times' or 2,520 years of Daniel 4 running their course to end from 1914 onwards. Historians appear to be in agreement with the Bible's chronology regarding the dating of the end of the 70 years' Captivity and the time of Cyrus.

Time from Creation to the Passover on April 15th 458 BC

Days	1,321,125
Solar Years	3,617 years, 43 days
Lunations	44,737 lunations, 15 days, 12 hours, 3 minutes*

---

* The above total of lunations includes the 10 hours by which lunar time became in advance of solar time because of the sign of Isaiah 38: 8 (see pages 143-144).

APPENDIX 6

The 500 years from Nehemiah to the Crucifixion of Christ

Seventy weeks, or 490 years, with 10 years of Jubilee

Solar Year	Years of Scripture	Event	Scripture Reference
458 BC	3694	Commandment to restore and rebuild Jerusalem	Neh. 2: 1-8
409 BC	3743	'Seven weeks' end – Jerusalem rebuilt	Dan. 9: 25
1 BC	4152	Incarnation of the Son of God	
AD 26	4177	John the Baptist's testimony opens	Luke 3: 1
AD 29	4180	Public Ministry of Jesus Christ opens	Luke 3: 23
AD 33	4184	Crucifixion and Resurrection of Christ	
		The Ascension and Day of Pentecost	Acts 1–2

Notes and Comments

1. The **Chronology of Redemption** records **10 Jubilee Cycles** of 49 years (with intercalation) from the Passover of 458 BC to the Crucifixion of Christ in AD 33. This period is called 'seventy weeks' in Daniel 9: 24.

2. The Commandment given by Artaxerxes, King of Persia, to Nehemiah to restore and rebuild Jerusalem was not, however, given at the Passover but 10 days later, as a close examination of the chronology shows — that is, in the evening of the 24th day of the 1st month (Nisan), April 25th 458 BC.

3. From this starting point exactly 483 solar years ran their course to April 25th AD 26, when John the Baptist commenced his testimony to 'Messiah the Prince' at the close of the days of unleavened bread (Nisan 21st).

Daniel's Seventieth 'Week'

These last seven years were lost to the Jews since they failed to see in Jesus of Nazareth the long-promised Messiah of Israel. Because of this, the prophecy of Daniel 9: 26 (RV) leaves them unreckoned and simply states 'and after the threescore and two weeks (making, with the previous seven, 69 weeks in all) shall the anointed one be cut off, and shall have nothing'*. The last seven years are, therefore, held over to be relived at

---

* See Chart 1 on page 186

the end of the Gentile age, as detailed in Revelation 4 to 19. But, for the believing Jews and the Church of God, the 490 years with their 10 Jubilees were, of course, seen to bring to a close the great *4,000 Years of Redemption* — to 'make an end of sins, and to make reconciliation for iniquity, and to bring in everlasting righteousness', etc. (verse 24), through the atoning death of Jesus on Calvary.

Time from Creation to the Crucifixion at the Jewish Passover in AD 33

Days	1,500,110
Solar Years	4,107 years, 51 days
Lunations	50,798 lunations, 15 days, 14 hours, 38 minutes

Note From the opening of the day of the Resurrection of Christ to the Ascension were 40 days and 14 hours. The *lunations at the Ascension* were, therefore, 1 lunation, 11 days, 1 hour and 16 minutes in advance of the above total, that is, 50,799 lunations, 26 days, 15 hours and 54 minutes. It must be remembered that 'the moon was turned to blood' — thus signifying that lunar recording was 'dead' and held at a standstill during the two complete days while the body of the Redeemer lay in the Sepulchre *(see pages 97, 125-128, 160, 164 and 170-171).*

APPENDIX 7

The 2,000 Bible years from AD 33 to 1933

The 4 x 490 years of 'The Times of the Gentiles'

Solar Years AD	Years of Scripture	Event	Scripture Reference
33	4184	The Ascension of Christ and Day of Pentecost	Acts 1–2
33	4184	Stephen martyred – 'the fig tree' cut down	Acts 7, Luke 13
36	4187	Conversion of Cornelius	Acts 10–11
66	4216	Jewish revolt – the Roman War opens	
70	4222	Jerusalem and the Temple destroyed – Dispersion of the Jews begins	Luke 21: 20-24
73	4225	Fall of Masada – Jewish resistance ends	
1917	6128	Balfour Declaration – Palestine liberated	
1923	6134	Palestine Mandate operates	
1933	6144	World Conference of all Nations opens in London on June 12th	

Notes and Comments

1. The **Chronology of Redemption** records **40 Jubilee Cycles** of 49 years (of 354 days) each, together with 40 Jubilee Years, between AD 33 and 1933. This era does not commence, however, until October 11th–12th in AD 33, when the year referred to as 'this year also' in Luke 13: 8 comes to its end with the killing of Stephen (see Acts 7). It is then that 'the Fig Tree' — Israel as a nation — is 'cut down' for the course of the Gentile age. This judicial sentence is passed in Heaven, and 1,960 x 354 days later, on June 12th 1933, the Gentile Nations also are 'cut off' from their place in 'the olive tree' into which they had been grafted in the place of Israel, as described in Romans 11.

2. 1,900 solar years ran their course from the Ascension of Christ on June 13th AD 33 to June 11th 1933. From hour to hour, this period was 1,900 years, 1 day and 10 hours, that is, from the morning of the Ascension (8 am) to 6 pm (3 pm GMT) on June 12th 1933.

Time from Creation to June 12th 1933 — Opening of World Conference

Days	2,194,114
Solar Years	6,007 years, 103 days
Lunations	74,299 lunations, 19 days, 6 hours, 17 minutes

APPENDIX 8

The Measurement of the 6,000 Julian Years

Time from Creation to 8 am April 25th AD 26	**4,100 solar yrs, 52 days, 14 hrs**
Time, as reckoned to sinful man, is held in suspense for the 7 years and 49 days between the opening of John the Baptist's Ministry on April 25th AD 26 and Jesus' Ascension on June 13th AD 33.	*(Time suspended)*
Time from Ascension to 6 pm June 12th* 1933	**1,900 solar yrs, 1 day, 10 hrs**
Total	**6,000 solar yrs, 54 days, 0 hrs**

* This would have been '14th June' but our present calendar is out by 2 days – see Appendix 1.

The 6,000 years of man commenced after the Sabbath of Creation — the day of the Fall of Adam remaining unreckoned. By taking these eight days away this reduces the above total to:

6,000 solar years and 46 days, or 6,000 Julian Years exactly

Note   A Julian Year is 365¼ days.
A solar year is 365 days, 5 hours, 49 minutes (mean over 6,000 years – *see page 171*).
Our current calendar is kept accurate by dropping three 'leap year days' in every 400 years.

EXPLANATORY NOTES

1. Seven 'Times' or 2,520 Years *(pages 13, 14, 18, 40-41 & 66)*

The Babylonian Year was 360 days, which was also known as a 'time'. 7 x 360 = 2,520, and the days were also used to represent years in prophecy. Seven 'times' was therefore 2,520 days or years. The 2,520 days related to Nebuchadnezzar; the various 2,520-year periods related to the prophecies about Israel's restoration. The use of a 360-day year as a 'time' is confirmed by comparing the 1,260 days of Revelation 11: 3 & 12: 6 with the 'time, times, and half a time' (3½ times) of Revelation 12: 14. 3½ x 360 days = 1,260 days. *(See also Daniel 12: 7.)*

2. The Consummation of The Age *(pages 22, 33, 75, 119 & 130)*

The 'consummation of the age' is a time of harvest at the end of the age (Matthew 13:39). W E Vine (in his Expository Dictionary of New Testament Words) says of the Greek word for consummation — *suntelia* — 'The word does not denote a termination, but the leading up of events to the appointed climax'.

3. The First (Day) of the Weeks *(pages 70-71, 91, 98, 106 & 113)*

Te mia ton sabbaton correctly translated should be 'the first (day) of the sabbaths'. The word 'day', correctly interpolated as *mia* (first), is feminine and requires a feminine noun, *sabbaton* being neuter. *Sabbaton* **cannot** be translated 'week' as it is a plural noun. The term 'sabbaths' refers to the seven sabbaths (or weeks) between the waving of the 'sheaf of the firstfruits' (see Leviticus 23: 9-21) and the waving of the two 'loaves' of 'the firstfruits' at Pentecost, fifty days later.

4. Silver Used to Signify Redemption *(page 74)*

Numbers 3: 44-51 gives instructions for the redemption of those 273 firstborn Israelite males whose number exceeded the number of 22,000 mentioned in verse 39; they were to be redeemed by the Levites. The money was to be paid 'after the shekel of the sanctuary' (verse 47), which was silver (see Leviticus 5: 15 & 27: 6, also Exodus 30: 11-16 & 38: 25-28).

In Exodus 26, the boards of shittim (acacia) wood overlaid with gold speak of the humanity of Christ and His Divinity (gold) resting on sockets of silver. The Divine glory must rest on silver (the ground of redemption) for man to be associated with Him.

5. The Saviour's Birth at 8 am *(pages 82 & 105)*

2 Kings 20 and Isaiah 38 tell us of a sign in the sun in the days of Hezekiah when the shadow of the sun was caused by God to return 'ten steps' (hours). The effect was to make time reckoned by the moon ten

hours ahead of that reckoned by the sun, so that each 24-hour period ended at 8 am rather than 6 pm. All sacred time is lunar, and the Lord's 'day' started at 8 am — the number so amazingly linked with Himself. *(See pages 143-147 for more detail on Hezekiah's sign.)*

6. Yom Kippur Prayer *(page 100)*

The prayer on this page originates from Rabbi Ammon of Mainz, a legendary figure and martyr, about the year 1000 AD. This prayer now forms part of the additional service for the Day of Atonement. For further details see the Encyclopædia Judaica.

7. The Six Day War of 1967 *(page 101)*

When all the letters for the Greek words for *'Son of God'* have been given their numerical equivalent and added together, they total 1,934. This is, therefore, the number of the *Son of God*. It can be proved that it was exactly, to the day, 1,934 solar years from the triumphant ascension of Jesus, the Son of God, into Heaven in June AD 33, to the ceasefire with Syria which came into effect in the evening of 10th June 1967, and brought the war to a close. So God has set His seal upon Israel's repossession of her land and holy city.

8. 280 Years Viewed as One Day *(page 112)*

280 days is the normal period of gestation. The ten curtains covering the Tabernacle were 28 cubits in length, a total of 280 cubits. The Bible associates gestation (the number 280) with a covering (see Psalm 139: 13).

Biblical chronology shows that from Isaiah's prophecy — 'Behold, a virgin shall conceive, and bear a son, and shall call His name Emmanuel' (Isaiah 7: 14) — given on 3rd May 742 BC — to 29th October 1 BC, when Jesus was born, was 280 x 888 days. (This measurement omits the days in which the Remnant of Judah were outside the land in captivity in Babylon, but this would need further elaboration than space permits here.) Time periods relating to Jesus' life are measured in 'days' of 888 days and years *(see pages 81, 92, 125 & 135).*

9. Originally 70 Nations *(page 114)*

After the Flood the seventy sons and grandsons of Ham, Shem and Japheth became the progenitors of the nations. See Genesis 10.

CHART 1

The 70 Weeks' Prophecy

'Seventy weeks are determined for your people' Daniel 9: 24 (NKJV)

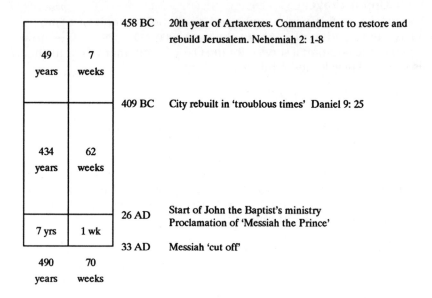

49 years	**7 weeks**	458 BC	20th year of Artaxerxes. Commandment to restore and rebuild Jerusalem. Nehemiah 2: 1-8
434 years	**62 weeks**	409 BC	City rebuilt in 'troublous times' Daniel 9: 25
7 yrs	**1 wk**	26 AD	Start of John the Baptist's ministry Proclamation of 'Messiah the Prince'
490 years	**70 weeks**	33 AD	Messiah 'cut off'

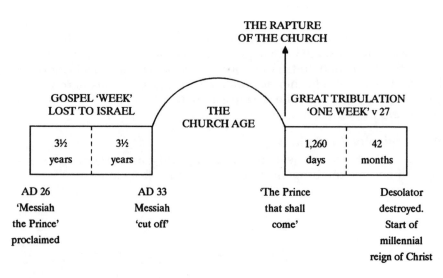

THE RAPTURE
OF THE CHURCH

GOSPEL 'WEEK' LOST TO ISRAEL		THE CHURCH AGE	GREAT TRIBULATION 'ONE WEEK' v 27	
3½ years	3½ years		1,260 days	42 months
AD 26 'Messiah the Prince' proclaimed	AD 33 Messiah 'cut off'		'The Prince that shall come'	Desolator destroyed. Start of millennial reign of Christ

(See Daniel 9: 24-27, and pages 27, 36, 61, 65, 95 & 180)

CHART 2

Abraham to the Exodus

The 490 years (10 Jubilee Cycles) in the Chronology of Redemption from the birth of Abraham to the Exodus

			Total Years	Unreckoned Years	Redemption Years
Birth of Abraham					
▪ Abraham leaves Haran and enters Canaan, aged 75	Gen 12: 4	75	75		75
Abraham enters Canaan					
▪ Ishmael conceived	Gen 16: 3-4	10	10		10
▪ Isaac born (Abraham 100)	Gen 21: 5	15	15	-15	60
▪ Esau & Jacob born (Isaac 60)	Gen 25: 24-26	60	60		60
▪ Joseph born; Jacob was 130 when Joseph was 40, so Jacob was 90 when Joseph was born		90 90	90		90
- Joseph was 40 in 3rd year of famine					
• Joseph before Pharoah	Gen 41: 46	30			
• 7 years of plenty	Gen 41: 29,53	7			
• 3rd year of famine	Gen 45: 6,11	3			
- Jacob's age later that year when Joseph was 40	Gen 47: 9	130			
▪ Joseph dies, aged 110	Gen 50: 22,26	110	110		110
▪ Moses born; 65 years makes up 430 years from Abraham entering Canaan to the Exodus		65	65		65
▪ Moses tries to help brethren	Acts 7: 23	40	40		40
▪ Moses dwells in Midian	Acts 7: 30	40	40		40
▪ Between Abraham entering Canaan and the Exodus is also described as:					
- between the promise to Abraham and the law	Gal 3: 16-17	430			
- the start of the sojourn to the Exodus	Ex 12: 40-41	430			
Exodus					
Total Years from Birth of Abraham to Exodus			505		
Unreckoned Years				-15	
Total Years in the Chronology of Redemption					**490**

(See pages 38 & 175)

CHART 3

The Exodus to Solomon's Temple

The 490 years (10 Jubilee Cycles) in the Chronology of Redemption from the Exodus to the Dedication of Solomon's Temple

			Total Years	Unreckoned Years	Redemption Years
Exodus					
▪ 40 years in the wilderness	Josh 5: 6		40		40
Enter Canaan					
▪ 7 years in Canaan to division of the land makes up 47 years from Exodus to division of the land			7		7
- from Exodus to sending spies	Num 10: 11-13	2			
- from sending forth the spies to division of the land	Josh 14: 6-10	45			
Start of the Judges		47			
▪ Division to Cushan-Rishathaim (1st captivity); 20 years makes up 450 years of Judges to Samuel the prophet	Acts 13: 20	20	20		20
▪ Cushan-Rishathaim, king of Mesopotamia	Judg 3: 8	8	8	-8	
▪ Othniel judges	Judg 3: 11	40	40		40
▪ Eglon, king of Moab	Judg 3: 14	18	18	-18	
▪ Ehud & Shamgar judge	Judg 3: 30-31	80	80		80
▪ Jabin, king of Canaan	Judg 4: 3	20	20	-20	
▪ Deborah and Barak judge	Judg 5: 31	40	40		40
▪ Midianites	Judg 6: 1	7	7	-7	
▪ Gideon judges	Judg 8: 28	40	40		40
▪ Abimelech judges	Judg 9: 22-23	3	3		3
▪ Tola judges	Judg 10: 2	23	23		23
▪ Jair judges	Judg 10: 3	22	22		22
▪ Philistines	Judg 10: 8	18	18	-18	
▪ Jephthah judges	Judg 12: 7	6	6		6
▪ Ibzan judges	Judg 12: 8-9	7	7		7
▪ Elon judges	Judg 12: 11	10	10		10
▪ Abdon judges	Judg 12: 14	8	8		8
▪ Philistines (Samson in this time)	Judg 13: 1	40	40	-40	
▪ Eli judges	1 Sam 4: 18	40	40		40
▪ 450 years of Judges to Samuel	Acts 13: 20	450			
Samuel					
▪ Samuel to Saul - 30 years make up the 480 years of Redemption from the Exodus to Solomon's 4th year	1 Ki 6: 1		30		30
- Philistines kept the ark for 20 of these 30 years	1 Sam 7: 2			-20	-20
▪ Saul	Acts 13: 21		40		40
▪ David	2 Sam 5: 4		40		40
▪ Solomon to 4th year of reign	1 Ki 6: 37		4		4
			611	-131	
▪ Exodus to Solomon's 4th year	1 Ki 6: 1	480			480
▪ Temple construction	1 Ki 6: 37-38	7	7		7
▪ Temple furnishing - 3 years make up the cycle of 490 years of Redemption	1 Ki 7: 13-51	3	3		3
Dedication of the Temple	1 Ki 8: 1-11				
Total from Exodus to Dedication of Temple			621		
Unreckoned Years				-131	
Total in the Chronology of Redemption		**490**			**490**

(See pages 36, 95 & 176-177)

CHART 4

The 7,000 Years of Redemption

This Chronology excludes stated periods of Divine chastisement and relates to time reckoned by the Jubilee Cycles of 'Forgiveness'

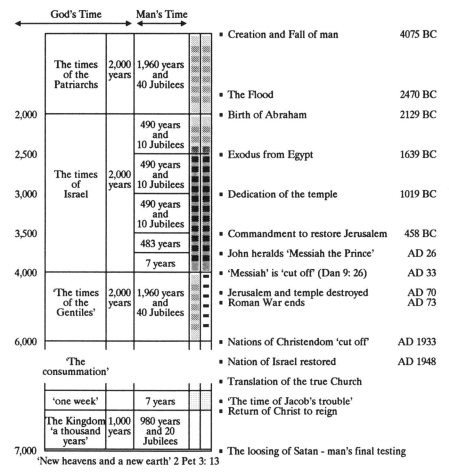

God's Time		Man's Time			
				• Creation and Fall of man	4075 BC
The times of the Patriarchs	2,000 years	1,960 years and 40 Jubilees			
				• The Flood	2470 BC
2,000				• Birth of Abraham	2129 BC
		490 years and 10 Jubilees			
2,500				• Exodus from Egypt	1639 BC
		490 years and 10 Jubilees			
The times of Israel	2,000 years				
3,000				• Dedication of the temple	1019 BC
		490 years and 10 Jubilees			
3,500				• Commandment to restore Jerusalem	458 BC
		483 years		• John heralds 'Messiah the Prince'	AD 26
		7 years			
4,000				• 'Messiah' is 'cut off' (Dan 9: 26)	AD 33
'The times of the Gentiles'	2,000 years	1,960 years and 40 Jubilees		• Jerusalem and temple destroyed • Roman War ends	AD 70 AD 73
6,000				• Nations of Christendom 'cut off'	AD 1933
'The consummation'				• Nation of Israel restored	AD 1948
				• Translation of the true Church	
'one week'		7 years		• 'The time of Jacob's trouble' • Return of Christ to reign	
The Kingdom 'a thousand years'	1,000 years	980 years and 20 Jubilees			
7,000				• The loosing of Satan - man's final testing	

'New heavens and a new earth' 2 Pet 3: 13

The Bible reckoning is in civil lunar years of 354 days until the Exodus, after which intercalation is included until AD 33.

There are four calendars in the Bible. The first shaded column in the chart shows which calendar operates in the Chronology of Redemption and the second shaded column shows which one is most evident on the surface of Scripture at any one time. The other calendars run concurrently, mostly below the surface. God told Israel in Exodus 12: 2 to change to the luni-solar year of 365¼ days, and so after the end of 'the Times of Israel' the Chronology of Redemption thus reverted to the civil lunar year of 354 days. However, the Gentile calendar of 365¼ days is the one found on the surface of Scripture after the Resurrection until the Tribulation.

 Civil lunar 354 days

 Luni-solar 365¼ days

 Gentile (Julian) 365¼ days

 Babylonian 360 days

(See pages 27, 44, 66 & 175)

CHART 5

The Jubilee Cycle

Leviticus 25

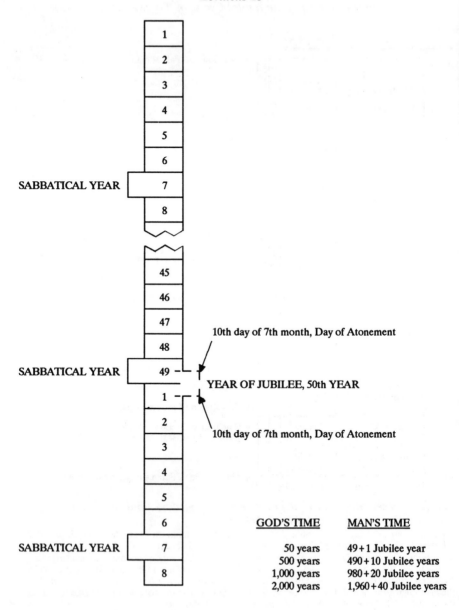

| 1 |
| 2 |
| 3 |
| 4 |
| 5 |
| 6 |
| SABBATICAL YEAR | 7 |
| 8 |

| 45 |
| 46 |
| 47 |
| 48 |
| SABBATICAL YEAR | 49 |

10th day of 7th month, Day of Atonement

YEAR OF JUBILEE, 50th YEAR

| 1 |
| 2 |
| 3 |
| 4 |
| 5 |
| 6 |
| SABBATICAL YEAR | 7 |
| 8 |

10th day of 7th month, Day of Atonement

GOD'S TIME	MAN'S TIME
50 years	49+1 Jubilee year
500 years	490+10 Jubilee years
1,000 years	980+20 Jubilee years
2,000 years	1,960+40 Jubilee years

(See pages 27, 35, 40, 44-45 & 169)

CHART 6

The Feasts of the Lord

Leviticus 23

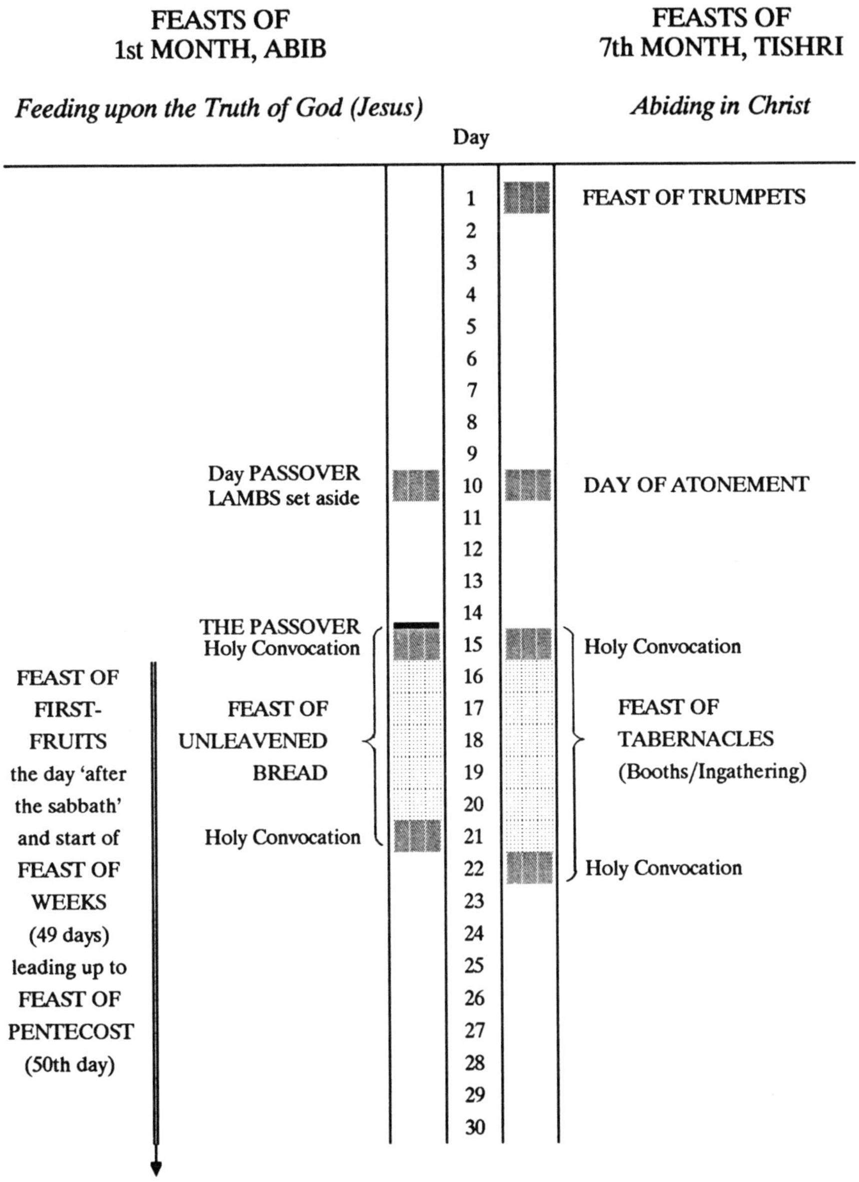

FEASTS OF 1st MONTH, ABIB		FEASTS OF 7th MONTH, TISHRI
Feeding upon the Truth of God (Jesus)		*Abiding in Christ*

Day

	Day	
	1	FEAST OF TRUMPETS
	2	
	3	
	4	
	5	
	6	
	7	
	8	
	9	
Day PASSOVER LAMBS set aside	10	DAY OF ATONEMENT
	11	
	12	
	13	
	14	
THE PASSOVER Holy Convocation	15	Holy Convocation
	16	
FEAST OF	17	FEAST OF
FIRST-FRUITS FEAST OF UNLEAVENED	18	TABERNACLES
the day 'after BREAD	19	(Booths/Ingathering)
the sabbath'	20	
and start of Holy Convocation	21	
FEAST OF	22	Holy Convocation
WEEKS	23	
(49 days)	24	
leading up to	25	
FEAST OF	26	
PENTECOST	27	
(50th day)	28	
	29	
	30	

(See pages 55, 80, 83, 107, 112 & 116)

CHART 7

Type and Antitype

The Days of the Exodus   **The Days around the Death of Jesus**

1639 BC			AD 33		
	(May 7)			(April 26)	
	Abib 10			Nisan 10	
	Sun			Sun	
6pm		'A lamb for a house'	6pm		The Lamb Chosen
	11			11	
	Mon			Mon	
6pm			6pm		
	12			12	
	Tues			Tues	
6pm			6pm		
	13			13	
	Wed			Wed	
6pm			6pm		
	(May 11)			(April 30)	
	14			14	
	Thurs			Thur	
6pm		Passover in Egypt	6pm		The Lord's Passover
	15	**Exodus**		15	**'His Exodus'**
	Fri		3pm	Fri	Death of Jesus
6pm		SUCCOTH	6pm		The Jews' Passover
	16			16	The Jews' Sabbath
	Sat			Sat	
6pm		ETHAM	6pm		
	17			17	The Jews' First Day of the Weeks
	Sun			Sun	
6pm		MIGDOL	6pm		
	(May 15)	The Red Sea Crossing	Midnight	(May 4)	The Resurrection
	18	The Morning Watch 'Morning' - The Song of Moses		18	'The First (Day) of the Weeks' 'He is Risen'
	Mon			Mon	
6pm					

(See pages 55, 59, 90, 107 & 109)   **Note** 'Abib' became 'Nisan' (See page 40)

CHART 8

The Seven Sabbaths to Pentecost, AD 33

SOLAR CALENDAR	JEWS' CALENDAR		SOLAR CALENDAR	JEWS' CALENDAR		SOLAR CALENDAR	JEWS' CALENDAR	
Thurs April 30th	NISAN 13	■ The Lord's Passover Crucifixion ■ Death of Jesus	Mon May 18th	ZIV 1	■ 3rd Meeting of Jesus with His Disciples John 21 & Matthew 28	Fri June 5th	ZIV 19	
Fri May 1st	14		Tues 19th	2		Sat 6th	20	
Sat 2nd	15		Wed 20th	3		Sun 7th	21	
Sun 3rd	16	■ Resurrection	Thurs 21st	4		Mon 8th	22	
Mon 4th	17 1st day of weeks	■ 1st Resurrection Meeting of Jesus with His Disciples	Fri 22nd	5		Tues 9th	23	
Tues 5th	18		Sat 23rd	6		Wed 10th	24	
Wed 6th	19		Sun 24th	7		Thurs 11th	25	
Thurs 7th	20		Mon 25th	8		Fri 12th	26	
Fri 8th	21		Tues 26th	9		Sat 13th	27	■ Ascension Acts 1: 9-12
Sat 9th	22		Wed 27th	10		Sun 14th	28	
Sun 10th	23		Thurs 28th	11		Mon 15th	29	
Mon 11th	24	■ 2nd Meeting of Jesus with His Disciples	Fri 29th	12		Tues 16th	SIVAN 1	
Tues 12th	25		Sat 30th	13		Wed 17th	2	
Wed 13th	26		Sun 31st	14		Thurs 18th	3	
Thurs 14th	27		Mon June 1st	15		Fri 19th	4	
Fri 15th	28		Tues 2nd	16		Sat 20th	5	
Sat 16th	29		Wed 3rd	17		Sun 21st	6 49th day of weeks	■ Divine Sabbath
Sun 17th	30		Thurs 4th	18		Mon 22nd	7 50th day of weeks	■ Divine Pentecost

JEWISH MONTHS

1st Nisan
2nd Ziv
3rd Sivan

KEY TO HATCHED SQUARES

Jews' Sabbaths

Divine Sabbaths

Jews' feast days not reckoned

(See pages 72 & 94)

CHART 9

Calendars in Operation in AD 33

	GENTILE SOLAR DATE	JEWS' NISAN	DIVINE NISAN	7th MONTH IN THE LORD'S OWN CALENDAR	EVENTS (see explanation opposite)
6pm 12mid	April 25 Sat	8 SABBATH	9 Sun	8	8am
6pm 12mid	26 Sun	9 Sun	10 Mon	9	8am 6pm ■ Jesus came to Bethany He is anointed by Mary
6pm 12mid	27 Mon	10 Mon	11 Tues	God's hidden Day of Atonement	8am 2pm ■ Triumphal entry to Jerusalem 'the hour is come'
6pm 12mid	28 Tues	11 Tues	12 Wed	11	8am ■ Fig tree cursed - 'your house is left unto you desolate'
6pm 12mid	29 Wed	12 Wed	13 Thurs	12	8am Jesus kept 4 days as the antitypical Passover Lamb
6pm 12mid	30 Thurs	13 Thurs	14 Fri	13	8am 6pm ■ Lord's Passover
6pm 12mid	May 1 Fri	14 Fri	15 SABBATH 1st day		8am ■ Crucifixion 12noon ■ Sun darkened for 3 hours 3pm ■ Death of Jesus. The moon is 'turned into blood' 6pm ■ Burial
6pm 12mid	2 Sat	JEWS' PASSOVER 15 SABBATH	1st night 2nd day	Time not counted to one dead	Two feasts of the Jews are turned into mourning
6pm 12mid	3 Sun	16 Sun JEWS' FIRST (DAY) OF THE WEEKS	2nd night 3rd day 3rd night		
6pm 12mid	4 Mon	17 Mon	FIRST (DAY) OF THE WEEKS	14	12mid ■ Resurrection ■ Presentation of the Firstfruits; 'I ascend' ■ Emmaus walk
6pm 12mid	5 Tues	18 Tues	II	15	12mid ■ 1st appearing of Jesus to His disciples; Holy convocation
6pm 12mid	6 Wed	19 Wed	III	16	12mid
6pm 12mid	7 Thurs	20 Thurs	IV	17	12mid Feast of Unleavened Bread and Feast of Tabernacles run concurrently as at the Exodus
6pm 12mid	8 Fri	21 Fri	V	18	12mid
6pm 12mid	9 Sat	22 SABBATH	VI	19	12mid
6pm 12mid	10 Sun	23 Sun	VII	20	12mid
6pm 12mid	11 Mon	24 Mon	VIII	21	12mid
	12 Tues	25 Tues		22	12mid ■ 2nd appearing of Jesus (Thomas recovered); Holy convocation

(See pages 83, 89, 105, 111 & 113)

CHART 10

The Seven Days of Unleavened Bread

following the Passover in Egypt in 1639 BC

6pm	Gentile Calendar	Jewish Calendar	RAMESES	
	May 11	Abib 14		
6pm 12mid			Passover / Unleavened Bread Midnight - death of the firstborn	
	12	15	The Exodus	
6pm			SUCCOTH	
	13	16		3½ days (see pages 59 & 68)
6pm			ETHAM	
	14	17		
6pm			MIGDOL (Pi-Hahiroth) Red Sea Crossing Song of Moses	
	15	18		
6pm			Three days in the wilderness Exodus 8: 27	
	16	19		3½ days
6pm				
	17	20		
6pm			MARAH - Exodus 15: 22-27	
	18	21		
6pm			ELIM	

(See pages 59, 68, 109 & 114)

A Brief Explanation of Chart 9

The left-hand column shows the days in April and May, with their weekdays, and the days of Israel's first month.

Viewing the day of Christ's Birth in 1 BC (October 29th) as reckoned from the evening of October 28th, it will be found that the 7th month of His 34th year of 354 days ran concurrently with Israel's NISAN in AD 33.

Therefore, when Jesus came to Bethany 'six days before the (Jews') Passover' it was on the 9th of this 7th month, and in the evening Mary anointed Him with her ointment.

CHART 11

God Shows His Hand in World War II

Many and wonderful are the exact time-patternings of God in the modern history of Israel. The diagram reveals the pattern from the opening of Christ's ministry in John 1 to the salvation of European Jewry at the close of World War II.

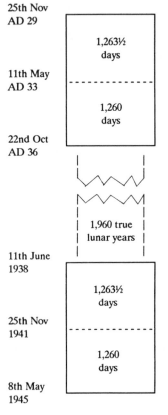

25th Nov
AD 29

1,263½ days

11th May
AD 33

1,260 days

22nd Oct
AD 36

1,960 true lunar years

11th June
1938

1,263½ days

25th Nov
1941

1,260 days

8th May
1945

- 'Behold the Lamb of God, which taketh away the sin of the world' (first recorded day in Gospel of John, John 1: 29)

- **The Apostles United**
  Jesus restores Thomas at His second appearing after His Resurrection (Anniversary of Exodus Midnight)

- **The Purpose of God for the Gentiles Revealed**
  'They glorified God' at the Acts 11 conference

- Four times 'seventy times seven' years or 1,960 true lunar years elapse

- **The Bible's Chronology Published in Brief**
  Meeting for press in London on November 25th 1937

- **Earthquake** in England at Noon

- 'The greatest recorded **earthquake**' (on Atlantic bed) starts series round the world before 'Pearl Harbour')
  'I will shake all nations' (Haggai 2: 7)

- VE Day. World War II ends in Europe at 12.01 am.
  Salvation of Israel's European Remnant Completed

'The Times of the Gentiles'

The Bible reveals that in its Chronology of Redemption God gave Israel exactly four periods of 'seventy weeks' (4 x 490 years) from the Birth of Abram to the Death of Christ.

The Chart demonstrates that from the first day Jesus appeared after the Temptation (John 1: 29) to the Acts 11 Conference in AD 36, just 1,263½ and 1,260 days had run their course, according to the pattern of time given in Revelation 11: 3 & 11 and 12: 6 & 14.

From that day God also gave the Gentiles exactly four periods of 'seventy weeks' (4 x 490 years) to June 11th 1938, marking the end of these 1,960 lunar years with an earthquake in Britain. Thereafter the 1,263½ + 1,260 days ran their course, ending to the hour when hostilities ceased in 1945, as far as Europe was concerned.

(See Chapter 20, especially pages 131-135)

Afterword

This book is offered humbly to show that God has lovingly kept His covenants and promises. He has not forsaken, and will not forsake, those whom He has chosen and loved.

In these days of turmoil and conflicting philosophies, uncertainty, fear and perplexity, God is still in control of events. Their apparently random and often ugly nature should not be allowed to obscure the perfect timing of Him who is truly King of Kings and Lord of Lords.

It is hoped that this book may help the reader to see the underlying plan of the ages and understand the Divine purposes of history, and that by this it may bring faith and hope afresh to Jew and Gentile alike. Nothing less was the heart's desire of the writer, and nothing less are the wonderful purposes of God in the way major events of the renaissance of the State of Israel can be exactly related to the Bible's plan of the ages.

Indeed it has occurred to many that the time is now near when there will once again be a great Divine intervention in the affairs of men. The culmination will be a time when the Messiah will come again to rule the world from Jerusalem and they will look upon Him 'whom they have pierced' (Zechariah 12: 10) and will recognise the Redeemer of the world.

Therefore let us behold the Bridegroom and go forward to meet Him, and may our hearts be stirred and quickened in our love for Him for, as Paul says in 2 Timothy 4: 8, there is 'a crown of righteousness, which the Lord, the righteous judge, shall give me at that day: and not to me only, but unto all them also that love His appearing'. Let us remember the closing words of Jesus in Revelation 22: 20 '"Surely I come quickly." Amen. Even so, come Lord Jesus'.

Books Referred To In The Text

DENNY, Sir Edward
Forgiveness Seventy and Sevenfold Companion to two prophetical charts
  – London 1849
The Seventy Weeks of Daniel (chart) – London 1849

GREEN, Jay P, Senior
The Interlinear Bible (Hebrew/Greek/English) – Hendrickson, Massachusetts,
  USA 1985

GUINNESS, Dr H Grattan
Light for the Last Days – London 1878

NAISH, Reginald T
Spiritual Arithmetic – 4th Edition, London 1930

SMITH, Sir William
A Dictionary of Greek and Roman Antiquities (Art. Calendarium) – London
  1842 and 1848

VELIKOVSKY, Immanuel
Ages in Chaos (Abacus Edition) – London 1973

VINE, W E
Expository Dictionary of New Testament Words – London 1940

WHISTON
Josephus – Wars of the Jews Book VII – London 1845

Encyclopædia Britannica – 14th Edition, London 1949

Encyclopædia Judaica – Keter 1971, under the name Rabbi Ammon of
  Mainz for the prayer on page 100

The Epistle of Barnabas found in 'Early Christian Writings – The Apostolic
  Fathers' translated by Maxwell Staniforth – Penguin Books 1968

Guideposts Magazine – New York October 1970, Guideposts Associates Inc.

Other items of interest

BULLINGER, E W
Number in Scripture – Kregal Publications, Michigan, USA repr 1990

PANIN, Ivan
The New Testament in the Original Greek printed privately for the Editor – University Press, Oxford 1934

The Miracle of Septenary Design in the Hebrew Scriptures Published by The Pentecostal Jewish Mission – 1975

Bible Studies on Audio Cassette:

PRICE, Roger

Biblical Chronology — STS 41-45
Biblical Numerology — STS 98-99
The Millennial Issue — STS 7-10
Fulfilled Prophecy — BBS 29-42
Unfulfilled Prophecy — BBS 43-63

Address for tape orders
(and a full Tape Catalogue):

> CCF Tapes
> Living Word Bookshop
> 30 Crescent Road
> BOGNOR REGIS   W. Sussex
> England   PO21 1QG
>
> Tel: 01 243-862621 or 01 243-828223

Scripture References

Index to Time Periods

Jubilee Periods *(40 Jubilees in each period)*

1. Times of the Patriarchs
Adam to the birth of Abraham   22, 45, 50-52, 66, 80, 173, 189

2. Times of Israel
Birth of Abraham to the Death of Christ   22, 38, 45, 66, 80, 108, 189
This period is divided into four periods each containing 10 Jubilees:

    A. Birth of Abraham to the Exodus   37-38, 45, 175, 187, 189

    B. Exodus to Dedication of Solomon's Temple   35-36, 45, 95, 176
        188-189

    C. Dedication of Solomon's Temple to Commandment
        to restore and rebuild Jerusalem   37, 45, 178, 189

    D. Commandment to restore and rebuild Jerusalem
        to the Crucifixion of Christ   36, 45, 61-63, 98, 180, 186, 189

3. Times of the Gentiles
AD 33-1933   19, 22, 28, 30, 66, 79, 119, 130, 168, 182, 189, 196

Other Time Periods

Adam to the Crucifixion   53-55, 87-88, 170

Exodus to the Crucifixion   37, 169

Creation to AD 33   156, 158, 162-163, 181, 183

Creation to 1933   182-183, 189

General Index

Further Information

Further copies of this book can be obtained from the address below, post free, at the price shown. Please write for multiple copy and trade discount rates.

Those desiring to study the subject of time in the Bible in detail may like to know that the text of this book is also available on computer disk (in ASCII code) from the same address. Please write for details.